THE ANCIENT ENEMY

'Contempt and hatred for another nation are nowhere united with more force and expression than in the English against the French ... but in a thousand instances the French return this contempt.'

JOHAN GEORG ZIMMERMANN, *Essay on National Pride*, tr. S. H. Wilcocke (London, 1797), pp. 116–17.

The Ancient Enemy

*England, France and Europe from the
Angevins to the Tudors 1154–1558*

Malcolm Vale

hambledon
continuum

Hambledon Continuum is an imprint of Continuum Books
Continuum UK, The Tower Building, 11 York Road, London SE1 7NX
Continuum US, 80 Maiden Lane, Suite 704, New York, NY 10038

www.continuumbooks.com

First published 2007

British Library Cataloguing-in-Publication Data
A catalogue record for this book is available from the British Library.

ISBN 978 1 84725 177 0

Typeset by Pindar New Zealand (Egan Reid), Auckland, New Zealand
Printed and bound by MPG Books Ltd, Cornwall, Great Britain

Contents

Illustrations

Plates

1. Henry I of England, Duke of Normandy, crossing the Channel in a hulk. *The Bridgeman Art Library.*

2. Map of Calais and the English Pale in the reign of Henry VIII (*Chronicle of Calais*). *The British Library.*

3. Computer-generated reconstruction of the former Plantagenet castle of the Ombrière at Bordeaux, now totally destroyed, set beside the modern adjoining buildings on the site today. *AXYZ Images. With the kind permission of the municipality of Bordeaux.*

4. View of Calais in the reign of Henry VIII (*Chronicle of Calais*). *The British Library.*

5. Town seal of Winchelsea, one of the Cinque Ports, early fourteenth century (National Maritime Museum, Greenwich). *The Bridgeman Art Library.*

Maps

To Pierre Capra (+) and Jacques Bernard
Anglo-Gascon historians
in gratitude
and in memory of le bon vieux temps *in Bordeaux*

This royal throne of kings, this scepter'd isle,
This earth of majesty, this seat of Mars,
This other Eden, demi-paradise;
This fortress built by Nature for herself
Against infection and the hand of war;
This happy breed of men, this little world;
This precious stone set in the silver sea,
Which serves it in the office of a wall,
Or as a moat defensive to a house,
Against the envy of less happier lands;
This blessed plot, this earth, this realm, this England...

William Shakespeare, *Richard II* (*c.* 1595–6), Act 2, scene 1

Gascony, and the other forts that our lord the king has over there, are and should be as barbicans to the kingdom of England; and if the barbicans are well guarded, with the safe-keeping of the sea, the kingdom will be in good enough peace; but otherwise we shall never have peace and quiet with our enemies. For they will then make war fiercely at the very doors of our houses, which God forfend; and also, by means of these same barbicans, our lord the king may have good ports and good points of entry to [the lands of] his enemies, to harm and damage them when he pleases.

Richard Scrope, reply to the Commons, in the Parliament of October 1378.[1]

Our greatest hereditary enemy was not Germany, it was England. From the Hundred Years War to Fashoda, she hardly ceased to struggle against us ... she is not naturally inclined to wish us well.

Charles de Gaulle, 27 June 1962.[2]

---

1 *Rotuli Parliamentorum*, iii, p. 36b.
2 Quoted in R. and I. Tombs, *That Sweet Enemy. The French and the British from the Sun King to the Present* (London, 2006), p. 605.

Preface

This book represents the outcome, as we now must call it, of a long-standing concern with medieval England's external relations with its closest European neighbours. It forms an attempt to trace continuities, as well as changes, over a long period. To range over a time-scale which encompasses the mid-twelfth to the mid-sixteenth centuries means that there can only be many omissions and imbalances in my treatment of so long a period. It also means that there is – inevitably – considerable use of, and reliance upon, the work of others. I hope that all such debts will be clearly evident, and fully acknowledged, in the text and notes of this book. But I have also attempted to introduce, and justify, a contention that the past of two European nation-states, however remote it may seem, is not without contemporary relevance. What we have been, to some degree, makes us what we are, and neither the English nor the French can escape that shared past. It has, however, become as much a subject of myth-making as of a search to discover historical truth, and one objective of this book is to try to seek origins and explanations for some of these myths.

To trace the course of the 'ancient enmity' with which the book deals necessarily involves a transposition of mindsets and assumptions common to the twenty-first century into a very different mental world. The political climate of a Europe in which the unitary nation-state was not the paradigm for state-formation which it later became was clearly vastly different from our own. An English kingdom which, for almost 500 years, was closely linked to continental Europe, where its rulers held territorial possessions and acted as a continental land power, was evidently not solely, nor even primarily, the island fortress extolled by later commentators and myth-makers. But the legacy of that protracted episode of direct continental government, administration and investment lived on. Why, for example, is the Joan of Arc story so potent and so formative of Anglo-French attitudes to this day? Why is the very notion of a closer union between Britain and France still greeted with deep scepticism and disbelief on both sides of the Channel? The answers can only lie in the past experience of the two nations, in which their earlier history – as well as the post-Reformation, post-Louis XIV, and post-colonial past – has a part to play. The Shakespearean 'scepter'd isle' (England) and the providentially-ordained hexagon (France) both have their proud and distinct senses of identity but, in both cases, these have more recently undergone profound re-examination, driven by both internal and external pressures. This may mean that similarities could, in the future, outweigh the historical differences between the two countries and their peoples – but the reasons for those differences must first of all be understood. It is to this end that this book forms a contribution.

I have incurred many debts in the course of researching and writing this book. First, I have benefited from periods of research leave generously granted by my College and by the Oxford History Faculty. Second, the unfailing helpfulness of the staffs of many institutional libraries and archives has been invaluable. I would especially single out those of the Bodleian Library, History Faculty Library, Taylorian Institution Library and St John's College Library at Oxford. The staff of the National Archives (ex-Public Record Office) at Kew and, over many years, the Departmental archivists of Pyrenees-Atlantiques (Pau), Gironde (Bordeaux), Nord (Lille), Pas-de-Calais (Arras) and Tarn-et-Garonne (Montauban) have helped to make working in their collections a pleasure. Among individuals, I wish to thank – for many kindnesses – my colleagues Jean Dunbabin, the late Rees Davies, Peter Lewis, Maurice Keen, Gervase Rosser, John Watts, Steven Gunn and William Whyte (Oxford); David D'Avray (London); Jean-Philippe Genet and Werner Paravicini (Paris); Jean-Bernard Marquette and Francoise Laine (Bordeaux); and, among a rising generation of scholars, Guilhem Pepin (Bordeaux and Oxford) and Hannah Wheeler (Oxford). An earlier draft of the book was kindly read and commented upon by John Watts. Timothy Vale also read parts of it and contributed helpful comments. For any errors or omissions which may remain in the book, I am entirely responsible.

St John's College, Oxford
27 March 2007

Abbreviations

AHG	*Archives Historiques de la Gironde*
AMB	*Archives Municipales de Bordeaux. Livre des Coutumes* ed. H. Barckhausen (Bordeaux, 1890)
AN	Archives Nationales (Paris)
Antiq. Journal	*Antiquaries' Journal*
ADG	Archives Departementales de la Gironde (Bordeaux)
APA	Archives Departementales des Pyrenees-Atlantiques (Pau)
ATG	Archives Departmentales de Tarn-et-Garonne (Montauban)
BEC	*Bibliotheque de l'Ecole des Chartes*
BIHR	*Bulletin of the Institute of Historical Research*
Cal. Charter Rolls	*Calendar of Charter Rolls*
CPR	*Calendar of Patent Rolls*
Cal. S. P. Dom.	*Calendar of State Papers, Domestic*
Cal. S. P. Foreign	*Calendar of State Papers, Foreign*
Cal. S. P. Venetian	*Calendar of State Papers, Venetian*
EcHR	*Economic History Review*
EHD	*English Historical Documents*
EHR	*English Historical Review*
Foedera	*Foedera, conventiones, litterae et cuiuscunque generic publica*, ed. T. Rymer, 20 vols (London, 1704–35)
JWCI	*Journal of the Warburg and Courtauld Institutes*
King's Works	*The King's Works*, ed. H. M. Colvin *et al.*, 6 vols (London, 1963–82)
Letters & Papers	*Letters and papers Illustrative of the Wars of the English in France during the Reign of Henry VI, King of England*, ed. J. Stevenson, 2 vols (London, 1861–4)
Libelle	*The Libelle of Engyshe Polycye. A Poem on the use of Sea-Power, 1436*, ed. G. F. Warner (Oxford, 1926)
Lisle Letters	*The Lisle Letters*, ed. M. St Clare Byrne, 6 vols (London and Chicago, 1981)
PPC	*Proceedings and Ordinances of the Privy Council of England*, ed. N. H. Nicolas, 7 vols (London, 1827–34)

RG	*Roles Gascons*, ed. F. Michel, C. Bemont, Y. Renouard, 4 vols (Paris and London, 1885–1964)
Rot. Parl.	*Rotuli Parliamentorum*, ed. J. Strachey *et al.*, 6 vols (London, 1783)
Saint-Sardos	*The War of Saint-Sardos (1323–1325). Gascon Correspondence and Diplomatic Documents*, ed. P. Chaplais (Camden third series, lxxxvii, London, 1954)
Treaty Rolls	*Treaty Rolls, preserved in the Public Record Office, i (1234–5)*, ed. P. Chaplais (London, 1955); *ii (1337–1339)*, ed. J. T. Ferguson (London, 1972)
TNA(PRO)	The National Archives (ex-Public Record Office), London

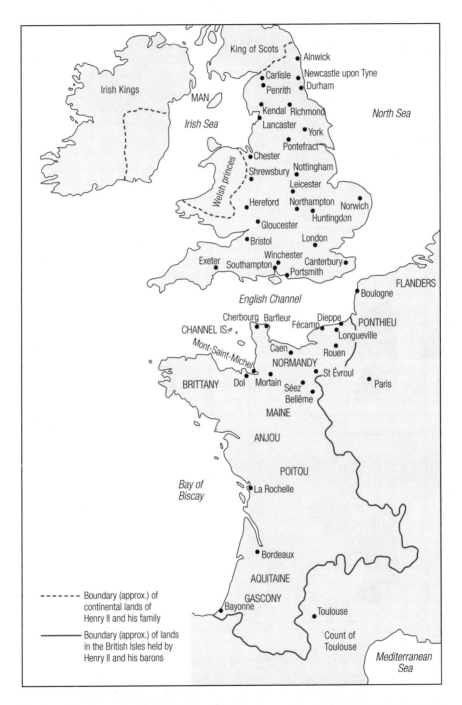

Map 1: The Angevin dominions, *c.* 1175. FRAME, *THE POLITICAL DEVELOPMENT OF THE BRITISH ISLES, 1100–1400* (OXFORD, 1990), MAP 2.

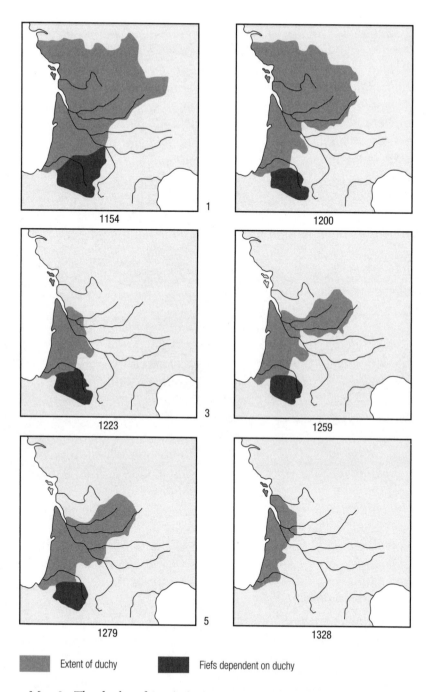

1154	1200
1223	1259
1279	1328

Extent of duchy   Fiefs dependent on duchy

Map 2: The duchy of Aquitaine, 1154–1328. *BORDEAUX SOUS LES ROIS D'ANGLETERRE (BORDEAUX MEDIEVAL, II)*, ED. Y. RENOUARD (BORDEAUX, 1965), CARTE 2.

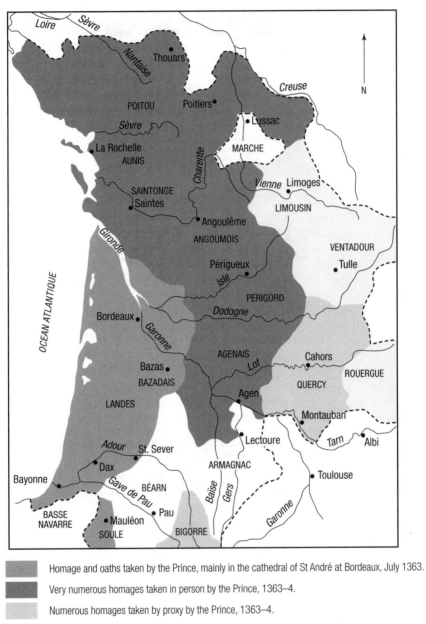

Map 3: The Black Prince's Principality of Aquitaine, 1362–1372. *BORDEAUX SOUS LES ROIS D'ANGLETERRE (BORDEAUX MEDIEVAL, II)*, ED. Y. RENOUARD (BORDEAUX, 1965), CARTE 9.

Map legend:

- Homage and oaths taken by the Prince, mainly in the cathedral of St André at Bordeaux, July 1363.
- Very numerous homages taken in person by the Prince, 1363–4.
- Numerous homages taken by proxy by the Prince, 1363–4.
- Few homages, 1363–4.
- - - - - Boundary of the lands of the count of Armagnac and vicomte of Béarn.

Map labels:

Loire, Sèvre, Nantaise, Thouars, Creuse, POITOU, Poitiers, Lussac, Sèvre, MARCHE, La Rochelle, AUNIS, Charente, Vienne, Limoges, SAINTONGE, Saintes, LIMOUSIN, Angoulême, ANGOUMOIS, VENTADOUR, Gironde, Périgueux, Tulle, Isle, PERIGORD, Dodogne, Bordeaux, Garonne, AGENAIS, Cahors, Bazas, Lot, ROUERGUE, BAZADAIS, QUERCY, Agen, LANDES, Montauban, Lectoure, Tarn, Albi, Adour, St. Sever, ARMAGNAC, Dax, Toulouse, Bayonne, BÉARN, Baïse, Gers, Gave de Pau, Pau, Garonne, BASSE NAVARRE, Mauléon, BIGORRE, SOULE, OCEAN ATLANTIQUE, N

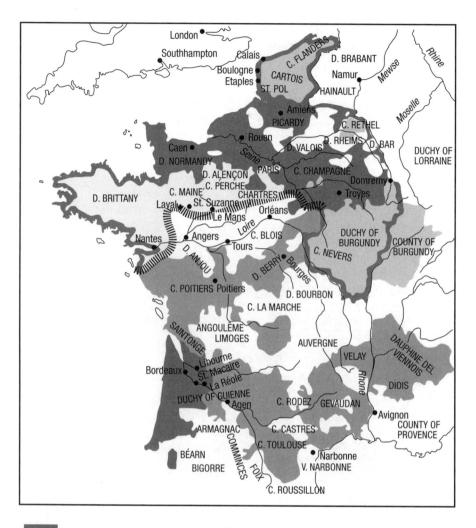

Lancastrian France and the duchies of Normandy and Aquitaine

Burgandian dominions

Brittany (acknowledging Henry VI's title)

Demesne lands of Charles VII

||||||||||||| Fluctuating frontier of Lancastrian France

Map 4: France at the time of Joan of Arc (1430). E.F. JACOB, *THE FIFTEENTH CENTURY, 1399–1485 (OXFORD HISTORY OF ENGLAND)*, (OXFORD, 1961), MAP 4.

England and its neighbours

The English and the French have never been good neighbours, or so it is often asserted.

The enmity between them, noted by independent observers in the eighteenth century, already had a long ancestry.[1] A Swiss essayist reported in 1768 that

> As to the word 'French', the national [English] antipathy against their opposite neighbours is so great, that to call a foreigner, *dog*, is not insulting enough, but he must be called *French dog*, to convey the highest degree of detestation.[2]

Neighbourly rivalry and its attendant animosity was placed in a more general scheme of things by fifteenth-century commentators, such as Philippe de Commynes, who thought that 'wars and divisions are ordained and permitted by God' as:

> God has created neither man nor beast in this world without making something which is opposed to them, to induce humility and fear in them … Nor is it only to this nation [Flanders] that God has given some kind of goad. For to the kingdom of France He has opposed the English; to the English the Scots; and to the kingdom of Spain, the Portuguese.[3]

Although the Anglo-French relationship acquired many other dimensions over the course of time, including colonial rivalry and, ultimately, uneasy and often mistrustful alliance, the old enmity has never been forgotten; in its more extreme manifestations, it was often to be found on the English side, but did not exclusively originate there. Its later incarnation was to be found in the words of Charles de Gaulle when, in June 1962, he declared

> Our greatest hereditary enemy was not Germany, it was England. From the Hundred Years War to Fashoda, she hardly ceased to struggle against us … She is not naturally inclined to wish us well.[4]

He was repeating a theme that had already appeared in the later Middle Ages. In January 1436, for instance, King Charles VII of France could refer, in a reply to a petition from his 'loyal subjects' in the Limousin, to 'our ancient enemies the English'.[5] It was to become a common and universal formula in letters issued

by the French Crown. 'Our ancient enemies and adversaries the English' was
the term normally used to describe them in the following decades until, and
after, their expulsion from all of their French possessions except Calais in 1453.[6]
During the entire period covered by this book (1154–1558), the rulers of the
medieval and early modern kingdom of England had held, or laid claim to, titles
and territories within the kingdom of France. These had been acquired by various
means – inheritance, marriage and other dynastic alliances, purchase, conquest
and occupation. For a significant part of the period – and until long after its end
– they had claimed the throne of France, as well as the right to hold inherited
lands within that kingdom. Even after the loss of its continental possessions,
England never formed a long-term and durable alliance with its closest European
neighbour. Their ancient enmity seemed to survive the vast political, religious
and cultural changes of subsequent centuries.

William Shakespeare wrote his *Richard II* about 40 years after England,
the 'scepter'd isle', had lost its last surviving possession on the mainland of
continental Europe. From that date, or so it transpired, England ceased to be
a continental land power. Calais had fallen to the French in 1558. It was the
last of those 'barbicans', or fortified outer defence-works, of England to which
Richard Scrope had alluded in his reply, on Richard II's behalf, to the Commons
in the Parliament of 1378.[7] The subsequent story of the island nation, anchored
like some great armoured battleship off the coast of north-west Europe, self-
contained, superior and invincible, has often been told and re-told.[8] But it is not
the only story. Another, alternative story has been constructed, especially during
recent decades. Britain – the archipelagic successor to the medieval kingdom of
England – is now linked to its continental neighbours by a tunnel, and is perhaps
more closely involved with them today than at any time since 1558. A common
history, and a common European culture, it is now argued, is shared with them.
That history is seen to inform, shape and mould the present. How that past is
to be represented and interpreted has also been swept up in a political debate
notable for its intensity, its divisive effects and, in its least appealing forms,
xenophobia. Is Britain, or is it not, a European country?[9] Upon what kinds of
historical evidence do these alternative narratives of Britain's evolution depend?
Above all, can a balance be struck between these conflicting accounts so that
history – which seeks something approximating to the truth – replaces myth,
which does not?

Britain's relationship to continental Europe at the present time has, inevitably,
been shaped by its past, and not merely by the recent past. 'Historically', it has
been said, 'Britain is a child of Europe' and, in its relationship to its European
partners, 'what we need is nothing less than a historic compromise with our
ancient enemy, France'.[10] Both the parentage of Britain and the origins of that
ancient enmity with France can be traced back to the Middle Ages – and to

issues well beyond the current (2007) preoccupation with Britain's national identity, post-imperial position, alliance with the United States of America, and past, present and future role within the European Union. European states, we are told, are essentially inter-connected, to a far greater extent than ever before. But this essential inter-connectedness is not a phenomenon of recent origin. In 1864, the editor of the first volume (1202–1509) of the *Calendar of State Papers and Manuscripts relating to English affairs, existing in the Archives and Collections of Venice* observed that 'as civilization advances, certain members of the European family are so closely inter-connected by community or antagonism of interests, that scarcely any event which materially affects the one can be uninteresting to the historian of the other'.[11] More recent claims and assertions about Britain's integrated or detached role in 'Europe', some of which employ historical, or pseudo-historical, arguments, at least have the merit of prompting pertinent historical questions. How close, or how distant, were relations with continental Europe over the centuries before the relatively tardy emergence of a United Kingdom of Great Britain and Ireland between 1707 and 1801? What consequences flowed from England's position as a continental land power, and what were the causes and effects of the loss of its overseas possessions? To what do we owe the myth of 'a thousand years of British sovereignty'?[12] To what extent has the Channel acted as a barrier, rather than as a highway, between continental Europe and the British Isles? How far did the island kingdom of England experience a different, distinct historical evolution and development from its nearest continental neighbours? Was that course of development in any way determined by its allegedly insular nature?

The medieval English kingdom in fact formed only part – albeit the greater part – of a group of offshore islands on the Atlantic seaboard of Europe. This cluster, ultimately to be linked with kindred immigrant peoples across the ocean, has been christened the 'Atlantic archipelago': that 'island group lying off the north-western coasts of geographic Europe, partly within and partly outside the oceanic limits of the Roman empire and of what is usually called "Europe" in the sense of the latter's successor states'.[13] Its unique geographical position and physical nature could not fail to have a significant effect upon its relations with other peoples and powers, both within the British Isles and on the European mainland. There was a Janus-like character to medieval England. The Roman god of entrances and exits, of bridges and portals, was represented as a two-faced image: one face depicted at the front and the other at the back of the head. So, like Janus, medieval England presented two faces: one gazed out on to the European continent, the other looked inward towards its Celtic neighbours – the Welsh, the Irish and the Scots. Its rulers and its people increasingly defined themselves in relation to both their British and continental neighbours, among the latter especially the French. But England's role and status as the dominant power within the British Isles also made it a major player in European power-politics, sought as an ally, feared (or, in periods of weakness, mocked and disparaged) as an enemy, enlisted as a sponsor or protector and accorded parity of status with the greatest powers of the continent. England became a Great Power, it has been observed, whose 'military power in the late Middle Ages was out of all proportion to her population or size'.[14] At a later date, the far-flung British Empire was to replicate that phenomenon of the disproportionate strength of a relatively small country, ruling even vaster overseas territories, out of all proportion to its size. Textbook accounts of the growth of British power proudly made the point, well expressed by H. E. Marshall's best-selling children's book *Our Island Story* of 1905.[15] It was assumed that the later Empire, for better or for worse, had medieval precedents.

Within the British Isles, English dominance led increasingly to the identification – by the English – of Britain with England.[16] The 'high kingship of the British Isles' was subsumed in the title 'king of England'.[17] But medieval England was unusual among the major western European powers in that its rulers also held substantial territories within a neighbouring kingdom, that of France. The fact that those territories were separated from England by stretches of water did not make it unique: the kingdom of Denmark, for example, directly held the flat plain of Scania, lying to the immediate south of the kingdom of Sweden, across the narrow Sound from Copenhagen. Similarly, Aragon ruled a Mediterranean sea-borne empire from the late thirteenth century onwards, including the Balearic Isles, Sardinia and Sicily. But the closest contemporary medieval parallel to England would be that of the kingdom of Naples, held from 1266 onwards by the French house of Anjou – who were *kings* in Naples but, from 1246 to 1291, also *counts* in their French dominions (Anjou, Maine).[18] The first two Angevin rulers of Naples – Charles I and Charles II – had to acknowledge the judicial sovereignty of the French crown over their French lands. Just as the Plantagenet kings of England were obliged to permit cases of appeal from their own courts in their duchy of Aquitaine to the French crown's Parlement at Paris, so the Angevin kings of Naples retained proctors there for the same purpose.[19] Like his contemporary, Edward I of England, Charles I of Anjou, though largely absent from his French possessions, was clearly concerned with their administration and was constantly in touch with his officers there;[20] there was thus no inherent or inevitable contradiction between the positions of rulers who were vassals of other rulers as well as kings in their own right.

It has been said that: 'the Norman Conquest [1066] inaugurated four centuries during which the history of the British Isles was intertwined with that of northern and western France'.[21] Not only was it inextricably intertwined with events and developments within France but, inevitably, with the rest of Europe. We might profitably extend that period to five centuries – from the late eleventh to the mid-sixteenth century – and examine both continuities and changes in England's relationship with these regions of France, as well as the impact of that relationship on dealings with other European powers. This 'intertwining' was to have a profound effect on the nature of political and institutional structures and on state formation. A large recent literature now exists on the subject of British national and regional identities, but it tends to confine itself to the British Isles. This book will, by contrast, emphasize the importance of a broader context, not only British but also European, in which to see England's self-definition, role and functions.

England's continental territories, however much reduced from their original extent they may have become in the course of time, naturally tended to form areas of considerable political and diplomatic sensitivity. That sensitivity continued long after the end of the Middle Ages, especially in the field of Anglo-French relations. On 25 June 1794, for instance, it was decreed by the French Revolutionary government that 'all documents recalling English domination in France were to be destroyed'.[22] Fortunately for the historian, that edict was never obeyed to the letter. During the Middle Ages, the rulers of England had played a dual, if often overlapping, role in European affairs: first, as sovereigns of their English kingdom and, second, as the lords of other territories, in many of which they did not initially, *de jure* – that is, by universally acknowledged legal right – possess fully sovereign status. How, and in what capacity, they negotiated, treated and did business with other European powers was therefore dependent upon their respective statuses and the nature of the matters and questions at issue. But the possession of lands which lay within the territorial limits of the French kingdom, whatever their precise status, gave rise to problems which were to provoke major crises in international – or inter-kingdom – relations. For example, it became increasingly apparent that ostensibly minor happenings within those continental possessions, and on their borders, could have very wide-ranging consequences. Pinprick incidents or – to change the metaphor – small fires could, if not contained, lead to major conflagrations. The mere existence of the English monarchy's continental possessions could therefore not only influence but also complicate and sometimes worsen relations with other powers, especially with the kingdom of France. For example, a relatively minor 'outrage' in south-west France, at a newly-founded *bastide* (planted town) of St-Sardos in the Agenais in October 1323, was one such incident, which was to lead to a major Anglo-French war. A band of armed men, in the pay of a local Gascon noble, allegedly in collusion with the Plantagenet regime, had raided the site of the projected French *bastide* and hanged the serjeant of the French crown, who was to proclaim the establishment of the new foundation, thereby insulting and defying the sovereignty of the king of France. Edward II of England's former representative in the duchy – the French-born seneschal of Aquitaine,

Amaury de Craon – could write at the time that if no reparation was made, then Anglo-French differences ('le contenz pereillous') 'poet gesir la tresgrant doute pereillouse de la plus grant partie de tote crestienete' ['could bring about the greatest peril for the greater part of the whole of Christendom'].[23] His fears, despite the dramatic and exaggerated tone in which they were couched, were not entirely unfounded.

The period addressed by this book ranges from the accession of Henry II Plantagenet to the throne of England, bringing extensive continental dominions with him, in 1154, to the final loss to the French of the last of those dominions – the town, March and Pale of Calais – in 1558. This is not a chronological span which has found much (if any) favour among historians. In an age of extreme specialization in the writing of history, to embark on the study of a 400-year period is to invite critical and adverse responses. We will nevertheless attempt to construct a general overview of this long period, noting continuities as well as changes in England's position within Europe. England had already become a continental land power in 1066, as a result of the Norman Conquest; or rather, it had become part of a cross-Channel union with the duchy of Normandy. The shape of English continental possessions, in the form which they would assume for most of the Middle Ages and beyond was, however, created by the Angevin succession to the English throne in 1154. From that date onwards, there was no time, until 1558, when the occupants of the English throne did not hold continental possessions. But the historiographics of the so-called 'Angevin Empire' (1154–1224) and that of the so-called (or mis-called) 'Hundred Years War' (1337–1453) have so often been treated apart that one might be forgiven for thinking that their practitioners seem to inhabit different historical and methodological worlds. It will, on the contrary, be argued here that the retention of continental possessions by the English crown provides one theme of continuity in the kingdom's external relations which was broken only in the mid-sixteenth, rather than the mid-fifteenth, century.[24] It has been concluded that, under the Yorkists and early Tudors, between 1461 and 1558:

> England reluctantly but finally abandoned her medieval ambition to win and hold dominions upon the continent of Europe, the 'continentalist' policy based upon land power which she had pursued through most of the Middle Ages. It was under their [the Tudors'] rule that she felt her way towards an insular policy based upon sea power and regarding herself as an island 'off' rather than 'of' Europe.[25]

The so-called 'logic of history' is said to have prevailed during the Tudor age, meaning that the loss of England's last remaining continental dominion – Calais – was inevitable. What has been described as the 'insularity' of the Tudors set the tone and pace for the future. 'A shrunken, post-imperial England', it has been said, 'faced an uncertain and vulnerable future on the margins of … Europe'.[26]

But the 'continentalist' policy did not die without a fight. Too teleological and deterministic a view of historical development can lead to distortions of interpretation. Henry VIII (1509–47), for example, with strong public support, was determined to cut an impressive and powerful figure by pursuing his claims to title and territory on the European scene. The English claim to the throne of France, moreover – however empty – was not finally abandoned by the British monarchy until 1802. And, given the ever-present danger of foreign invasion, the English could never afford to stand and watch on the sidelines as continental European powers and superpowers struggled for territorial gain and political supremacy.

Any consideration of England's relations with other peoples and powers must necessarily focus upon two areas: the kingdom's immediate Celtic neighbours, on one hand, and the European continent on the other. To some extent these were inter-related and interdependent: throughout the Middle Ages (and beyond) England's surrounding and protective sea encountered British coastlines – Irish, Welsh and Scottish – which harboured hostile and turbulent peoples in their hinterlands. Scottish alliance with France from the later thirteenth century onwards, and the incomplete annexation of Ireland by the English crown, served to heighten awareness of England's vulnerability to rearguard action from its Celtic neighbours, often in league with foreign foes. The English knight, Sir Thomas Gray, writing in c. 1355–62, could allude to the Franco-Scottish practice of border raiding, masquerading as an invasion to force the king of England to return from France to save his own kingdom.[27] English conquests and annexations of 'Celtic' regions within the British Isles could therefore provide one means of defence against continental enemies. England has accordingly been described as an 'imperial' power during the Middle Ages, but the nature of that imperialism prompts further questions. How, for example, did the relationship between England and the continental inheritances and conquests of its ruling house resemble, or differ from, that with its immediate Celtic neighbours? And to what extent did the relationship with its continental possessions ever 'develop, substantively or historiographically, into an integrative one'?[28]

The conquered and settled lands (Wales, Ireland) could be contrasted with the inherited and acquired lordships (continental dominions) for in many ways the Celtic lands were much more alien to 'English' (that is, Anglo-Norman, Angevin and Plantagenet) rulers, their customs and culture, than the overseas territories. These latter had, after all, constituted the original heartlands of those dynasties which ruled England after 1066. Indeed, it could be argued that many rulers of England at this time were as 'French' as they were 'English', accustomed to the Anglo-Norman language, as well as the 'French of Paris', sharing with their continental European neighbours a cosmopolitan and chivalric culture. They often had as much, if not more, in common with their continental peers and vassals than with many of their English subjects. Sometimes, however, English officers sent to administer the continental lands thought otherwise and were distinctly unflattering in their comments upon their inhabitants. In December 1323, the admittedly rather dyspeptic Master Adam Lymbergh, constable of Bordeaux (1322–4), told Edward II that:

'Sire, il bosoignereit molt qe vous eussez pris les homages de voz gentz de Gascoigne, qi ne se poont faire par autre qe par vous meismes, et vous les averez molt le plus enclyns et obeissantz a vous, *car ils sont ore touz le plus come sauvages et ne conissent point ceo qe seignurie est a regard de ceo qils feroient apres ce qils vous eussent veu et fait lour homages.*'[29]

['My lord, it would be very advantageous for you to receive, in person, the homages of your people in Gascony, which cannot be done by anyone but yourself, and you will find them much more inclined and obedient towards you, because they are presently just like savages and do not know what lordship is when compared with what they will do once they have seen you and performed their homages'.]

His view was not unlike those of countless British colonial officers, sent to govern unruly or disaffected populations in a later Empire. It was, more significantly, supported by Sir Ralph Basset of Drayton, seneschal of Aquitaine,[30] as the king-duke's ordinary representative in the duchy at the time. On 15 December 1323, Hugh the Despenser the Younger, Edward II's favourite, accordingly notified the king's Gascon officers of the king's intention to come to the duchy – an intention which, in the event, remained unfulfilled.[31] It became the normal practice, after Edward I's (1272–1307) second and last visit to his Gascon dominions in 1288–9, for the king-duke to be represented by a lieutenant or viceroy of high status in Aquitaine – until Edward III (1327–77) created a (temporary) principality or apanage there for the Black Prince, his eldest son, in 1362. The Prince certainly received homages, from over one thousand of his Gascon vassals, in person, at Bordeaux and elsewhere. But to see their sovereign in person, after Edward III's assumption of the title to the French crown in 1340, the Gascon subjects of the English crown had to come to England, or to other places in France, or elsewhere on the European mainland, wherever the king happened to be. Yet if he was represented in the duchy by an Englishman of sufficient standing, there was little evidence of Gascon dissatisfaction or resentment. Too close a royal presence might have proved unwelcome. Nor was there any attempt, before the mid-fourteenth century, to colonize any of the continental possessions. Attempts to export English settlers, customs, laws or institutions were confined largely to the Celtic lands, and were not applied to the territories in France. But some movements began to take place in that direction from the mid-fourteenth century onwards: with the capture and resettlement of Calais as an 'English' town (1347–8); then the full-scale conquest of Normandy and Lancastrian (northern) France in the fifteenth century (1417–24). The consequences of these developments will be assessed later.

It will be argued in this book that two significant watersheds in the relationship between the English kingdom and continental Europe occurred: in 1294 and, most significantly, in 1340.

Edward I and Philip the Fair had gone to war in 1294 for the first time in over half a century, and relations between the two ruling houses of Plantagenet and Capet were never the same again. In 1340, all feudal and vassalic ties with the Valois crown of France were severed by Edward III. Before that date, there had been a fundamental difference between the position and status of the English crown in its Celtic lands on the one hand, and in its continental domains on the other. In Wales and Ireland, ultimate lordship and jurisdiction 'in the last resort' lay with the king of England; in Aquitaine and the rest of the continental possessions, before 1340, it lay, theoretically and technically, with the king of France.[32] This, potentially, had serious implications for the degree of freedom of action which could be exercised by the Plantagenets in foreign affairs. As a vassal of the French crown, the king of England could, at least in theory, neither be an entirely free agent in his own domains, nor in his dealings with other European powers. A major aim of the Plantagenet administration was thus to render the king-duke and his officers as independent as possible of French royal jurisdiction in Aquitaine. Edward I undertook a series of reforming measures in 1289 which were, in large part, to determine the government of the Plantagenets' longest-held continental territory until its final loss in the mid-fifteenth century. No such considerations applied to Wales or Ireland. Hence the king of England, as immediate, but not sovereign, lord of his continental lands, stood in a similar relationship to the king of France (especially after his acknowledgement of a feudal, vassalic relationship in 1259) as did the king of Scotland to himself. The Scottish rulers were in fact vassals of the English crown for those lands which they held within the kingdom of England. Similarly, between 1259 and 1340 the English king-duke-count was in effect a French prince, theoretically holding land within the kingdom of France from the Capetian, and then the Valois, crown, for which he was required to render a form of homage. This, as we have seen, was not a unique situation, but its implications for both Anglo-French relations and European politics were profound.

But how far does the traditionally anglocentric view espoused by historians tend to distort our sense of perspective, especially when applied to the Angevin and Plantagenet 'empires', both within the British Isles and on the European mainland? This view puts the English kingdom firmly at the centre of the variable and fluctuating assemblage of lands which constituted those empires. Modern historical writing about empires has tended to formulate models. One of the most pervasive and potent is the notion of empires comprising a 'metropole' and 'peripheries'[33] or 'core' and 'colonies'. The parent state, or imperial power, becomes a 'metropole'. According to this argument, England fulfilled that function. But to what extent can such a concept be profitably applied to our period? Similarly, how far do models, derived largely from political and social theory, of 'tribute states', 'domain states', 'tax states' and 'fiscal states' illuminate these political constructs? We might seek alternative hypotheses, such as ideas of composite monarchy and polycentric empires,[34] or of political structures which resisted 'centralizing' tendencies and were compatible with a high degree of both devolution and itineration by rulers. At what stage, for instance (outside the minds of modern historians), were the 'Crown's possessions beyond England … seen as annexes of an England-centred world'?[35] The English crown's continued continental ambitions and involvements might suggest that England remained a European-centred power in an essentially Europe-centred world. We will therefore attempt to see 'Europe in England' as much as 'England in Europe'. The extent to which England and its inhabitants shared a common culture with their continental neighbours forms the subject of a later chapter. The English kingdom was without doubt an independent entity, but it was bound by many ties to the continental mainland, not simply by territorial holdings and by claims to both lands and titles. But those claims, and the very nature and location of its territories, brought it into particularly close relationships with other neighbouring and adjacent European powers – above all, France, the principalities of the Low Countries, the German empire, the Iberian kingdoms and the papacy. Such relationships could only shape and determine the status and behaviour of England on the wider European stage.

From an Anglo-centric standpoint, it could be argued that the continental possessions of the English crown were leeches and parasites – they formed a drain on resources, and a distraction of energies, which could have been devoted to establishing permanent, stable English hegemony over the rest of the British Isles. At its simplest, the common view is that their loss was beneficial to the English nation, its language, its sense of identity and its control over its own destiny. The children's author H. E. Marshall put it well in 1905:

> The loss of Normandy, which was caused by [King] John's cruelty, proved to be a blessing to England. Norman lords no longer came to England, expecting to fill the best places in the land. French was spoken less and less, until only a few French words remained, which we still use, and which now form part of the English language. The hatred between Norman and English died out, because the differences disappeared, and the Norman lords became English barons.[36]

However, if another perspective is adopted, we might ask whether any tangible advantages were conferred upon England as a result of its continental inheritances and acquisitions. First, as Richard Scrope pointed out in 1378, the very location of England's continental possessions made them important forts, bases or bridgeheads with which to defend the kingdom, and from which to launch campaigns against adjacent powers. They formed an essential part of the 'wide belt of possessions and friendly or satellite territories across the Channel that … served [England] as a land buffer against invasion'.[37] Aquitaine provided a relatively secure, if distant, point from which to conduct raids and expeditions into neighbouring enemy territories, in both France and the Iberian Peninsula. The Black Prince's expeditions of 1355–6 and 1364–5 set out from Bordeaux and from other strong-points in the duchy – subsequently the principality – of Aquitaine. Although communications with England itself were necessarily made more difficult by sheer distance, the degree of local support and the quantity of local resources which could be gathered and mobilized in south-west France made it a viable launch-pad for campaigns of both territorial reconquest and great plundering *chevauchées* south of the Loire. Similarly, the possession of the county of Ponthieu in north-west France, between 1279 and 1337, 1360 and 1369 and, after 1347–8, of the town and march of Calais, offered bridgeheads into northern France which were much closer to the southern coast of England. Lastly, the occasional occupation of parts of the Breton coastline enabled English and allied shipping to negotiate the dangerous sea-passage to Bordeaux and Bayonne in relative security. Brest was held by English forces between 1342 and 1362 and again between 1372 and 1397.[38] Brittany's significance for England's relations with its possessions in south-west France has been compared with that of Egypt – also positioned on a vital sea route – for the British Empire of a later epoch.[39]

Second, apart from their military and strategic role, the continental dominions could serve as useful bases for speedier communication with nearby countries: Aquitaine for the Iberian kingdoms; and Ponthieu and Calais for northern France and the Low Countries. In the 1280s and 1290s, Edward I was using Gascon couriers to carry most of his correspondence with the king of Aragon. A letter of that date reported that the use of a Gascon agent was very advantageous and it was desirable that 'littera sibi celeriter presentetur, ita quod negocium non pereat per defectum boni et prudentis nuncii in hac parte'[40] ['the letter should be delivered to him (Alfonso of Aragon) quickly, so that the negotiations do not fail through lack of a good and prudent envoy in this matter']. At a later date, the personnel on the establishment at Calais could perform similar functions: thus William Pirton, lieutenant of the fortress of Gunes in the march of Calais, was dispatched as an envoy with Edward Grimston, esquire, to the duchess of Burgundy in March 1449.[41] Calais became a normal staging-post for English envoys to foreign courts. In the 1530s, a constant stream of ambassadors and messengers passed through the town. In October 1533, Henry VIII's courtier and favourite Sir Francis Bryan wrote from Marseilles, where he had seen Pope

Clement VII, to the Lord Deputy at Calais, telling him in two bantering letters that he and other English envoys would soon be arriving there:

> against which time, I, Sir Francis Bryan, desire you to make more ready for me a soft bed than an hard harlot. We would that ye had part of the wines that we drink here, and then we doubt not ye would pity us … Sir, whereas in your last letter I perceive that in Calais ye have sufficient of courtezans to furnish and accomplish my desires, I do thank you of your good provision, but this shall be to advertise you that since my coming hither I have called to my remembrance the misliving that ye and such other hath brought me to; for the which, being repented, have had absolution of the Pope.[42]

Bryan recommended, jestingly, that the Lord Deputy, an old friend and 'loving brother of old', should follow his example and forthwith come to seek papal absolution. Calais thus served not only as a staging-post but as a meeting-place for those engaged on the king's business (and their own), drawing to it a resident population who ministered to their needs and pleasures.

Routes taken by both English and foreign envoys to and from England sometimes avoided the kingdom of 'royal' France altogether, especially, but not always, in time of war, and the continental possessions played an important role in that process.[43] They could also act as sources of revenue from which to pay expenses incurred by the English crown in its relations with neighbouring powers. Pensions and fees granted by English kings to subjects of the crown of Aragon, for example, were often paid from the receipts of the constableship of Bordeaux. The duchy of Aquitaine could also be used as a base for diplomatic mediation and negotiation with neighbouring powers – thus Edward I operated from Aquitaine during his mediation of issues concerning France, Castile and Aragon in the late 1280s. Edward offered mediation to Philip III of France and Alfonso X of Castile as, in a credence to be spoken by his envoys to Philip III:

> Il [Edward] ad entendu de novel ke le Roys de Castele bee aprucher as parties de Gascoygne, si il y ueit, il vos maunde, sire, ke si il vos plest volentires se travayelera, ou de pes ou de trewe entre vos … le graunt desir ke il ad de purchacer ceste chose, le fet emprendre cest travayil si vostre volente y est, pur le graunt profit de la creistiente, e pur ceo ke il est tenuz a vos e au Reis de Castele, si com vos savez, e especialment a vos.[44]

> [He has recently heard that the king of Castile intends to be near to the region of Gascony and, if he comes there, he (Edward) informs you, sire, that if it pleases you, he will willingly work to achieve either peace or truce between you … (as) the great desire that he has to achieve this end urges him to undertake this task, if you should wish it, for the greater profit of Christendom and because he is beholden to you and to the king of Castile, as you know, and especially to you.]

Such *démarches* on the king-duke's part also gave him the potential to upstage the crown of France – Edward, after all, was technically Philip's vassal for his fief of Aquitaine. Relations with Philip's son and successor – Philip the Fair – were not improved by such a legacy, especially after Edward's arbitration of the Anjou-Aragon dispute in 1288–9.

These relationships could in turn, as we shall see, carry cultural as well as political and diplomatic implications. The cosmopolitanism of court culture stemmed in part from the presence of an international aristocratic and clerical elite at the courts of European rulers. In England, it was common to grant membership of both the king's council and household to 'foreigners' – they were retained as *familiares* or as *secretarii*, and were drawn from France, the Low Countries, the German Empire, Italy, the Iberian kingdoms and elsewhere. They proved useful as essential intermediaries – as negotiators and representatives at foreign courts – to conclude alliances and represent English interests, for example against France or to keep the peace with France.[45] Among them were noblemen such as Maurice de Craon, Amaury de Craon, Henri de Sully, William and Aymer de Valence, under Edward I and Edward II alone. A particularly good instance is the case of the French noble Amaury de Craon, lord of Craon and Sable, last hereditary seneschal of Anjou, Maine and Touraine (for the French crown) as well as seneschal of Aquitaine, in 1313–16 and 1320–22, for Edward II of England. As we have seen, on 4 November 1323 Amaury wrote to the king expressing his concern about the state of Anglo-French relations and alluded to the

> very great unease which I have about the disagreement between you and your brother the king of France [Charles IV], our lord, and the desire to find ways, according to my limited ability, to prevent it.

> [la tresgrant mesaise de cuer qe je averois en la discencioun dentre vous et vostre frere le roi de France, nostre sire, et laffeccion de trover les voies de mon petit entendement a la eschuer.][46]

In his letter to the king on the incident at St-Sardos, he went on to mention two members of the court of France known to be especially favourable to Edward II: Alphonse d'Espagne, lord of Lunel and Mathieu de Trie, marshal of France. Amaury wrote 'that I truly think that they wish for your good and your honour … that they are grieved by this, fearing that, if remedy is not soon found, great evil will come of it' ['qe je pense veroiement qils voudroient vostre bien et vostre honur … qe molt lour en pesoit, dotauntz, si brief remede ny estoit mis, qe grant mal en venist'.][47]

Some of these go-betweens were of high status at foreign courts – again, in the crisis of 1323–4, Edward II could rely on the services and good offices of such men as Henri de Sully, hereditary *bouteiller* of France, close to the seat of Capetian power.[48] Sully was appointed seneschal of the confiscated duchy of Aquitaine by Charles IV of France and was instrumental in securing and implementing the peaceful and speedy restoration of the duchy to Edward II. Hence the employment of foreign councillors, knights and clerks as intermediaries, with double or multiple loyalties and linguistic accomplishments, especially for the transmission of secret messages, proved beneficial to the English crown in its dealings with other powers.[49] As we shall see, cultural 'hybridity' and eclecticism was promoted and furthered by these connections, above all among the upper echelons of English society.[50] Such cosmopolitanism could be promoted and furthered by the itinerant and peripatetic nature both of rulers' courts and nobles' households. The constant journeying undertaken by these intermediaries, both clerical and secular, served to keep the English court, its associated and dependent households, and the members of the upper echelons of English society in close and regular contact with their continental European contemporaries. It could also act as a counter-balance to hostile behaviour, especially towards France. The implications of this consistent characteristic of England's relations with its neighbours will be examined later.

In 1751, the French scientist and geographer Nicolas Desmarets (1725–1815) composed a short treatise entitled *L'ancienne jonction de l'Angleterre à la France ou le Détroit de Calais. Sa Formation par la Rupture de l'Isthme* [*The former connection of England to France, or the Straits of Calais. Its formation by the breach of the Isthmus*]. He argued that the British Isles and the European continent had once been joined together and, in the course of his discussion, noted that:

> the majority of islands are very close to continents: for if we study a world-map, and consider attentively the economy and disposition of those spits of dry land which lie above the waters, we see that they are not strewn about quite as irregularly as may appear at first sight. This observation gives rise to the suspicion that they were once joined together.[51]

England, he argued, had once been joined to France by an isthmus – a strip, neck or tongue of land – between Dover and Calais. His treatise was reprinted in 1875 and formed part of a published collection of documents intended to support a projected Channel Tunnel – not, in the event, to be realized for another hundred years. But Desmarets's views had wider implications: England was a continental European country, physically divided from its closest continental neighbour only by an accident of marine geology.

Surrounded as it was on three sides by the sea, the medieval English kingdom was often described and depicted by contemporaries as an island. In the Wilton Diptych, Richard II's magnificent portable altarpiece of *c.* 1395–6, a tiny orb is shown surmounting a staff, held by an angel, on which a banner of St George's cross is flown. Within the orb, a tiny representation of a green island, with trees and a twin-towered castle, is visible, set in a sea, once made of silver leaf, on which a masted ship in full sail is shown.[52] Given its context, this may well be a symbolic representation of the English kingdom, which Richard offers to the Virgin Mary as her 'dowry'. The significance of England's status and position as an island had been commented upon by writers since an early date. Bede quoted Pliny, Gildas and Orosius on the subject, stating that: 'Britain, once called Albion, is an *island of the ocean* and lies to the north-west, being opposite Germany, Gaul and Spain, which form the greater part of Europe, though at a considerable distance from them'.[53] Six hundred or so years later, a monk of St Peter's abbey, Gloucester, could emphasize England's island status in his Middle English metrical chronicle (*c.* 1294–1300). With a clear sense of pride in his native land, the monk wrote:

> England is a right good land, I think of lands the best;
> Set at the far end of the world, all in the west;
> The sea runs round about it, it stands as in an isle;
> Its foes it need not fear, unless it be through guile ...[54]

This was robust, patriotic sentiment – of the kind that was to give rise to Shakespeare's 'this scepter'd isle' speech in *Richard II*. The theme was taken up by the anonymous author of the polemical tract known as the *Libel of English Policy* (*c.* 1436), who exhorted 'alle Englande to kepe the see enviroun and namelye the narowe see':

> Kepe than the see aboght in speciall,
> Whiche of England is the rounde wall,
> As thoughe England were lykened to a cite
> And the wall environ were the see.
> Kepe than the see, that is the wall of Englond,
> And than is Englond kepte by Goddes hond ...[55]

On the other side of England's 'wall' or 'moat' lay her outer defences, or 'barbicans', which could also act as England's watchful and vigilant 'eyes', from which the movements and intentions of her enemies could be observed and anticipated. The author of the *Libel* echoed the remarks attributed to the Emperor Sigismund who, during his visit to Henry V in 1416 had supposedly told the king that Dover and Calais were vital to England's security, exhorting him to

> Kepe these too townes sure to youre mageste
> As youre tweyne eyne [eyes] to kepe the narowe see.[56]

England was thus portrayed as a sea-girt isle, safe from her enemies by reason of her 'moat' – unless betrayed by guile and treachery, or endangered by lack of vigilance and neglect of the 'keeping of the sea'. But how, if at all, did this insular character and stance influence the formation of the English state and the growth of a sense of national identity? An extreme statement of the view that the English had become an island nation by the fourteenth century was put forward by

G. M. Trevelyan in his best-selling and influential *English Social History* (first published, significantly, in the dark days of 1942 in the USA and Canada; subsequently in Britain, in 1944). England, wrote Trevelyan, then began to 'emerge as a distinct nation, no longer a mere oversea extension of Franco-Latin Europe'.[57] The ultimate failure of its attempted conquest of France in the fifteenth century, he asserted, left England 'as a strange island, anchored off the Continent, no longer a mere offshoot or extension of the European world'.[58] But it has been argued more recently that England was already a nation-state by 1066, both as an actual and imagined community.[59]

As a kingdom, the English regnal state certainly possessed a marked and early sense of its own identity and particularity, and that identity came to be more sharply defined as a result of the relative absence of its rulers and the precocious growth of its institutions between 1066 and 1204. It also began to define itself in relation to its neighbours, both British and continental. But the kingdom also formed part of a wider network of territories – which historians have christened an 'empire' – both within the British Isles and overseas. Was the 'first English empire' in any way similar to later empires, and can the expansion of English authority be helpfully described as 'imperialism' in this period?[60] The status of the insular English kingdom was, it seems, enhanced by its position within the Angevin 'empire' – and it was largely to this enhanced status that it owed its rise from a middle-range to higher-echelon European power. The marriage alliances of the English crown served as a reliable barometer of its status in European politics, and could be contrasted with those made, for example, by the Scottish royal line. Between 1216 and 1327, English kings had married only into the Spanish and French royal houses. In the twelfth and thirteenth centuries, Scotland emerged only as a middle-ranking European power, forging marriage alliances, not with other royal houses, but with greater duchies and counties such as Flanders or Brittany.[61]

The medieval English kingdom, like its Tudor successor, was not in fact an island. Reporting to the Doge and Senate of Venice from Rome in March 1588, their ambassador there told them that Pope Sixtus V had described Elizabeth I of England as 'a great Queen', but 'mistress of only half an island' ('et non e patrona si non di meza Isola').[62] England had a land frontier with the kingdom of Scotland and, before 1282, with Wales, which rendered its political society in the North and West more like that which could be found in the frontier zones of continental Europe. Scotland was to pose the most serious and constant threat to English ambitions both at home and abroad. Yet, surrounded on three sides by water, the English kingdom was already perceived by contemporaries to be a defensible fortress, for whom, as we have seen, its continental possessions acted as 'barbicans' or outworks. A petition dating from the 1320s already described Aquitaine as a 'barbican and defence of England'.[63] In his speech to the Parliament of 1378, the Chancellor had referred to 'Calais, Bordeaux, Bayonne and the other places that we have on the other side of the sea' in just this manner.[64]

It was imperative that the coastline of northern France and the Low Countries, from Brest and Boulogne to Bruges and Antwerp, should be closely watched and, where feasible, acquired, occupied, or at the very least neutralized through alliances with the English monarchy. But, since the Norman Conquest of 1066, England's 'moat' was a navigable sea as well as a defence-work, forming a highway rather than a barrier to the transmission of people, goods and ideas. The sea-girt isle developed modes of defence, transport, exchange and communication which reflected its essential orientation towards the European continent. Under the Anglo-Norman kings the regularity and frequency of what has been called cross-Channel transfretation was indicative of the extent to which the rulers of England and their subjects, both landed and mercantile, had strong material interests in Normandy and other parts of western and northern France. Until its loss in 1204, tenure of the Norman duchy determined much of the activity of those rulers and, as we shall see, efforts to regain it or, failing that, to sustain a continental presence in other parts of the kingdom of France, continued to absorb both their imagination and energies.

It was imperative to keep open the sea-ways between England and its continental territories. The author of the *Libel of English Policy* dwelt at tedious length on the need for English mastery of the sea, so as to ensure the free passage of 'commoditees' in both directions, 'for whiche grete nede is well to kepe the sees'.[65] This, as all subsequent English governments found to their cost, was a very difficult, if not impossible, objective to achieve. England suffered from the handicap of prevailing winds which, in the Western Approaches and English Channel, often blew from the south-west, thereby penning ships in the ports of the south coast for considerable periods. The same winds which brought hostile or invading fleets from France or the Iberian Peninsula onward could trap English fleets in their own harbours. It was therefore all the more vital for England's security that the coastline of northern France and the Low Countries should provide bases, or at least footholds, from which to launch counter-attacks, as well as to conduct campaigns for the conquest or recovery of continental possessions.

It was often necessary for English vessels, attempting to intercept enemy fleets or convoys, to position themselves to windward of the approaching forces. Naval defence – such as it was – of the south coast of England was undertaken by the association of towns known, since the late twelfth century, as the Cinque Ports.[66] They had become part of an elaborate system of naval defence under the admirals of the eastern and western fleets by the early fourteenth century.[67] The five ports were Hastings, Dover, Hythe, Romney and Sandwich, to which the two 'ancient towns' of Winchelsea and Rye were added in the early thirteenth century. At the height of their power, the Liberty of the Cinque Ports included 39 satellite towns and villages, extending from Sussex to Essex. In return for the provision of ships, in the form of armed merchantmen, to the crown, they received extensive privileges. Yet this did not ensure their loyalty, nor did it prevent them indulging in piracy and raiding, sometimes directed against other English ports.[68] The ships which they sporadically provided were merchantmen and, with two notable exceptions – Richard I and Henry V – no English medieval king had a force of vessels specifically designed for naval warfare at his disposal. There was no permanent squadron, let alone a fleet, of professional, dedicated warships, unlike the galleys and other vessels maintained by Castile, Genoa, France, Portugal and Monaco.[69] It has recently been concluded that, for the naval historian, medieval England's greatest weakness was 'the lack of any reliable means of putting a force of warships at the disposal of the crown'.[70]

Ships were therefore considered by English monarchs and their counsellors to be essentially an ancillary to their primary aim: the defence of their continental possessions and, subsequently, the invasion of France, supported by allies in the Low Countries. English armies, as well as traders, depended upon fleets and convoys of (normally) requisitioned and armed merchantmen to transport them and their merchandise. The Channel was a mere 22 miles (33 km) wide at its narrowest point and voyages could be readily and, when the prevailing winds and tides were favourable, speedily undertaken. It could in effect be easier for the Anglo-Norman and Angevin kings to journey to, and communicate with, their continental possessions than with many parts of their English kingdom. While the sea passage from Dover to Wissant, just north of Boulogne, might take no more than a day, the overland journey to York or Durham could not be completed in less than three weeks – which was also far longer than the time taken for a sea voyage to Bordeaux. This could take no more than seven days, in optimum conditions and with favourable winds.[71] On 10 July 1442, for example, Thomas Beckington, Henry VI's secretary, sailed from Plymouth in the *Catherine* of Bayonne, arriving at Bordeaux on 16 July. The Channel crossing from Dover to Wissant was the shortest and most frequently used route.

In May 1286, an agreement was reached between Edward I and the men of both Dover and Wissant over transfretation costs and loading: each ship employed to transport the king and his retinue or army was to carry 24 horses' tonnage and different terms were set out for travel in times of peace, truce and war.[72] Although the sea passage to Aquitaine was frequently employed in times of war and tension with France, and for the carriage of armies, bulky merchandise and cargoes of wine, the overland route via Dover, Wissant, Paris, Poitiers and Angouleme or St-Jean d'Angely was often taken by the king-duke's administrators, clerks and messengers.[73] It had the merit of allowing them to deliver letters to, and to communicate with, the king-duke's representatives at the court of France and his proctors at the Paris Parlement. The total overland journey time from Westminster to Bordeaux, with favourable winds for the Channel crossing, was about 26 to 28 days. With the capture of Calais in 1347, the speed of communication between England, northern France and the Low Countries was considerably improved. In the 1530s, towards the end of English rule there, it was reported that news from Calais was 'with speed known in the Court' at Westminster, and that when a proclamation was made at Calais on a Saturday 'the King's Grace had word of it by 9 of the clock the Monday'.[74] Travelling post-haste, Thomas Howard, duke of Norfolk, 'scribbled in haste' from Amiens on Thursday 28 August 1533, at three in the afternoon, to the Lord Deputy at Calais telling him that he expected to arrive there, via Abbeville, by 12 noon the next day (Friday). He would then embark immediately for England as 'my going to the King doth require such diligence that, God willing, I will not tarry with you one half hour if the wind and tide may serve, trusting to be with his Highness on Saturday' (30 August). He in fact achieved his aim and reached London on that day, averaging over 60 miles per day between Lyon, where he had begun his journey, and Westminster.[75] This represented a one-day journey, with a favourable wind and tide, between Calais and London.

It is sometimes possible to calculate more or less exactly how long an exchange by correspondence between England and a continental dominion could take. On 16 October 1324, John Travers, constable of Bordeaux, sent a letter to Edward II, to which the king, a notoriously tardy correspondent, replied by letter from Cheshunt, dated 24 November of that year.[76] Yet the sea passage was not without its dangers. In 1120 Henry I had lost his only legitimate male heir in the White Ship disaster and the succession to the Anglo-Norman realm was thrown into jeopardy. It became a common practice to make and send multiple copies of letters 'on account of the dangers of the sea' and sealing processes could be dictated by the 'dangers of the roads'.[77] Sometimes closed or especially secret letters would be sealed with an inappropriate seal in order to disguise their contents. Dangers of interception of the diplomatic bag led Edward II and Edward III, for instance, to use the postal service provided by Italian merchant banking houses such as the Bardi for especially important correspondence. Thus, in May 1326, the Florentine firms of Bardi and Peruzzi were acting as agents and couriers for both the English crown and the Venetian republic. Letters patent of Edward II, relating to the settlement of a dispute over an 'affray' involving Venetian merchants at Southampton, were delivered by the Bardi and Peruzzi to the Doge who, in turn, ordered them to direct a copy of the letter to the republic.[78]

It was vital to keep open all lines of communication with the European mainland, and this south-eastwards and south-westwards orientation of the English kingdom after 1066 continued into the later Middle Ages, periodically and episodically offset by ventures into the Celtic lands. The subject island lordship of Ireland was also linked to England by the sea, and it has been justly observed that, by the early thirteenth century, 'the waters between Britain and Ireland, like the English Channel, had become an Anglo-French aristocratic highway'.[79] Despite the loss of Normandy and much of the rest of the Angevin dominions after 1204 and 1224, this remained the case. The sea and overland passages to Aquitaine had always to be kept open and constant diplomatic missions to and from both France and the Low Countries necessitated free passage of the 'narrow seas'.

England's 'off-shore island' position and status also had implications for the identity and character of the kingdom and its institutions. How far was England 'different' from continental Europe and to what extent can any sense of 'insularity' be detected there?

There was little doubt that the legacy of Anglo-Saxon kingship made England unique among both the Anglo-Norman and Angevin dominions. It was, above all, a kingdom – unlike the rest of the continental dominions which remained duchies, counties and other lordships largely within the kingdom of France. The regnal status of the Anglo-Norman monarchs in England conferred powers upon them, exercised within their kingdom, which they did not possess, by virtue of non-regal titles, overseas. In England they could levy a national tax – the geld; they could enforce the criminal law so that the king's writ ran in all parts of the kingdom, except where such powers had been specifically devolved upon lords with franchisal jurisdiction; and they could outlaw private war, prohibit baronial minting of currency and deny other rights possessed by Norman lords in the duchy of Normandy or county of Maine. But before 1340, the English crown's wearer was obliged to act not as king but as duke, count or other lord in his continental domains. The mere fact of conquest in 1066 had rendered England, in the first instance, a conquered 'colony' of the Norman dukes.[80] A Francocentric perspective would therefore make Normandy the 'metropole' and England the 'periphery' in the so-called Norman Empire.[81] At its inception, that Empire embodied a 'cross-Channel state', formed by 'the union of the adjacent heartlands of the Norman dukes and West Saxon kings'.[82] This had important strategic implications for the security of the English kingdom. The heartlands of the West Saxon kings became a conquered land, but that land had strong indigenous institutions, formed in part by conflict with other foreign invaders – the Danes. The kingdom was not yet the heartland of the new Norman dynasty and became essentially an annexe of the duchy. It provided a valuable reservoir of men and money with which to wage continental campaigns of an increasingly defensive kind.[83]

The wealth of conquered England fell into the hands of a Norman baronage, a lesser aristocracy and the Church. Endowment of Norman monasteries with English land by Anglo-Norman barons and knights became an important instrument of dispossession and colonization. The abbeys of Fécamp, Séez,

Bec, Holy Trinity at Caen and so forth became significant English landholders. The position of those Norman monasteries who held English land remained an issue until the dissolution and expropriation of those houses – the so-called 'alien priories' – in the later fourteenth and early fifteenth centuries.[84] Under subsequent Angevin rule after 1154 this Francocentricity of England's rulers became even more marked – until the *débâcle* of 1202–4 in Normandy served to check continental expansion along traditional lines. Angevin rule was not, initially, England-centred. Its only real power-centre lay with the ruler – surrounded, as he constantly was, by his itinerant court. It is all too easy to succumb to the temptation to impose a 'centralist' pattern on the political and governmental structures of this period. We need perhaps to concentrate on the idea of a polycentric administrative and fiscal apparatus, in which there was clearly transfer and exchange of both personnel and (to some extent) funds and resources across the Channel, but which retained a high level of provincial, local and seigneurial autonomy. Without observance of regional and tenurial characteristics (laws, customs, privileges, liberties, immunities) within the discrete territories there could be no effective rule and no durable empire.

Side by side with the Francocentric regime of Henry II, Richard I and John, however, a sense of English racial and ethnic identity developed which was, in part, a reaction to the prolonged and intensive preoccupation of these rulers with their continental dominions. Royal absences prompted the growth of offices and institutions which could function effectively in the king's absence.[85] Justiciarships, lieutenancies and vice-regal positions had of necessity to be employed in the government of the English kingdom. Even before 1154, English self-government was becoming more clearly visible – and there was little or no attempt to export English forms to the continental possessions. If anything, Norman and Angevin practices, urban franchises, 'assizes' and other judicial practices, may have influenced English developments. It has been suggested that the English common law could be seen as one of the western group of French customary laws.[86] But, beneath the surface of institutional life, there were also signs of a cultural shift whereby a sense of 'Englishness' began to characterize the middle and lower ranks of English society. Although often expressed in the Anglo-Norman form of the French language, this recognition of a vernacular culture and specific identity was in many ways an inevitable consequence of the Norman Conquest. As land became hereditary and was passed on from one generation to the next, a class of exclusively 'English' landholders arose, who held no territory in continental Europe. This was particularly marked among the lesser baronage, knighthood and free tenantry.[87] The political consequences of this tendency were clear for all to see in the events which led to John's downfall in 1215–16. Yet the tenacious determination of the crown to retain and, if possible, to recover, its lost French lands remained a feature of English relations with

Europe until the mid-thirteenth century. It was to be rekindled in the fourteenth and early fifteenth centuries under opportunist monarchs, but with a rather different strategy and political agenda. This book will trace those changes over a long period. We will now consider the origins, means of acquisition and nature of the 'empire' which the Angevin rulers both inherited and created between 1154 and 1204. What were the major issues and problems confronting them and how did they attempt to solve them?

2

The Angevin Empire and the Kingdom of France

As we have seen, the succession of Henry II to the throne of England in 1154 brought another essentially Francocentric dynasty to power.[1] Angevin kingship succeeded to the Anglo-Norman complex of territories which had been divided since the death of Henry I in 1135. An interrupted and broken succession was to some extent restored with the accession of Henry's grandson to both the English throne and the duchy of Normandy. The marriage of Henry's only surviving legitimate heir – the ex-empress Maud – to Geoffrey Plantagenet, count of Anjou, was to bring the lineage which had posed the most serious threats to the Anglo-Norman monarchy in its continental dominions to power over a much-enlarged polity. The re-creation and enlargement of the Norman Empire replaced the fragile regime of Stephen of Blois (1135–54) with a vast cross-Channel lordship, stretching from Normandy to Aquitaine and from Brittany to the Massif Central. The Anglo-Norman baronage was now joined by the nobilities of the other Angevin lands, all of them vassals of Henry II Plantagenet. These men – from Anjou, Touraine, Poitou, Limousin, Angoumois, Saintonge, Périgord, Aquitaine and Gascony – held little or no land in England, unlike many of their Norman peers and contemporaries.[2] The ultimate allegiance of many of them was, in theory, not to the Plantagenet ruler but to the Capetian crown of France. In many cases this feudal superiority was more apparent than real, and the Plantagenet king-duke-count in effect exercised a degree of pragmatic power over the lands and inhabitants of western France which excluded Capetian authority altogether.[3] But this duality of allegiance posed potentially significant problems for the Angevins. The implications of the potential clash between Angevin territorial lordship and Capetian claims to suzerainty were wide-ranging: they could not fail to influence the mutual relationships between the kings of England and their neighbours in Brittany, Flanders and other regions of the French kingdom. The English monarch was obliged to act in a number of different capacities and his behaviour towards the other great magnates of France could not ignore the fact that he was in effect one of their number, as well as the ruler of an independent and free-standing kingdom.[4]

How, if at all, did Angevin rule differ from that of the Anglo-Norman past? Did it build upon pre-existing tendencies under the Normans towards the 'Europeanization' of England? A study of the itineraries of the Angevin rulers

confirms their essentially Francocentric focus – under Henry II, the king spent
more time in his continental possessions than in his English kingdom, and
Richard I was an absentee, both on Crusade and in France, for the greater part of
his reign.[5] Preoccupation with affairs which were external to England encouraged
and furthered a number of tendencies within English government. The outward
orientation of Angevin power engendered a diplomatic archive, especially
under Richard and John, and the precociousness of English administrative
development and its record-keeping was in striking contrast to the relatively
tardy emergence of a *Trésor des Chartes* (royal archive) in Capetian France.[6]
The proliferation of both archival repositories and castle treasuries reflected
the itinerant and mobile style of Angevin government which was commented
upon by contemporaries, sometimes – as in the writings of the *curialis* Walter
Map – in distinctly unfavourable terms.[7] There is, however, an imbalance in the
surviving documentary evidence for Angevin government – in England, the
records of Chancery and Exchequer enable the historian to chart governmental,
administrative and financial activities in great detail, especially with the institution
of the great series of Chancery enrolments under Hubert Walter after 1199. For
the continental possessions the surviving evidence is far less plentiful and this
may sometimes give a distorted impression of the nature and scope of Angevin
administration there. Just because we do not possess records of the activities
of Plantagenet seneschals and other officers in Poitou or Aquitaine does not
necessarily mean that they were inactive or that the government of these regions
was 'chaotic' or 'underdeveloped'. Just because they did not account to the
English or Norman Exchequers does not mean that these territories were not
productive of revenue, nor were they 'feudal backwaters' which were in effect
ungovernable. The historian of the Angevin 'empire' has always to take account
of these fundamental problems in the sources.

Within the English kingdom, signs of divergence from the other Angevin
possessions were becoming more marked. Although its beginnings can be traced
back to the Anglo-Norman past, a growing sense of English identity among
landed society seems to have evolved more rapidly under the Angevins. 'During
the ... twelfth century', it has been argued, 'and at an accelerating pace, the sense
of a separate Norman or French identity among the ruling elites of England
wilted, to be replaced by a single, undifferentiated English identity.'[8] Recently it
has been argued that it was during the reign of Henry II that 'ethnic boundaries
finally broke down', and that the Church was a prime mover in cultural assimilation.[9] The 1170s appear to have witnessed the passing of the last vestiges of ethnic
distinctions. This sense of an English identity may well have been accelerated
by the Angevin succession. Few members of the continental Angevin nobilities
– outside the duchy of Normandy – also held land in England. There was no more
conquered English land to distribute, and such acquisitions as were made lay in

the Celtic regions, already the prey of existing Anglo-Norman families. Members of the Angevin baronial elite outside the duchy of Normandy formed no part of the English ruling elites. A sense of English identity was thus more likely to emerge among those families of middling rank in the landed hierarchy,[10] who held fiefs exclusively in England. An incipient division within the English ruling classes between those who held 'cross-Channel' lordships – often the greater families – and those whose landed endowments lay only in England and Ireland had begun to form. Some of the latter certainly had kinsmen in Normandy, but the formation of specifically 'English' branches of these Norman clans – such as the Mandevilles, Bassets or Harcourts – was clearly evident by the mid-twelfth century, especially among those of lesser baronial and knightly rank.[11] An English gentry was in the process of formation. It could be argued, therefore, that much of the impetus towards a sense of English identity during this period came from below. It was not espoused, nor was it imposed, by higher authority at this time because the Angevin rulers had little to gain – and potentially much to lose – from identification with an ideology which exclusively stressed their Englishness. Their interest lay in promoting and encouraging a sense of regnal, rather than ethnic, identity. As rulers of multiple and disparate peoples, and of vast dominions on the European mainland, it was essential for them to be regarded as continental princes whose *de facto* authority was evidently supported and, to a degree, bolstered by their regnal status and by the resources of their island kingdom. But their title to rule over their French territories in no way depended upon that status.

It was imperative for Henry II, Richard and John to present themselves to their continental vassals and subjects as immediate lords, conscious of the customs and privileges of a given region, rather than as suzerains whose authority might be exercised in a regal manner. They were regarded by those vassals very much as the counts of Champagne or Flanders were perceived by their own men.[12] In England, on the contrary, the authority of the monarch amounted in effect to sovereignty over the entire kingdom, and it was to a king rather than merely a lord that men paid homage and swore their oaths of fealty and personal loyalty. But the upper ranks of the 'English' baronage, and some lesser barons and knights, still held Norman lands and lordships right up to the *débacle* of 1204. This very fact conferred upon them a distinctive status and sense of separate identity. Cross-Channel, or trans-Channel, landholding served to sustain this sense. Their holdings in the heartlands of the Norman dynasty identified them as lords in the duchy, subject not to English law but to the *Coutume de Normandie*.[13] They shared a common 'French' culture and language, with strong links to continental Europe, both northern and southern. This meant that a former Norman or French identity in effect became an *Anglo*-French, rather than a specifically *English*, identity among the upper ranks of English society. It is therefore possible to witness the emergence of an Anglo-French court nobility in twelfth-century England, as in contemporary Scotland.[14]

The major difference between the Norman and Angevin empires lay in the much greater size and scale of the Angevin inheritance.[15] Its power-base and centre of political gravity was grounded not in Normandy – although the duchy was a valuable possession – but in west and south-west France. The heartlands of the dynasty lay in the Loire valley and in the vast southern inheritance of Eleanor of Aquitaine. Her great dowry of Poitou, Aquitaine and Gascony gave the whole complex a distinctly south-western orientation.[16] As Yves Renouard pointed out, however, the Angevins introduced a number of practices stemming from their Norman and western French inheritance into the South-west, such as the forms of urban government set out in the *Etablissements* of Rouen.[17] The 'assizes' of the region also derived from more northerly customs, and the *sénéchaussées* and *bailliages* of Poitou, Aquitaine and Gascony owed something to the institutional structures of Normandy, Anjou, Maine and Touraine.[18] The whole complex tended to look outwards, towards the sea and towards England. A continuous coastline lay in Angevin hands. From Bayonne, Bordeaux and La Rochelle to Nantes, Caen and Rouen, the coastal and river ports of the Angevin empire served to give some degree of unity to a network, or patchwork, of lands and lordships which have often been described as 'incoherent' or 'over-extended'. It has, however, never been clear what the optimum size for a twelfth-century political unit is deemed to be. Yet the concept of an 'empire' begs a number of important questions, and the consequences and implications of the English kingdom's place and function within this larger political grouping warrants further investigation. This was a French-centred and French-dominated society and culture, in which there was little or no room for vernacular writing, or other modes of expression, in the English language. This, as we shall see, remained the case for a long time. English identity at this period initially expressed itself in French – or in the Anglo-Norman forms of that tongue.

The 'Frenchness' of the Angevin rulers of England (1154–1216) and their continental inheritance has often been commented upon: there is no evidence, for example, that any of them spoke any English; nor, indeed that they needed to do so. Henry II was clearly conversant with the Anglo-Norman tongue, with the French of the Ile-de-France which became known as *francien*, and with the Provençal, or Occitan, language of the Languedoc.In his continental dominions he acted as a French prince, issuing written instruments according to essentially 'French' formulae and conventions. This continued into the reigns of his sons – in 1194, for instance, Richard I's treaty with Philip Augustus of France was entirely French in its diplomatic form.[19] The languages in which sentiments of 'English' identity were expressed – in narrative and imaginative literature, for example – remained Latin and French, in its Anglo-Norman form, in for instance, the

Brut, the works of Geoffrey of Monmouth and Wace. At the Plantagenet court, or courts, the French and Provençal-based literature of both epic (*chanson de geste*) and romance flourished, setting the court of Henry II and Eleanor of Aquitaine into a cultural context which was shared with other French principalities.[20] It was from the Anglo-Norman and Plantagenet households that the Arthurian legend emerged, and the influence of the secular, troubadour literature of Aquitaine and Provence was far more marked at the court of Henry II than at that of Louis VII. Clerks, minstrels, poets and performers of all kinds throve in this milieu and the revision of theses which accord automatic primacy to Capetian France in the culture of the twelfth century are now well under way.[21]

Yet it has been claimed that the Plantagenets were eclipsed and upstaged by the Capetians as cultural patrons and as royal propagandists. One purpose of that propaganda was to inculcate a sense of inferiority in rival dynasties. Twelfth-century royal France saw the rise of a Capetian ideology orchestrated by 'the sophisticated propaganda-machine based in Paris, a glittering centre of learning that the Angevin lands could not begin to rival, which promoted their royal status and the idea of France'.[22] It is certainly true that the evolution of the schools of Paris resulted in the creation of a *studium generale* which was to become the intellectual centre of northern Europe, if not of western Christendom, during the thirteenth century. The work of abbot Suger at St-Denis under Louis VI put that great monastery on the cultural and intellectual map for the rest of the Middle Ages. A tradition of triumphalist historical writing at St-Denis – in Latin and then, after 1279, in French – which was broadly eulogistic of the Capetian dynasty, began. The Latin chronicle of St-Denis was to give birth to the vernacular *Grandes Chroniques* in the thirteenth century.[23] There was no real equivalent of that chronicle in the Angevin lands, and the monastic writers who composed historical narratives under Henry II, Richard and John were more often critics than apologists of the regime. Yet Capetian power, unlike Angevin power, possessed more form than substance. Outside their demesne, confined largely to the Ile-de-France and Paris basin, the Capetians exercised very little real and tangible authority. The Angevins, on the contrary, were the direct and immediate lords of a vast array of territories, but possessed relatively little directly-held demesne, outside the royal forests, either in England or in their continental possessions. It was a very different style of monarchy, and the circumstances of the Angevin succession and inheritance need to be taken into account in order to explain its nature. The ideologies and mythologies of kingship took different forms in the two kingdoms. This had a direct influence upon the ways in which the two monarchies were regarded by their vassals and subjects; and by their European peers and contemporaries.

In 1154, Henry Plantagenet, count of Anjou, duke of Normandy and duke of Aquitaine, had succeeded to the English throne. His father, Geoffrey Plantagenet,

count of Anjou, had been the consort of the ex-empress Maud, after the death
of her first husband, the emperor Henry V, in 1125. Geoffrey had been knighted
in 1128 during an elaborate ceremony held at Rouen by Henry I of England and
Normandy, and a Norman–Angevin alliance was eventually cemented by the marriage with Maud. This was in effect the origin of the future Angevin empire. The
power of the house of Anjou threatened to eclipse that of the Norman dukes, and
in 1144 Geoffrey Plantagenet had taken Normandy. His authority was expressed
in many ways: not least in the monumental enamelled plaque (dated 1151–60),
made for his tomb in the cathedral of Le Mans which celebrated his deeds as a
warrior and giver of justice.[24] This was a dynasty which, especially when in alliance with other magnates, could pose real and serious threats to its neighbours.
Henry II thus inherited the power-base of the house of Anjou in western France,
with its spiritual home at the abbey of Fontevrault where he was to be buried in
1189. His English kingdom, inherited from his grandfather and his mother (for
Geoffrey Plantagenet had no claim on the English throne), was not the centre of
gravity of his dominions. That lay between Tours and Poitiers. Despite his Anglo-
Norman parentage and affiliations, this was a ruler who was just as foreign to
England as his forebears had been. His itinerary is revealing.[25] Transfretation in
both directions – across the English Channel – was a constant feature of his reign.
Continental campaigns, the need to be seen among his vassals and to hold full
court at specific times and places, meant that the king–duke–count ruled over a
polycentric polity. There was no true 'capital' of the Angevin empire and no good
reason why there should have been one. Each major lordship and region had
its power centres and it was incumbent on the ruler to visit them, summoning
his vassals to him in order to exchange oaths and transact all kinds of business.
The court therefore met throughout the Angevin dominions, from Woodstock
and Clarendon to Angers and Tours. This peripatetic regime imparted a certain
character to Angevin government. Although the Capetians were also itinerant
rulers, their area of circulation was more restricted and they tended to confine
themselves to the safe haven of their demesne. No Capetian king had been as far
as Toulouse before the reign of Louis VII. The first two Angevins, on the contrary,
journeyed far and wide and it was in the southern parts of his inheritance – in the
Limousin – that Richard I met his death at Chalus in 1199. Angevin government
was one of roads, rivers and sea-passages.

The Angevins, unlike their Capetian rivals, have sometimes been thought not
to have created an ideology or mythology of their own which might sustain and
enhance their rule. One reason for the disintegration of the Angevin empire (or
Anglo-Norman realm) after 1204, it has been argued, was the relative lack of a
Plantagenet ideology in the face of Capetian propaganda under Philip Augustus.[26]
Yet the Angevin's dynastic saga combined a number of foundation myths and
pseudo-historical accounts of their origins and genealogical descent.[27] They laid

claim to thaumaturgic, healing powers, just as their Capetian contemporaries did, but the style of their rule was essentially different. The elevated stance of the sacral Capetian monarch was not for them. Angevin kingship and lordship, at its best, tended to stress the more companionable, open-handed, convivial nature of rulership. Henry II's initial liking for Thomas Becket stemmed in part from the chancellor's willing acceptance of the styles of behaviour found in Henry's household and his apparent tolerance at that stage of the peccadilloes of its members.[28] In many ways, the Angevin courts and households represented and celebrated secular culture, while the Capetians were concerned to present themselves as sacred – though accessible – kings, often in apparently close alliance with the clergy. The way towards Louis IX's religiosity was well paved by his predecessors. There was a distance between them and even their greatest vassals and subjects, and the Capetian court, despite its propaganda, was not always the most convivial or lively of places. In their attitudes towards such essentially gregarious and convivial events as the court feast, often accompanied by tournaments, the two dynasties also differed. While Henry II and Richard I had few, if any, objections to the tournament – in an attempt to exercise some degree of control over it Richard licensed tournament sites in his English kingdom in 1194 – the Capetian kings of France issued ordinances prohibiting that most chivalric of encounters. It was too closely linked to private war, and had the ban of the Church upon it. No Capetian participated in the dangerous sport. Some of the most accomplished frequenters of tournaments and jousts were thus to be found in the Angevin lands, and the career of William Marshal provides excellent evidence.[29] The Angevin partnership between ruler and secular vassals paralleled that between the Capetians and the higher clergy, but it was to break down in the reign of John.

Why, then, did the Angevin empire disintegrate into fragments between 1204 and 1242? Internal divisions had always been apparent but they were the stuff of twelfth-century family politics. Multiple loyalties were the norm for the political society of the age. External forces were, however, also at work. The fragmentation of the inheritance which Henry II had brought to his dynasty carried profound implications for the kingdom of England, both in terms of its internal as well as external condition. Equally profound implications for the subsequent history of relations with Capetian France also flowed from these events. Between 1201 and 1204, a crisis erupted in the continental dominions of the Angevin dynasty which was, in the longer term, to lead to the loss of the greater part of those dominions. The appeals launched by the Lusignans, the greatest barons of the county of Poitou, against their king-count, John of England, were received in the court of Philip Augustus of France and the confiscation of John's major French fief, the duchy of Normandy, was decreed. Angevin resistance, and John's defiance of Philip, as his overlord, gave a pretext to the latter to reduce the recalcitrant vassal's duchy to obedience by armed force. It is the results, rather than the causes, of the loss of Normandy which concern us here.[30] Some of John's non-English subjects refused to pay homage to Philip Augustus – above all, the inhabitants of the Channel Islands, who retained their loyalty to the English crown. But first, and most obviously, the loss of Normandy spelt the end of cross-Channel landholding by the Anglo-Norman baronage.[31] Only the Norman monasteries managed to retain their English lands, while the cross-Channel landholding aristocracy were forced by Philip Augustus to make a decisive choice.[32] Either they were to acknowledge their homage and fealty to him for their Norman fiefs; or they were to opt for their English lands, abandoning their Norman holdings. Allegiance to both overlords was not feasible, although there were a few exceptions to this rule. It was not surprising that those who held more land and income in Normandy entered Philip's direct homage, while those whose lordships lay primarily in England chose John – some with great reluctance – as their lord. William Marshal (d. 1219) was almost alone in securing an agreement with Philip Augustus whereby he retained his Norman lands of Orbec and Longueville but remained a liegeman and subject of John for his earldom of Pembroke and other English lordships. There may have been a few others, but they were very few, and in 1244 a definitive end to the practice was decreed by Louis IX. But, for the majority of the Anglo-Norman baronage and knightly class, the loss of the duchy of Normandy produced a tenurial crisis. It could only lead, in the long term, to the rise of a far greater sense of anglocentricity and identification with their English (and Irish) holdings among most of them.

Second, the 'manifest disinheritance' of John in 1204 could not fail to change the configuration and balance of the Angevin empire and its constituent territories. For the first time since the accession of Henry II in 1154, the continental possessions of the ruling house were not geographically adjacent to their English kingdom. No longer were the 'adjacent heartlands' of the Norman dukes and English kings joined together in a cross-Channel state divided only by a relatively narrow stretch of water.[33] If Normandy were not recovered, this could only lead to a reorientation and re-alignment of the remaining Angevin dominions towards the south. Hence John's apparent determination to regain his Norman inheritance, and the means whereby he did so were, in part, to engender a crisis of similar if not greater proportions in England. The close connections between the south coast ports of England and the Norman ports were severely disrupted and the economic disadvantages of the exercise of Capetian lordship over the duchy, especially French control of the Seine estuary, redounded to their disfavour. The conquest of Normandy gave Philip Augustus a direct outlet to the sea – Paris was no longer a land-locked city, cut off from the maritime trade routes of Northern Europe by the mere fact of Angevin lordship and its toll-taking activities in Normandy. In economic terms alone, it was a valuable acquisition.

What were the effects of the loss of Normandy on the rest of the Angevin dominions? Its consequences for England are well-known: the imposition of harsh fiscal measures for its recovery, and a significant increase in the manipulation and exploitation of royal rights and patronage, under both John and his successor, Henry III. Sweeping claims have been made for the long-term effects of the crisis. It could be said to have played a substantial part in initiating a sequence of events which was to lead to the concession of Magna Carta in 1215. Powicke could conclude that:

> after the annexation Normandy became a province. As a result of the separation, England became a kingdom. The loss of Normandy hastened the two-fold development of the English state. The king strengthened his position as the source of justice; the people, under the leadership of the baronage, gradually acquired the power of making the law.[34]

It could be argued that England was already 'a kingdom' long before 1204, and that many other reasons might be adduced for the developments in justice and law-making which Powicke identified. The crucial significance of the loss of Normandy lay largely in the increasingly southward gravitation of Angevin power in the continental dominions, and in the admittedly gradual development of an anglocentric monarchy, baronage and knightly class in England. This tendency to concentrate upon the south-western inheritance of the Plantagenets was to characterize English relations with France until the reign of Henry V. It has been claimed that 'Angevin supremacy ... [was] a shadow of its former self' after 1204.[35] But this may exaggerate and accelerate the steady eclipse of John's and Henry III's authority unduly: the attempted recovery of lost territory, and the retention of existing lands, remained their primary concern until 1259. In this process, the more southerly lordships of the Plantagenets assumed even greater significance. The major theatre of Anglo-French war, after John had defied Philip Augustus and renounced his homage, was the county of Poitou. With the *de facto* loss of Normandy, Maine, Anjou and Touraine, Poitou became the northernmost power-base of the Plantagenets in France. Until its final loss in 1242, Poitou formed the main area of warfare between Henry III, Louis VIII and Louis IX.[36] It was not to experience direct Plantagenet lordship again, between 1362 and 1372, until the reign of Edward III. It was a well-fortified and defended region, studded with both comital and seigneurial fortresses, many of them of advanced design.[37] The southward orientation of the Angevin lands was therefore accentuated and furthered by the loss of Normandy. Aquitaine and Gascony assumed a more vital and critical role in the maintenance of a continental presence by the king-dukes and, with the sole exception of the acquisition of the county of Ponthieu in northern France in 1279 this tendency, as we shall see, continued up to the reign of Edward III.

The loss of Normandy was followed by the loss of Poitou. In 1224, La Rochelle fell to the French. Until that date much of the wine imported from France into England had been transported via La Rochelle and much of it was in fact Poitevin, Limousin and Angoumois. After that date, the economic privileges enjoyed by these regions in the trade with England disappeared. The southward shift of economic as well as political gravity within the continental dominions of the Plantagenet monarchy was furthered by this development. Economically, the future now lay with Aquitaine and Gascony, and especially with the city of Bordeaux as the major centre of the trade in wine.[38] The hinterland of Bordeaux, and the so-called *haut pays*, stretching as far east and south as Quercy and the Toulousain, now both produced and marketed the greater part of the wine exported to England. As we shall see, this economic fact tended to strengthen the remaining links between the kingdom of England and the residual continental possessions of the crown. England was now divided from those continental territories not only by the sea, but by the greater part of northern and western France. The implications of this tendency for the emergence of a more anglocentric 'empire' were far-reaching. Without strong-points, bases and entrepots in Normandy, Brittany, Anjou or Poitou, the Plantagenet regime was bound to operate in a different manner from its Norman and Angevin predecessors. French occupation of Poitou led to the dispossession of those Poitevin lords who had either remained loyal to the Plantagenet cause or supported the rebellion of Hugh of Lusignan, count of La Marche, against the Capetians in 1242. Some of them became exiles in England, closely linked by kinship and other ties to the ruling house.[39] The Poitevin/Lusignan presence in England under Henry III was represented by such clans as the Valençe, and some of them precipitated the unleashing of a tide of hostility towards 'aliens'. English xenophobia was easily stimulated and a more marked sense of 'English' identity among the middle ranks of English landed and urban society may be detected at this time.[40] Henry III's alleged favouritism towards them led to the downfall of some 'alien' families, but (as will be seen) their presence was by no means completely eliminated. They joined Henry's Savoyard relatives as objects and targets of hostility for, it was claimed, they were displacing the king's 'natural' counsellors and receiving undue shares of royal patronage. The final loss of Poitou in 1242 was a severe blow to Plantagenet authority and prestige among European powers and made the retention of the last remaining continental dominion – the duchy of Aquitaine – all the more pressing an objective for Henry III's government.

Between the confiscation of Normandy in the spring of 1202 and the final fall of Poitou in 1242, all feudal relations between England and France had been suspended. This situation was to be continued until the agreement reached at Paris between Henry and Louis IX in 1259. Until that date, Henry was not a Capetian vassal, having renounced his homage, thus permitting independent action in the duchy of Aquitaine. The stormy and troubled lieutenancy there of Simon de Montfort strove to retain as much authority over the duchy as was compatible with the loyalties of its inhabitants. But the treaty of Paris (1259) was to change this state of war, followed by armed truce, into an *entente* between the rulers of France and England that was to last until 1294. The acknowledgement of French sovereignty, which the treaty entailed, endorsed and formalized the practice of Gascon appeals to Louis IX's court at Paris. This was by no means a unique situation, as other French peers and princes – the counts of Flanders, dukes of Burgundy or counts of Champagne – found themselves in similar positions. After 1259, the king-duke of Aquitaine was not even a *de facto* source of legitimate supreme authority in his duchy. It became imperative, especially after the succession of Henry III's heir, Edward I – who had not initially consented to the treaty – to find ways and means whereby the worst and most damaging implications and effects of the liege homage stipulated in the agreement could be averted. The Gascon issue posed many problems to those Plantagenet officers responsible for the conduct and negotiation of Gascon affairs. One of them could write (in 1314): 'for those embarking [on a voyage] on this great sea, God alone determines its beginning, steers its course, and conducts it to the end. Gascon business is rightly called a great sea, full of shipwrecks, with no safe haven.'[41] The effects of this 'renunciation' by Henry III of his title to all remaining Angevin lands bar Aquitaine had many ramifications. First, there was a marked and increasing emphasis on the inseparability of both Aquitaine and Ireland from the English crown. As we shall see, in 1252 the annexation of the duchy to the English crown had been secured.[42] The practice then developed of creating what was in effect an *apanage* for a close relative of the monarch, such as the Lord Edward, to be held for a term of years. This looked back to Henry II's custom of endowing his sons with parts of the Angevin inheritance, and forward to Edward III's creation of a principality of Aquitaine for the Black Prince.

It could also pose problems of power-distribution and the potential growth of alternative power-centres. Simon de Montfort's regime in Aquitaine in some ways demonstrated the potential dangers of endowing a great magnate with such a degree of vice-regal authority. It was hardly surprising that the quasi-*apanagiste* policy subsequently adopted by both Henry III (in favour of the Lord Edward) and Edward himself, as king-duke, should insist that only the king-duke's eldest surviving son should act in this manner on a long-term basis. Edward adopted a very similar practice in Wales, giving the conquered principality to his eldest male heir, and therefore heir-apparent to the throne. The risks of installing a rival source of authority, around which dissent and discontent might gather, were too great, and even the king-duke's heir was required to acknowledge the superiority of his father. This remained the practice into the reigns of Edward III and Henry IV. Granting Aquitaine as an *apanage* to John of Gaunt, for example, who was not his eldest surviving son, cost Richard II dearly in terms of Gascon disaffection. But for most of the period of English rule, tenure by a quasi-viceroy of the duchy of Aquitaine did not pose any perceptible threat to the security of the reigning monarch. The king-duke's ordinary representatives there – the lieutenants and seneschals – had more than enough to do simply maintaining their authority and were, in any case, never appointed for periods long enough for a viable focus of opposition to form. But in the territorially much-reduced Angevin dominions after 1259, continuance of a Plantagenet presence now obliged the king-dukes and their officers to recognize, but attempt to limit, the sovereignty of the Capetian crown. If English rulers were to continue to hold any part of their continental inheritance after its dismemberment, they had to concentrate their attention and efforts upon what survived, namely Aquitaine. It is to that duchy, and its nature and role in power-politics, that we must now turn.

3

Aquitaine and the French Wars

An early fourteenth-century description of the lordships held by the king of England as duke of Aquitaine in south-west France, composed at the abbey of St Seurin at Bordeaux, left little doubt about their substantial and wide-ranging nature.[1] Apart from what had recently been lost to the north of the river Dordogne, the king-duke was thought to be in rightful possession of all the land as far south as the Pyrenees and as far east as the river Garonne. As it stood in *c.* 1303, the king-duke's dominion broadly coincided with the territorial limits of the ancient duchy of Gascony, before its fusion with the duchy of Aquitaine proper, in 1063.[2] This was not the 'coastal strip' to which, it is sometimes alleged, the Plantagenet dominions had been reduced by the early fourteenth century. On the contrary, it consisted of two archbishoprics, nine bishoprics, four comtés, and 15 vicomtés. The Anglo-Gascon connection stemmed from a twelfth-century dynastic acquisition through marriage – the duchy, unlike Ireland or Wales, was a legitimate inheritance, not the product of imperialist conquest and occupation. It has been justly said that 'the habit which English historical atlases have of colouring the king-duke [of Aquitaine's] lands red, as though they were part of some medieval British Empire, gives a very wrong impression'.[3] A common feature of popular historical writing, especially in France, is the notion that an 'English occupation' or 'English domination' of the south-west took place during the Middle Ages.[4] In the mid-fifteenth century, the duchy of Aquitaine was therefore 'liberated' by the French, it is claimed, from the 'English yoke'. Nothing could be further from the truth. The Gascons did not consider themselves to be 'liberated' from anything in 1453, least of all from some imagined servitude to their English masters. But a teleological, deterministic approach of this kind to French history has rendered it more or less axiomatic that the inexorable onward march of the unitary nation-state should be mythologized in this way.

Although the kings of England might also lay claim to the duchy of Normandy, their conquest and occupation of that province (only undertaken in the fifteenth century) bore little resemblance to the regime that was already in place in south-west France. Normandy was, to some degree, 'colonized' by the English under Henry V. Aquitaine did not have to be conquered, nor colonized, by him for it to remain united with the English crown. Is there, therefore, any evidence for the 'colonial' status of Aquitaine? A good, popular work on its history under English

rule by Margaret Wade Labarge entitled *Gascony, England's First Colony, 1204–1453*
appeared in 1980. It may well be true that, in the duchy of Aquitaine, 'England
experimented for the first time with the government of an overseas possession
where it was essential to keep the loyalty and support of its inhabitants'.[5] But that
did not make it a colony. The duchy clearly does *not* fall easily into the category
of 'English colonies beyond England', exemplified by Wales, Ireland and the Pale
around Calais. It ranks as a lordship, or dominion, rather than a colony. There
is no evidence for the purposeful creation of a colonial body of 'Englishry', as in
Wales, Ireland or Calais, with their populations of planted English settlers. The
lack of any marked English influence on Gascon institutions was striking, and
there was little evidence there for the development of customs and usages which
were not to be found in other parts of western and southern France. Institutional
parallels can more plausibly be drawn between Aquitaine and the other great fiefs
or principalities of France: Burgundy, Artois, Flanders or Brittany.

Nor is there much evidence, in Aquitaine, for an agenda of occupation,
settlement or 'centralization'. The relative lack of English settlement, and the
relatively short terms served by the principal English administrators in the
duchy, meant that those born in England remained foreigners and expatriates
there, as they did in India at a much later date. There was a tiny minority of
'Englishmen' who held lands and goods in Aquitaine. Examples can be found
at Bordeaux, or among occasional English residents elsewhere, such as William
of Norwich, *anglicus*, burgess of St-Jean d'Angély, who held 'houses, lands and
vines and other goods' in that northernmost point of the duchy in *c.* 1327.[6]
This rendered it, again, quite unlike Calais, or parts of occupied Normandy and
Lancastrian France in the fifteenth century. The sheer distance between England
and Aquitaine had always to be reckoned with: England's defensively effective
'moat' was in fact at its widest point between Plymouth and Brest. The Bay of
Biscay and the Gironde estuary were some days' sailing time from the Channel
and the Western Approaches. The Gascon ports and figurative 'barbicans' were
very distant outworks indeed of England's defensive system, in so far as they
played any role in that system. In an age in which, unlike the nineteenth century,
science had not yet annihilated distance, the government and administration of
these more remote and distant overseas territories had necessarily to be adjusted
to take account of long delays and sluggish rates of response. The journey from
Westminster to Bordeaux, averaging 28 or so days overland, was roughly equal
to that from London to Bombay by sea after the opening of the Suez Canal in
1869.[7] It was only with the introduction of the electric telegraph, followed by
cable and wireless telegraphy after 1870, that communications within the British
Empire were transformed.[8] It was extremely difficult before that date to achieve
any degree of unity, whether material or cultural, between the discrete parts of
an imperial network of territories. This, as we have already seen, necessitated

considerable devolution of authority and decision-making to the king-duke's representatives in the duchy of Aquitaine.

The rise of a more anglocentric, Westminster-based English polity in the course of the thirteenth and fourteenth centuries has been a common theme in recent historical writing, witnessed by the work of Rees Davies, Mark Ormrod and Michael Prestwich. In the sphere of fiscal and financial administration, much has been made, for example, of the question of accountability for receipts and expenses to the Westminster exchequer, especially in the later years of Edward I. This has been considered as one means whereby a measure of centralization, focused on Westminster, was applied to the continental possessions of the English crown. But was this a truly centralizing policy or mere pragmatism? The creation of an apparently more secure and unitary financial administration in Aquitaine began with the setting up, under the Lord Edward's lieutenancy in October 1255 of an embryonic exchequer at Bordeaux. This was soon to be superseded by the office of constable of Bordeaux as the major financial institution of the duchy by 1270.[9] The constable, performing duties similar to those discharged by the constables and castellans of castles (and castle treasuries) in thirteenth-century England, rendered account – at Bordeaux – at the end of his term of office. But the erratic and unsatisfactory nature of this arrangement led to Edward I's decision, taken at the post-Easter Parliament of 1293, that 'henceforth, every year, once per year, the accounts of Gascony and Ireland shall be rendered by the constable of Bordeaux and the Treasurer of Ireland at the English Exchequer, and audited there by the Treasurer and Barons'.[10]

This measure was intended to put the finances of the duchy of Aquitaine on to a basis comparable with those of Ireland, North and South Wales and (temporarily) Scotland, where exchequers at Dublin, Caernarfon, Carmarthen and Berwick were accountable to the 'parent' institution at Westminster.[11] The Berwick exchequer, established in March 1297, was to follow the practices of the Westminster exchequer exactly, according to Edward I's wishes: 'the king's will is that the same order, in every matter, which is in his exchequer at Westminster shall henceforth be observed in his exchequer at Berwick' ['voluntas ipsius regis existit quod idem ordo per omnia qui est in scaccario suo Westmonasterii in dicto scaccario suo Berewici de caetero habeatur'].[12] This made good administrative sense. Although the order of 1293 concerning Gascon finances met an immediate need, its effectiveness might be questioned. The constable at the time – Master Robert de Leysseth – was soon to lose all his books and papers as a result of the French occupation of the duchy in 1294, and was still petitioning Edward II for respite from pursuit by the Exchequer in the Parliament of 1314–15.[13] Subsequent constables of Bordeaux were, however, required to present themselves and their accounts once per year at the Exchequer, although many evidently did not do so. The rendering of accounts at Westminster tended, as before, to fall at the end of each constable's term of office. It was a pragmatic means whereby some measure of supervision and control was attempted over the finances of a distant territory. But the practice of local receipt and accounting did not, and could not, cease: one function of the constable's subordinate – the controller of Bordeaux, first mentioned in 1280 – was to oversee and record the revenue from the all-important customs levied on wine and other goods at Bordeaux, as well as the receipts and expenses of lesser officers in the duchy. He, just like the controller under the chamberlains of North Wales after 1284, kept the 'counter-roll' on which all of the constable's transactions were recorded, and which played an essential part in the final accounting procedure.[14]

The latter part of the thirteenth century witnessed a number of attempts to render the Gascon dominions of the English crown as free as possible from interference by the Capetian monarchy of France. This freedom would be furthered by financial autonomy. It was necessary to create local and regional receipts, accounting-offices and financial officers in the duchy, such as the constables and controllers of Bordeaux. The ordinances made for the government of Aquitaine by Edward I in 1289 thus emphasized the accountability of local officers – sub-seneschals, prévôts, bayles, castellans and others – not to the Westminster exchequer but to the constable and controller of Bordeaux. Their accounts were to be presented and audited in the castle of the Ombrière at Bordeaux at fixed terms of the year. Each bailliage was to have a clerk or scribe who was to be qualified as a public notary, while the controller at Bordeaux was to employ two clerks competent in the drawing up and transcribing of accounts.[15] Distant and remote dominions could only be effectively governed and administered by delegated authority on the spot. The evident and apparent need to gain some degree of overview of the crown's finances from the mid-thirteenth century onwards, as has been suggested, could – in part – be related to the use of Gascon, Irish and Welsh revenues by the English crown as securities for large loans (e.g. from Italian banking houses). There was certainly a need for an 'integrated system of accounting … if the resources of the peripheries were to be used to repay the debts of the core'.[16] But this hardly represented a surrender of 'peripheral' revenues to Italian merchant bankers such as the Riccardi, Frescobaldi or Bardi. Such practices were also applied to many other sources of revenue, including the English customs, upon which loans were constantly assigned for repayment. The 'peripheries', such as Aquitaine, were also responsible for the repayment of their own debts, as any analysis of a constable of Bordeaux's account reveals.[17] No tallies of assignment were kept in the Ombrière at Bordeaux (unlike the English exchequer) but plenty of warrants, quittances, receipts and vouchers, which were subsequently totalled and summarized in the enrolled accounts, survive. These were ultimately audited, often very tardily, following the expiry of the accounting officer's term of office, at Westminster.

Aquitaine therefore enjoyed the fiscal status of a relatively autonomous province within the complex of Plantagenet lands bordered by other lordships technically owing allegiance to the French crown. It could also produce a surplus. The wine trade and the carrying trade proved profitable not only to the regime, by means of customs and tolls, but to individuals among the wine-growers, middlemen, vintners, ship-owners and mariners whose livelihood depended upon those trades. It has been estimated, for example, that a return of something approaching 100 per cent per annum on capital could be gained from the Southampton–Bordeaux trade in the early fourteenth century. Even in the less prosperous, and more risky, years later in the century, the building costs of a Southampton ship might be fully recovered in two or three voyages to Aquitaine, that is, within a year or less.[18] The trade in wine and its shipping was a very lucrative one. In 1308–9, the export of wine from Bordeaux attained its highest recorded figure in the Middle Ages, reaching 102,000 tuns paying customs duty there.[19] An average annual total of 83,000 tuns of wine was exported between 1305 and 1336.[20] Similarly, an estimate of revenues derived by the English crown from the duchy in 1324 gave a clear receipt of £13,000 st., surpassing the annual return from the English shires by over £1000 st.[21] In 1306–7, revenues from the duchy totalled £17,000 st., of which almost half derived from Bordeaux and the Bordelais. In turn, almost 80 per cent of the latter stemmed from the customs levied there.[22] Aquitaine was certainly worth defending and fighting for in economic terms alone. Substantial payments were derived from producers, middlemen and suppliers, both within the duchy and outside its immediate frontiers, while corn, tin, timber, furs, cloth, leather and other commodities were lucratively exported from England. Commercial reciprocity, moreover, rather than colonial exploitation, would better characterize the Anglo-Gascon union. As we saw earlier, the Gascon trade ranked highly among the priorities of English ports. There was a very active commerce between the ports of the West Country, Bristol, Southampton, London and Bordeaux. Bayonne – unlike Bordeaux – was a ship-building and ship-owning centre, playing a major role in the carrying trade, especially in wine, between Aquitaine and England. It was often listed along with the Cinque Ports, despite its ongoing rivalry with them, in petitions representing the interests of England's maritime traders.[23] The relative prosperity of the region also meant that, in the last quarter of the thirteenth century, it could become the object of others' acquisitive attentions. By making the issue of Aquitaine a *casus belli*, Philip the Fair of France was to take Anglo-French relations to the brink of war, and over the brink, in the 1290s. In 1294, England was to come very close to losing its residual continental possessions for ever.

That year saw the outbreak of an Anglo-French war, the first since the defeat of Henry III in Poitou just over 50 years earlier. It was in many ways a product of the terms of the treaty of Paris in 1259. The issue of appeals to the French crown from some of the Gascon subjects of the Plantagenet king-duke, and the allegedly outrageous behaviour of others among his subjects towards the sovereignty of France and its representatives, lay at the heart of the conflict. The Capetian monarchy was flexing its muscles against its greatest vassals – the count of Flanders as well as the duke of Aquitaine – and, bolstered by the propaganda of its lawyers and polemicists as well as by the self-interest of others among the great magnates, was determinedly on the offensive. The consequences of the war (1294–1303) between Edward I and Philip the Fair continued to reverberate until the outbreak of the Hundred Years War in 1337. It could be claimed that a new era in Anglo-French relations began at that time. On a wider European stage, many other powers became embroiled, or at least implicated, in the Anglo-French conflict. Flanders, Scotland, the German Empire and the Iberian kingdoms were drawn into the imbroglio. The following decades witnessed a sequence of con-flictual and increasingly confrontational episodes which pitted the Plantagenets against both the Capetians and, after 1328, their Valois successors. Despite accom-modations and intermarriages between the dynasties, fundamental irritants continued to influence relations, and the situation in Aquitaine continued to promote tension between the two monarchies. Yet both powers had to work out a *modus vivendi*. There were many means of attempting to keep the peace. Legal process, diplomacy, arbitration, mediation and what might be called 'sociability' all contributed to reducing the heat generated by such issues as frontier disputes, and by the consequences of a disinclination to perform homage on the English side, or to discharge obligations such as redressing grievances on the French. In these processes, the role of intermediaries between England and France was crucial. As we have seen, these go-betweens were drawn from various classes and categories: at the top, the popes and cardinals played mediating roles, while at lower levels, clerks, nobles, knights and other members of the courts and households of both rulers played a vital part. Much has been written about Anglo-French conflict at this time, but there is also evidence of strenuous efforts to keep the peace and preserve amicable relations between the two powers, often initiated and promoted by those in the immediate entourages of the rulers.

In many respects, the 1290s formed a watershed in the process whereby *entente* between England and France gradually turned sour, towards a more hostile stance; or rather, towards a resumption of the hostility which had been evident in the period before 1259. In 1294, neither side was anticipating a long-drawn-out conflict – yet no Anglo-French peace treaty was made until 1303; and a second conflict erupted in 1324–5. Neither side could in effect afford to go to war and sustain that war for any appreciable length of time.[24] The costs of protracted warfare were prohibitively high and they were, in part, met from the human and material resources of the areas – Flanders and Aquitaine – in which most of the fighting took place. One of those regions had, in the course of the thirteenth century, become more closely linked to the English crown. Henry III's annexation of the duchy of Aquitaine as a personal fief to the ruler of the kingdom of England in 1252 ensured that it became part of the inseparable and inalienable inheritance of the Plantagenets and that it could not be held by anyone other than the king himself, as duke, or by his eldest son. On 27 April 1252, Henry had conferred the duchy on his son, the Lord Edward, to be held inalienably from him during his lifetime, but indissolubly linked in perpetuity to the wearers of the English crown. The 'land of Gascony' and the isle of Oléron were given to Edward and his heirs, 'saving to the king the allegiance [*lyjancia*] of the same ... provided that the said Edward would not alienate them from the crown, but that they shall always be united thereto'.[25] On 8 June 1252, Henry confirmed the grant and addressed copies of the charter to a number of Gascon lords, as well as the towns of Bordeaux, Dax, St Sever, Bayonne, La Réole and Bazas.[26] The prohibition on alienation was never revoked. Aquitaine had become part of the king-duke's demesne, never to be separated from his inheritance.

Beside this increasing emphasis on inalienability, the mid-thirteenth century witnessed the embryonic beginnings of a tendency to 'centralize' and concentrate overall responsibility for government, and for the administration of both justice and finance, in one place, each under a single officer within each of the remaining continental possessions of the English crown. Yet how far did 'centralizing' tendencies (if they existed) under Edward I, Edward II and Edward III change the position of the continental possessions (Aquitaine and, after 1279, Ponthieu) within the Plantagenet dominions? Did the English 'state' resemble a 'phenomenon that could transcend the boundaries of the kingdom of England and genuinely integrate the dependencies of the crown into a cohesive unit'?[27] The conquest of Wales (1282–4) and the further integration of Ireland into the English polity certainly expanded the borders and the scope of English authority. The 'anglicization', with its attendant colonization, of the British Isles between the late eleventh and early fourteenth centuries has recently attracted considerable attention from historians.[28] Edward I's reign has been said to have witnessed an 'English take-over of the British Isles' – however short-lived that 'empire' may have been.[29] By the early fourteenth century, for example, the Celtic areas were expected to contribute to the general war effort against the French in Aquitaine. The wrongs allegedly inflicted by the French on Edward II were to be publicly proclaimed not only in Aquitaine itself, but also in Wales and Ireland. An English council memorandum dating from the autumn or winter of 1324 declared that: 'soient les choses declarees par decea la mier en Gales et en Irlande a la fin qe tut homme se adresse de bon corage de aider au roi en sa bone querele' ['matters should be proclaimed on this side of the sea in Wales and Ireland so that everyone should apply themselves with good heart to assist the king in his just quarrel'].[30] It was thought that as 'nothing can be done of which the people do not have knowledge', the king's cause should be explained to them, and the more recalcitrant among the Welsh and Irish should be rebuked for their 'negligence' and reminded that they could be accused of aiding in the 'disinheritance of the king and his crown'. The signs of the emergence of, at least, the rhetoric of a more fully-integrated English 'state' appear, on the surface, to be visible.

It has therefore been argued that the 'pragmatic but aggressive expansionism to which Edward I and Edward III committed the kingdom of England ... created a fundamentally new political geography of empire in the form of a great arc radiating out from the emergent capital at Westminster to incorporate the whole of the British Isles and significant parts of northern and south-western France'.[31] Following this interpretation, the map of that 'great arc' could again, as was the later British Empire in school atlases, be colour-coded in red. It looks like a re-creation of the Angevin empire, but with its centre of gravity firmly located in England. It is tempting to see this new 'political geography of empire' in a quasi-Napoleonic light. Analogies might be found with later developments, such as the creation of French administrative *départements* in the colonial possessions of the later French state, or the incorporation of dominions and dependencies into the British Empire. Yet it is not clear that a degree of 'centralization' of this kind was either feasible or desirable in the later Middle Ages, especially for the continental possessions of the English crown. We have seen how financial matters were necessarily devolved and locally administered in Aquitaine.[32] Measures of financial supervision, control and accountancy can be compared with other forms of administration. There was an evident and ever-present need for measures of delegation and local devolution, as there was in Ireland, Wales and Scotland, especially in view of the inevitable time-lags and delays in communication.[33] How, then, did this tendency to delegate and devolve relate to the apparent rise of a more 'Westminster-centred' polity? The views of the inhabitants of Aquitaine itself deserve to be heard in this context. In November 1324, for example, John Felton, captain of Saintes, wrote that 'les gens du pays diount qe pur defaute de bons ministres la tere est perdue' ['the men of the country say that the land will be lost for lack of good officers'].[34] By 'bons ministres' he was referring above all to the seneschals of Aquitaine and constables of Bordeaux, as well as to the more local officers. There was often a Gascon preference (sometimes forcefully expressed) for English (or Anglo-French) officers rather than Gascons – they were less likely to become embroiled in the conflicts and feuds of the area, and had no vested territorial or other interests in the duchy. Whatever degree of institutional 'centralization' and accountability to Westminster had taken place, the vital importance of the day-to-day behaviour of the king-duke's officers in the duchy itself was here underlined.

The extent to which English sovereign and 'imperial' power came to dominate a more integrated polity in what still remained a 'composite, pluralistic realm' may be disputed, but it raises questions about the relative status and levels of deputed government in the various dependencies of the English crown.[35] If a desire to reconstitute and recover lost continental lands characterized the behaviour of the Plantagenets after the setbacks of the early and mid-thirteenth century, then their title to those territories, and the manner in which they were to be held, is significant. If 1294 was one watershed, the years 1337–40, when Edward III formally assumed the title to the throne of France, formed another. We can therefore divide our discussion into two parts: the first relating to the period up to 1340, and the second tracing developments up to the Treaty of Troyes of 1420. Before 1340, the status of the continental possessions of the English crown differed in important respects from that of the territories over which dominion was exercised – or merely claimed – within the British Isles. With Edward III's assumption of the claim to the throne of France in 1340, however, full sovereignty over the continental lands was established although, as we shall see, that did not necessarily or exclusively depend upon the French regal title: a title which Edward III was, indeed, prepared to suspend between 1360 and 1369. The high-water mark of English ambitions to exercise full sovereign authority over French lands was reached in 1420 and, for Henry V, the claim to the throne of France was an essential element in that process. The most far-reaching attempt to unite the two kingdoms was to lead, in the longer term, only to their greater separation.

The reign of Edward I (1272–1307) has been seen as a time in which opportunities, and the king's own determination to exploit them to the full, came together to produce a consciousness of English *superioritas* ['superiority'] which extended over the whole of the British Isles. Something of a high-water mark in the tide of English 'empire' was reached during the early years of the fourteenth century. By 1305, it has been said, 'the omens for the establishment of a high kingship of the British Isles seemed altogether promising'.[36] Edward's reign also witnessed the beginnings of a protracted contest over effective lordship and, ultimately, sovereign authority, in the continental possessions of the English crown. In the course of the latter process, the manner in which the remaining French lands were treated began to change. An age which placed increasing emphasis on written instruments of government has left us substantial evidence of such tendencies. They were directly reflected in the ways in which the documents recording the workings of English administrations abroad, as well as within the British Isles, were issued and authenticated. The study of these processes is important, because it can tell us much about concepts of legitimacy, status and entitlement to rule. Documentary formats and formulae were not empty shells, devoid of meaning and significance for the exercise and transmission of power. Before Edward I's accession (1272), there was little evident sign of hard-edged definition and

sharpness of focus in the means whereby the more distant territories subject
to the English crown were treated and governed – although the beginnings of
that process can be detected under Henry III. The marked expansion of written
documentation – evidenced by the inception of the great series of Chancery
enrolments after 1199 – can mislead, but it was nonetheless highly significant as
an index of change. Until the 1270s, for instance, the business enrolled on the
Chancery rolls (Patent, Close, Charter, Fine Rolls) concerned the undifferentiated
affairs of all the constituent parts of the Plantagenet dominions. Hence the so-
called 'Gascon Rolls' of 1242–3 and 1253–4 simply contained all letters issued
by Henry III and his administration when the king was in Aquitaine, whether
they related to Gascon affairs or not.[37] These were issued under a seal which
was described as 'the seal which we use in Gascony' or 'our small seal which we
carry with us in Gascony', bearing an equestrian figure of the king on the obverse
and a shield of the arms of England on the reverse side.[38] This was in effect one
of the first of the 'deputed' great seals used by English monarchs. But, with the
exception of the Norman Rolls (*Rotuli Normannie*), there were no separate classes
of Chancery enrolment – that is, the procedure whereby letters, writs and other
documents were copied and registered – for the continental possessions until
the reign of Edward I. Even then, the documents enrolled on the Norman Rolls
were issued in Normandy under the great seal of England. The appearance of the
Gascon Rolls (*Rotuli Vasconie*) proper stems from November 1274, followed by
the Welsh Rolls (*Rotuli Wallie*) in November 1277 and the short-lived Scottish
Rolls (*Rotuli Scotie*) in June 1291.[39] Apart from the obvious administrative
and archival convenience that the practice conferred, the creation of separate
classes of enrolment for each of the constituent territories of the English crown's
imperium might also represent a devolution of authority and the promotion
of notions of semi-autonomy. This was especially the case in Ireland, where
a separate chancery with its own deputed great seal can be traced to the years
1227–32.[40] 'Imperialism' did not necessarily imply centralization. If there was a
medieval English empire, it was a 'ramshackle' one.[41] All roads did not lead to
and from Westminster.

Yet before the breaking by Edward III of all feudal ties with Valois France in
1340, the essential differences between the status of the English crown's British
and continental lands were evident. In the context of chancery administration,
for example, it has been said that 'the fundamental difference between the Irish
and Gascon dominions lay in the fact that the King of England was sovereign lord
of Ireland, whereas the ultimate sovereignty of Guyenne [Aquitaine] belonged to
the King of France'.[42] This meant that the duchy of Aquitaine could not acquire
a deputed royal great seal or a proper royal chancery. The king-duke's authority
in Aquitaine was exercised by virtue of his non-sovereign ducal, not royal, title.
In Ireland, a special great seal of sovereign lordship was made and entrusted to

a chancellor of Ireland between 1227 and 1232.[43] There was also an exchequer, which had its own deputed seal, at Dublin.[44] In Wales, the 1284 statute set up a deputed chancery, and new exchequers were created at Caernarfon and Carmarthen.[45] In the deputed chanceries of Ireland and Wales, and in the short-lived provision for a seal 'ad regimen regni Scotie deputatum' ('deputed for the rule of the kingdom of Scotland') under Edward I and Edward II, royal letters and other documents were issued in the king's name. They were sealed with a large, double-sided seal resembling the great seal of England, and attested by the king's normal representative – the lieutenant or justiciar – in the dominion concerned. These bore an image of the king enthroned in majesty on one side and a shield of arms of England on the other, and were 'proper' deputed great seals.[46] The exchequer seal for Ireland bore the unique representation of the king enthroned in a boat on the sea – a conscious and telling reference to the 'overseas' status of the lordship and to the practice of *transfretacio* ('transfretation').[47] Here the sovereign status of the Plantagenet monarchy, whether as king or lord, was embodied in the image of enthroned and sceptred majesty. In Aquitaine, on the other hand, the written instruments emanating from the secretariat at Bordeaux were issued in the name of the king-duke's ordinary representative in the duchy – the lieutenant or seneschal of Aquitaine – and authenticated with the smaller, one-sided seal of Gascony.[48] This displayed a shield of arms of England accompanied by a crescent and, in some examples, a fleur-de-lis.[49] The Plantagenet administration, especially after Edward I's reforming ordinance of 1289, was thus adopting the practice whereby all Gascon business conducted from Bordeaux purported to be done in the name of the lieutenant or seneschal, not of the king-duke himself. In this way, the king of England was not personally involved in any cases of appeal from his officers' courts in the duchy to the French crown's Parlement of Paris. He could retain his freedom of action and manoeuvre, because all subordinate officers in the duchy were deemed to be appointed under the seneschal's or lieutenant's seal of office. Direct confrontational clashes between the two monarchs – of England and France – could thus, it was hoped, be averted.

Yet, at first sight, the formal basis upon which the English crown's authority rested in both Ireland and Aquitaine was in effect quite comparable. Ireland was not part of the regnal dominions of the English crown: the king ruled there as lord (*dominus*) not as king, just as in Aquitaine he ruled as duke. But in Ireland he had no feudal suzerain: he was in effect a sovereign lord.[50] Similar conditions applied in Wales, and during the short-lived attempts at exercising English domination over Scotland.[51] Such niceties might again be dismissed as merely technical matters of diplomatic form, chancery practice or protocol – were it not for the fact that power and status were justified, expressed and exercised in this manner. It was in the nature of composite realms for a ruler to adopt what were in effect different personae in his various dominions. In Aquitaine, the king of England was, before 1340, regarded by his subjects there as their 'natural lord' – a non-sovereign duke who was also king of England; in Ireland, he was sovereign lord; in Wales he was also sovereign but had delegated his authority to a prince, normally his eldest son; in Scotland, despite claims to sovereignty, he was ultimately forced to recognize the separate identity of that kingdom's indigenous monarchy. Thus the composition of the Plantagenet dominions did not lend itself to 'centralized' authority, nor to 'integration' of the kind witnessed by nineteenth- and twentieth-century polities.

It has been said of the English 'empire' of Edward I within the British Isles that 'this was certainly no unitary British state':

> Scotland retained a governmental framework of its own; English Ireland had, at least outwardly, a pattern of institutions, including a parliament, which consciously mimicked those of England but were separate from them; while Wales was an anomalous and incongruous assemblage of quasi-independent marcher lordships on the one hand and recently created royal counties on the other.[52]

This was even more the case in the continental possessions of the English crown – at all times in their history – because, although held by the wearer of that crown, they were institutionally no more part of the kingdom of England than was the lordship of Ireland. Annexation to the crown of England did not imply the introduction of government, administration or judicial machinery derived in any way from English practice or precedent. The English common law (and its local Irish and Welsh variations) did not apply in Aquitaine, Ponthieu, Normandy nor even in the most uncompromisingly anglicized French possession, Calais. English 'imperialism' was forced to come to terms with the pluralistic and disparate nature of its constituent territories – if it was to survive at all.

Yet the notion that the English monarchy, from Edward I's reign onwards, took such opportunities as arose to re-create an 'empire' by extending and expanding its continental possessions carries with it a certain credibility. Under Edward I, the acquisition in 1279 of the Agenais in the south, and of the county of Ponthieu in the north, pointed the way and, after the subsequent setbacks of Edward II's reign, the possibility of a restoration of a much larger portion of the lost Angevin empire presented itself. 'Edward [III]', it has rightly been observed, 'was conscious of the Angevin past: in the 1350s and 1360s the British Isles seemed on the point of forming part of a restored and reshaped European *imperium*, bound together by a clutch of Plantagenet princes'.[53] In April 1340, Edward's envoy to the republic of Venice had informed the Doge and Commonwealth that Philip of Valois, 'styling himself king of France', was unjustly occupying what amounted to the greater part of the former Angevin empire, including Normandy, 'the greater and more fertile part of the duchy of Aquitaine', Anjou, Saintonge with the Isle of Oléron, and Ponthieu 'all of which from time out of mind appertained to the kingdom of England'.[54] Despite some historical inaccuracy, the claim was significant as a measure of Edward's ambitions. Initially, the reshaping of this empire depended upon his claim to the throne of France, but the terms agreed with the French at Bretigny-Calais in 1360–1 set up a sovereign duchy of Aquitaine, outside the homage of the crown of France. This was to incorporate substantial areas of the former Angevin dominions – Poitou, Limousin, Perigord, Quercy, Rouergue and so forth. A reconstituted Plantagenet *imperium* of this kind in effect involved the dismemberment (or at least the partition) of the kingdom of France and the deformation of the French monarchical state. To that extent, it differed from the earlier Angevin assemblage, held – as it had been (in theory) – by the performance of liege homage to the crown of France for the greater bulk of the Angevin holdings. It was to be inextricably linked to the so-called '*apanage*' policy of Edward III and the matrimonial strategies which were devised for his house. This made it comparable with other French princely states of the fourteenth century: Anjou, Orléans, Berry, Brittany and Burgundy.

It has been justly observed that the years 1337–40 saw 'a fundamental reorientation in England's territorial and political ambitions'.[55] The quasi-Arthurian 'dream' of a 'single monarchy of the British Isles' no longer corresponded with realities by the mid-fourteenth century. The outbreak of war with France, and Edward III's assumption of the title to the French throne in January 1340, marked something of a return to a former conception of English 'empire': based firmly on the mainland of continental Europe. The reverses suffered in Scotland and Ireland during the reign of Edward II had left a lasting and bitter legacy. The progressive weakening of bonds between the English of England and the English of Ireland, and the emergence of a distinctive sense of Scottish identity, belligerently expressed in the Declaration of Arbroath (1320), spelt the decline of English ambitions towards a 'high kingship' of the British Isles.[56] In their letter to Pope John XXII, dated at the monastery of Arbroath on 6 April 1320, the 'barons, … freeholders and whole community of the realm of Scotland' stated that: 'For as long as a hundred men are left, we will never submit in the slightest to the dominion of the English. It is not for glory, riches and honours we fight, but only for liberty, for which every good man is ready to die.'[57]

It was a resounding declaration from a 'less mighty neighbour' which was to set strict limits upon English expansionism within the British Isles for centuries to come. The English had more than one ancient enemy.

The proximity of the former Norman and Angevin territorial holdings in northern France – Normandy, Ponthieu – to the English kingdom made their loss acutely felt. In the reorientation of English ambitions which, with hindsight, we can see taking place gradually after 1340, the siege and capture of Calais in

1347–8 was crucial. Since the loss of the county of Ponthieu to the French, after its confiscation in 1337, the need for a bridgehead or gateway into northern France was paramount for the advancement of English continental strategies. A secure, defensible point of disembarkation for English forces was required, as well as a protected *entrepot* for the passage of merchandise, especially for that destined for the Low Countries. Calais offered an ideal base for these purposes. It could be effectively defended, by both sea and land, and offered a relatively safe haven for shipping. Edward III's assumption of the throne of France had legitimized intervention and attack anywhere within the French kingdom, in pursuit of his 'rightful' claim. The essentially defensive wars of the past half-century or so were to be eclipsed by a conflict which was ultimately to lead to a conquest and re-occupation of French territory on a scale which had not been seen since the very early thirteenth century. Calais and the 'March' around it provided a fortress and redoubt, a 'barbican' or outwork for England, which required regular and sustained expenditure on its garrisons and defences. The town and port was surrounded on its landward side by an area of about 120 square miles (180 square km) which, by 1436, was officially known as the 'Pale'.[58] An analogy with Ireland's English Pale, distinguished from the 'Greater Irishry', is apt. The Pale of Calais (anglicized as 'Callice') included 25 rural parishes, and was studded with forts and garrisons: apart from the castle and the fort of the Rysbank in Calais itself, there were heavily fortified strong-points at Guînes, Marke, Oye, Newneham Bridge, Sangatte and Hammes.[59] These absorbed substantial sums of money, mainly for fortifications and, as we shall see, water-defences.[60] At full peace-time strength, the Calais garrisons could total about 700 men, doubled in times of war and crisis, and they were to represent 'the largest concentration of military manpower in the dominions of the English king' after the loss of all other continental possessions in the second half of the fifteenth century.[61]

An English settlement was created there, after the expulsion of the native French population – it was in fact England's first major experiment in colonialism. Its place-names and street-names were English, or anglicized versions of French or Flemish topographical names – Summers Brook, Sandingfield, the Sprury, the Fenne, the Fleete, Fuller Street, Cow Lane, Chequer Street, Duke Street and so on.[62] Although Calais and the Pale were not formally incorporated into the English realm until the Calais Act of 1536, the effective frontier of the English kingdom, between 1347 and 1558, was not the south coast of England, but ran along the boundary of the Calais Pale. It stretched from Escalles (Scales) and Saint-Inglevert (Sandingfield, Santingheveldt) on its western edge, past Ardres and Vieille Eglise (Old Kerk) to Gravelines, in the county of Flanders, at its north-eastern extremity. Calais was a true barbican, an outwork on the other side of England's moat. The liberties and privileges granted to the town were derived from English municipal custom. A mayor and 11 aldermen were appointed, redolent of English incorporated boroughs. The king's representatives there – the captain of Calais and his lieutenant – were granted wide-reaching powers, including the granting of safe-conducts and, in effect, controlled the passage of people and merchandise.[63] Calais was soon to become England's major gateway to northern Europe. In 1363, a wool and cloth Staple was established there, which was to endure until 1558, and whose members – the Staplers – were to assume the responsibility for financing the garrison and to become a major source of loans to the English crown. Like other English dominions, its finances were administered by a treasurer and controller, with an exchequer and a special seal and, in the French manner, a counter-seal. A surviving example from Edward III's reign bore the legend 'Sigillum provisum pro terris et [...] in partibus Calesie dimittendis' ['seal provided for the demising of lands and [...] in the parts of Calais'].[64] This (the small counter-seal) bore the image of a castle or battlemented gateway, while the larger seal carried the equestrian figure of the king, caparisoned with a horse-trapper bearing the arms of England and France, and the legend 'Edward, by the grace of God, king of France and England'. This was modelled closely on the representation of the king on the reverse of the Great Seal of England. There was no question of anything less than a claim to full sovereignty in this case. This remained the norm until the reign of Mary I (1553–8).

The re-orientation of English ambitions and energies towards France in the second quarter of the fourteenth century could have led, as we have seen, to that kingdom's permanent, complete disintegration and dismemberment. Although relatively short-lived in comparison with the experience of Germany or the Italian peninsula, France's 'age of principalities' spanned the century from *c.* 1340 to 1440 and was profoundly influenced by a war with England which was also a French civil war.[65] Edward III's undermining of the authority of the Valois crown in 'provinces' such as Brittany was furthered by the creation of a Plantagenet principality of Aquitaine (1362). The new principality was to be 'an independent entity, with its own ruler, under no more than nominal control from England'.[66] It was in effect governed and administered from Bordeaux; during the life-span of the principality: 'the affairs of Aquitaine never depended on central administrative authorities over the Channel. Aquitaine had a true government'.[67]

This was not necessarily an instance of English 'imperialism', because it was consistent with other contemporaneous developments within France itself. Edward of Woodstock (the Black Prince), Edward III's eldest son, was invested for life on 19 July 1362 not with the ancient duchy, but with a radically re-defined principality, of Aquitaine. It seems that the principality was conceived as one means of implementing the terms of the Anglo-French peace treaty agreed at Brétigny and Calais in 1360–1.[68] Edward III was to suspend his claim to the French throne pending the fulfilment of the territorial clauses of the treaty. In the meantime, the Prince was to act not only as his father's lieutenant but as the independent ruler of what was, in effect, an apanage. This was to be held from his father, to whom sovereignty (*superioritas*) and ressort in cases of appeal were reserved. The new principality had its own chancery, chancellor – a clerk of relatively high decanal or Episcopal rank – a great seal, and a greatly enlarged financial administration under the constable of Bordeaux.[69] The Prince held court at Bordeaux, exercising deputed, but very extensive, authority over a vastly-increased area of the South-West.[70] The pattern observed in Aquitaine was not, however, out of line with other developments within France: the title of 'prince' (princeps) was increasingly accorded to dukes within the French kingdom from the latter years of Charles V (*c.* 1370–80) onward. The difference lay in the fact that, in this case, ultimate sovereignty lay not with the house of Valois but with that of Plantagenet. The creation of what amounted to autonomous princely states or 'kingdoms in miniature', exemplified by Brittany and Burgundy, was well advanced by the later fourteenth century and was to be furthered as a result of the onset of Charles VI's mental incapacity after 1392. The implications of this tendency were manifold, giving rise to opportunities for intervention in France by the English monarchy which were to be fully exploited under Henry V.

The principality of Aquitaine lasted only for a decade, and was resigned by the Prince on 5 October 1372. It was stated that the reasons for that resignation lay largely in the inadequate financial resources of the principality which, it was argued, were insufficient for the Prince to sustain his estate and dignity and to pursue the aims which lay behind its original creation. A fundamental feature of the grant of the principality to the Prince was the stipulation that it was to be financially independent: apart from some substantial initial outlay, the English exchequer was not subsequently to fund the costs of its defence, government and administration.[71] The existing financial officer in post in the duchy – the constable of Bordeaux – was made responsible for the receipt of revenues from the greatly expanded territory which made up the principality, as had been agreed with John II of France in the treaty of Brétigny-Calais. In 1360, Plantagenet Aquitaine had consisted of three sénéchaussées; by July 1362, it had expanded to 11 sénéchaussées. Each of these newly acquired regions had its own seneschal, receiver and council. The financial administrations of each area (Saintonge, Aunis, Périgord, Angoumois, Poitou, Poitou-Limousin, Agenais, Bigorre, Rouergue and Quercy) were made accountable to the Prince's successive constables or treasurers of Bordeaux – John Harewell, Alexander de Dalby, Alan Stokes and Richard Filongley – and it was evident that 'the vast possessions acquired in 1361, although each had its own coherent organization, depended – apart from the ultimate [sovereign] authority, exercised from London – on control from Bordeaux'.[72] That control was exercised by a commission of auditors, consisting of a triumvirate, all experienced in Gascon and Poitevin matters.[73] A treasury, or receipt general, was set up at Bordeaux for all the financial sub-divisions – including receiverships of mints, profits from sealing and writing offices, and *fouages* (hearth taxes) – of the principality. Richard Filongley, treasurer of Bordeaux, could thus produce an 'imposing dossier' or balance sheet of the prince's revenues and expenses, on an Exchequer model, from 1363 to 1372.[74] If the principality had lasted longer, it is possible that a more fully developed Exchequer, rather than a French-style Chambre des Comptes, might have materialized at Bordeaux, but the Prince's council seems to have been content to expand the functions of the constable-treasurers at Bordeaux, supplemented by a commission of auditors.[75] There was no attempt to transform institutions which were deemed adequate to fulfil the administrations' needs.[76]

The notion of the kingdom of France as an assemblage, or even a federation, of princely apanages, co-existing with other princely states and royal domain lands, contrasts sharply with the traditional and time-honoured idea of a unitary monarchical state as a dominant theme in French political and institutional development. Brittany, Flanders, Burgundy, Foix, Armagnac, Béarn, and many others achieved the *de facto* – and in some cases *de jure* – status of autonomous principalities. A comparison with English developments over a similar period would reveal some striking affinities as well as differences – the principality of Wales, or the palatine earldoms of Chester and Lancaster reveal some similarities.[77] Sovereignty and its devolution in the English crown's continental possessions, as well as evidence for the 'centralization' of power, can be studied through an examination of the Black Prince's government in Aquitaine between 1362 and 1372. This is not a simple task, owing to the relative scarcity of material, but this can be exaggerated. A corpus of documentation for the Prince's regime can be put together from very scattered sources. Some obvious questions present themselves: how realizable were the aims that lay behind the grant of the principality? Why did the experiment in changing the status of Aquitaine ultimately fail, leading to a resumption of the Anglo-French war after appeals against the Prince in 1368–9, and a restoration of the *status quo ante* after 1372? What were the effects of the experiment on Anglo-French relationships and rivalries? Some of the answers may be found in the very terms by which the principality was originally created.

The territorial composition of the new principality rested on potentially insecure foundations. The Prince was to hold all lands and rights in an expanded 'Aquitaine and Gascony' (*Aquitanie et Vasconie*) 'both by reason of the transfer (*transport*) which the king of France, our brother, has made to us according to the peace [treaty], drawn up between us and him, as otherwise'.[78] These comprised lands, rights, revenues and fiefs in Poitou, Saintonge, Aunis, Agenais, Périgord, Limousin, Quercy, Bigorre, Gaure, Angoumois and Rouergue, as well as all places within the current limits of the duchy of Aquitaine. Some of these territories had not been held by the Plantagenet regime for a very long time, nor had the territorial stipulations of the treaty of Brétigny-Calais, to which the grant referred, been fully implemented. It was in many ways striking that the Prince was, at least initially, able to command the number and range of homages from clergy, nobles and towns that he did: between 9 July 1363 and 6 April 1364, he received oaths of homage and fealty from no less than 1,747 lords and towns throughout the principality.[79] A substantial number of these came from Poitou, which had not been held by the Plantagenets since 1224. For the first time since Edward I had visited Aquitaine (1289), the closest male kinsman to the reigning king-duke – the heir to the English throne – was to reside and take homages in the south-western French possessions of the English crown. The likely beneficial effects of such personal and direct involvement, which successive English officers in Aquitaine had identified in the past, no doubt played some part in the thinking behind the new creation. Not only was the Black Prince to act, as others had done, as his father's lieutenant in Aquitaine, but as a *verus princeps* ('true prince'), enjoying the 'honour, title, appellation, and name' of prince rather than duke, with what amounted to vice-regal powers. The principality was conceived as a self-sufficient entity in fiscal and administrative terms, and all the prince's subjects there were to render and pay rents, dues, revenues and profits directly to his administration.[80] That some difficulties were anticipated in the willingness of some of the inhabitants of this vast dominion to obey the prince and perform homage, was evident from an injunction to them from Edward III to obey him 'everywhere, vigorously constraining all those ... who shall delay or refuse, by all ways and means that shall seem good to them'.[81] In order to meet the expenses incurred in the defence and administration of the principality, resort to extraordinary taxation in the form of fouages (hearth-taxes) became increasingly necessary. There are hints of problems to come in a petition of October 1366 in which the lady of Surgères in Poitou complained to Edward III and his council at Westminster about the behaviour of the Prince's officers, including the charge that they were levying unjustified taxes on wine 'notwithstanding the fouage paid to my lord the prince'.[82] Yet the prince's officers were not imposing unknown or 'English' forms of levy, without consultation, upon these regions – the fouage already had a long history in France, and other princes, as well as the Valois crown itself, were levying them in their lordships. Charles V of France was, significantly, to attempt their abolition on his deathbed in 1380. Many areas included in the Black Prince's principality had previously been subjected to subsidies such as the fouages, aides and tailles levied by the French crown and its agents.[83] It was the heavy incidence and frequency of the impositions, rather than the impositions themselves, which were resented, especially by those members of the higher Gascon nobility whose appeals against the Prince were to lead to a resumption of the more general Anglo-French war in 1369.[84]

The problems which were to result in the Prince's surrender of the principality to his father in October 1372 were partly of his own making and partly the work of others. The decision to embark on a Spanish expedition in 1366, and its subsequent draining of financial resources, undermined the solvency of the regime. Meanwhile, the fact that the lords of Albret, Armagnac, Comminges and Fézensaguet had been subjected to huge ransoms, totalling 600,000 florins, by Armagnac's traditional enemy – the house of Foix-Béarn, in the person of Gaston Phoebus – after their defeat at Launac in December 1362, made any request for subvention from the Prince's administration very unwelcome to them.[85] The imposition of a fouage by the Prince on their lands and subjects in January 1368, after consultation with the Estates of the principality, meeting at Angoulême met with their obdurate resistance and subsequent appeals to Charles V of France. Arnaud-Amanieu d'Albret and Jean I of Armagnac had experienced very great difficulties in paying their ransoms to Gaston Phoebus.[86] Lesser lords, such as Jean d'Armagnac, vicomte of Fézensaguet, raised the sum demanded (5,000 florins) and received remissions from the fines imposed on him by the Prince's officers, while continuing to serve him in war.[87] By May 1368 the tide of opposition to taxation had risen to the extent that the Prince was recruiting loyal nobles to coerce others into payment of the subsidies which had been granted by his 'great council and assembly' at Angouleme in January of that year.[88] Yet the complaints do not seem to have spread very far beyond the vassals, clients and allies of Albret and Armagnac. Despite these problems, the principality survived, at least in name, even after the Prince's return to England and the subsequent appointment of John, Earl of Pembroke, as lieutenant there by Edward III on 20 April 1372. Pembroke was to hold the lieutenancy 'saving … the estate and the rights of our very dear eldest son, the Prince, according to the tenor of the transfer (transport) that we have made him of the said principality' ['sauvant … lestat et les droitz de nostre trescher eisnee filz, le Prince, selonc le tenour du transport que nous lui avons fait de la dite principalte'].[89] By March 1373, Edward III was no longer referring to a principality of Aquitaine, but to the duchy, when he appointed Thomas Felton seneschal there.[90] The prince had surrendered the principality into his father's hands on 5 October 1372, in the presence of the king, the prelates and the secular peers.

The end of the short-lived principality had been hastened by many factors – not least, the deterioration in the Prince's health. Although he attempted to lead an expedition from England to recover the strongpoint of Thouars in Poitou in August 1372, the force never set sail.[91] It has also been argued that 'anglicization' of the principality's administrative personnel played a central role in its demise. It was certainly true that many of the key positions in the greatly-expanded dominion were held by Englishmen: William Felton was seneschal of Poitou, Richard Totesham served as seneschal of Angoumois and governor of La Rochelle and Thomas Wetenhale as seneschal of Rouergue.[92] But it had been a constant refrain of the Gascon subjects of the English crown in the past that English officers were to be preferred to local men – largely because it was believed that they were less likely to be swayed by vested interest and *partis pris* in feuds, quarrels and private wars.[93] The Prince's policy was thus consistent with some past precedent and practice, as well as serving to reward his own loyal retainers and followers. Some indigenous families were, however, appointed to administrative and judicial positions in the principality.[94] The extension of the territorial limits of the Prince's dominions necessitated the appointment of officers conversant with the previous administration of those areas under French, Valois rule. A good example was Guillaume de Seris, 'knight, of La Rochelle' who had served John the Good of France's government in Auvergne and Poitou. He had been at the Brétigny-Calais peace talks in 1360–1, on the French side.[95] He then changed his allegiance and was recruited to the Prince's service as a member of the commission of auditors appointed to oversee the finances of the principality.[96] By June 1371 he had reverted to French obedience and was created a first president of the Parlement of Paris by Charles V.[97] The Prince also undertook to assist members of the nobility of the region in payment of their debts, and both Armagnac and Albret – the two major protagonists in the appeals to Charles V of France in 1368–9 – benefited from this politic behaviour on his part. The explanation for the principality's collapse between 1369 and 1372 thus may lie in the reasons which the Prince himself gave: the 'revenues and profits deriving and issuing from the lands of the said principality could not suffice to maintain his estate and govern the country, nor to support the wars against the French enemies, and other charges that he had to bear, without provision of very great aid and [the meeting of] costs by the king his father'.[98] Ultimately, the balance tipped against the Prince as a result of bribery: the lavish sums offered to members of the principality's nobilities by Charles V proved irresistible.[99] Arnaud-Amanieu d'Albret, for example, received the enormous sum of 87,000 francs between August 1368 and August 1372, including compensation from Charles V for a debt of 'about 42,000 francs' owed by Albret to Edward III and the Prince.[100] A list of payments, all secured on the products of taxation, largely in the Languedoc, referred to the 'sums which, by the king's (Charles V's) order, have been paid to the lord of Albret since he came into the king's obedience and changed his allegiance'. It was a technique which had worked well in the past and was to do so again in the future.

We have already seen that Edward III's assumption of the title to the French crown after 1340 could be used by its apologists to justify aggression against France, *anywhere within the kingdom*, rather than to underpin the more limited and confined aim of defending existing continental possessions. This alone put the conflict on to a different footing. Under Henry V (1413–22), the opportunity to intervene in France was greatly enhanced by the prevalence of lethal conflicts among the highest echelons of the French nobility. War was now waged, especially after 1419, in pursuit of Henry's claim to the French throne, and the primary theatre of war now lay in Normandy and northern France. The Lancastrians, unlike their Plantagenet predecessors, came very close to implementing and stabilizing a durable 'double monarchy' of England and France under one dynasty. A partitioned realm of France became a distinct possibility, and the two allegiances – Lancastrian and Valois – assumed territorial embodiment between 1420 and 1450. The Lancastrian kingdom of France was not conceived, initially, as an annexe or dependency of England – it was a separate realm. The Lancastrian administration of both Normandy and the rest of its conquered and occupied French kingdom (the *pays de conquête*) conformed exactly to that recommended by Montesquieu in *L'Esprit des lois*: 'In this sort of conquest, things must be left as they were found: the same tribunals, the same laws, the same customs, the same privileges. Nothing should be changed but the army and the sovereign's name.[101]

The treaty concluded at Troyes between Henry V and Charles VI in 1420 made this plain – Lancastrian France was to be governed according to its own laws and customs. Plantagenet France had been similarly ruled, although its sway, after 1204, had been largely confined to the south-western regions. Even after Edward III's assumption of the French throne in 1340, English territorial gains in northern and central France – the heartlands of the Capetian and Valois dynasties – had remained minimal. But Henry V's war of conquest and occupation changed all that. It transformed the English 'presence' within France into a polity with its centre of gravity located in the north and centre of the kingdom. With the death of both Charles VI and Henry V, and the succession of the infant Henry VI to the Lancastrian French throne in 1422, the conquered duchy of Normandy which, until that date, had been administered separately by its English administration, was reunited to the crown of France under the terms of the Troyes treaty. Henceforth, the Exchequer (*scaccarium*) which Henry V had established at Harfleur was suppressed, as was the chambre des comptes at Caen, and the duchy's finances came under the direct control of the Paris chambre des comptes.[102] Normandy and the other conquered areas of Lancastrian France gained their own treasurers and receivers-general, who accounted not to the Westminster exchequer but to Paris. Henry V's, and Henry VI's, administration of Lancastrian France was thus 'French' in a manner that was not the case, and never would be, in Aquitaine. There, the affinities in this respect continued to lie more with Wales and Ireland, for the duchy remained annexed to the English crown with its own customs, liberties, privileges and immunities. The point was made heraldically in, for example, the *Rous Roll* (*c.* 1484) where the array of crested helms accompanying the images of Richard III of England (1483–5) represent England, Ireland, Wales, St Edward the Confessor, France and 'Gascoyn and Gyan' [Gascony and Guyenne] – which has its own vine-plant crest.[103] Under English rule, Parisian institutions – the Parlement and the chambre des comptes – had no authority over, or jurisdiction in, Aquitaine, which enjoyed its own court of sovereignty and independent financial structure. Gascon petitions continued to be received at Westminster, not at Paris.

The idea of a Lancastrian *condominium* under a single sovereign was certainly formulated, but direct government of both kingdoms by the king in person was out of the question. In Lancastrian France, a regent, lieutenant- or governor-general had always to be appointed to act in a vice-regal capacity according to the laws and customs of the French, not English, kingdom and its constituent principalities and lordships. Such an office became all the more critical during the minority of Henry VI (1422–37). John, Duke of Bedford; Humphrey, Duke of Gloucester; Richard Beauchamp, Earl of Warwick; William de la Pole, Duke of Suffolk; Edmund Beaufort, Duke of Somerset and Richard, Duke of York were all at various times to act in this capacity in all or part of the Lancastrian kingdom of France. After his death in 1439, for example, the inscription on Richard Beauchamp's magnificent tomb-chest (constructed between 1447 and 1449) in his chantry chapel at St Mary's, Warwick, commemorated his service in Lancastrian France. The inscription recalled that the earl

> visited with longe siknes in the castel of Roan [Rouen] therinne decessed ful cristenly the last day of April the yer of oure lord God anno MCCCCXXXIX he being at that tyme lieutenant general and governer of the roialme of Fraunce and of the duchie of Normandie, by sufficient autoritie of oure soveraigne lord the king Harry the vj. The whuch body with grete deliberacion and ful worshipful conduit bi see and by lond was broght to Warewik the iij. Day of October the yer aboveseide and was leide in a feir chest made of stone in this Chirche.[104]

In the history of the earls of Warwick by John Rous (*c.* 1484), Richard Beauchamp was similarly praised for his deeds:

> at Guines when he was captain of Calais, and in many other lands and in the wars of France … This Earl Richard died at Rouen in Normandy, he then being there Regent and the king's lieutenant, and is buried at Warwick in one of the fairest chapels of England, of his foundation.[105]

From the reign of Henry V onwards, a long-term career in Lancastrian France, accompanied by grants of land, title and office, was now offered to members of the English nobility, knighthood and gentry. This represented a fundamental and major shift in the nature of the war effort and in the character of English involvement in continental ventures. Henry V was to a degree exceptional among

English medieval kings for many reasons – not least for his appreciation of the value of sea power. The successful conquest of Normandy led to the elimination of French naval power in the Narrow Seas, an objective achieved by 1419–20.[106] By 1417, Henry had 34 warships available to patrol the Channel and protect English shipping, and had also succeeded in suppressing piracy. Among his ships, the *Grace Dieu*, which began building at Southampton in 1416, was the English answer to the carracks hired by the French from the Genoese and used in Channel raids against English south coast ports.[107] It was remarkable for its very large size (with a keel length of 38 m (127 ft), and a mainmast height of 61 m (200 ft)) and was a genuine warship, armed with three guns. Its wreck survives in the River Hamble. Once the whole of the Norman coastline had been secured by conquest and occupation, the immediate need for a permanent naval force was deemed to be less pressing and, under Henry VI, Henry's fleet was dispersed or broken up. But between 1417 and 1450, the progressive acquisition of most of the northern French coastline from Cherbourg to Calais by English arms meant that England's south coast now, once again, faced friendly territory across the Channel.

The Lancastrian conquest of Normandy and parts of northern France also reflected, and accompanied, a further ebbing away of English 'colonization' in the Celtic lands and a continued inability – and perhaps unwillingness – to achieve substantial gains over the independent kingdom of Scotland. The land settlement in Normandy and Lancastrian France in effect created a form of 'colonial' regime there – a kind of English 'ascendancy' comparable with the later, Irish pattern. Quite unlike the position in Aquitaine and in the more southerly parts of the English possessions, the occupiers of Normandy, Maine, Anjou and the Breton frontier formed an English community beyond England, broadly comparable with their contemporaries in Ireland. There was now considerable evidence for the re-emergence in England, for the first time since the loss of Normandy in 1204, of a Cross-Channel landholding group. These were men of noble, knightly and gentry status, many of whom, as a result of Henry V's and Bedford's conquests, held land and office in both England and Lancastrian France.[108] Among them were Walter, Lord Fitzwalter, Robert, Lord Willoughby, Sir John Handford, Sir John Fastolf, Sir William Oldhall, Sir Andrew Ogard, William Glasdale, Bertram Entwistle, Matthew Gough, Fulk Eyton, Sir Alan Buxhill, Sir Thomas Dring, Sir Richard Frogenhall, Sir Thomas Rampston, Sir John Popham and many others.[109] But their involvement in English political life, some as parliamentary representatives (Oldhall, Popham), and their investment in English land, tended to set many of them apart from the Anglo-Irish gentry who, by 1400, 'were a self-conscious group, with a distinctive set of concerns and attitudes formed amidst the stresses created by border war and the general economic difficulties of the period'.[110] A body of 'English of France', comparable to the 'English of Ireland', certainly emerged between 1417 and 1424, finally to be expelled and evicted from their holdings in 1449–50. Yet many of the more circumspect of them maintained strong and – ultimately – more lasting links with their English roots.[111]

By 1420, therefore, the promise of a successful fulfilment of the most extreme of English territorial ambitions on the European mainland – the conquest and occupation of the kingdom of France – was alluringly held out. These ambitions depended on many things, not least the making of alliances within France itself. English aggression exploited French civil war (above all, the feud between the houses of Orléans/Armagnac and Burgundy) in order to render such a prospect realizable. Henry V's (and his heir's) claim to the French throne justified and legitimated highly aggressive moves against Valois (or 'dauphinist') France, made feasible through the deft exploitation of divisions among the higher reaches of the French nobility which, as in the past, were reflected and echoed in the localities. Here we may discern an extension of Edward III's 'provincial' policy of undermining the Valois cause, especially in 'peripheral' and frontier regions, to the very centre of French political life under Henry V and the regent Bedford. The alliance and allegiance of the French higher nobility was critical – hence the securing of the oaths of Burgundy and Brittany to the treaty of Troyes (1420), however flawed that agreement proved to be, was an essential cornerstone in building the edifice of Lancastrian France. Burgundy's role was fundamental to the success of the double monarchy. The shift of English strategy away from the defence of existing continental holdings, accompanied as it so often was by sporadic raiding deep into Valois territory, towards a sustained war of conquest and occupation, had wider implications. Henry V's espousal of the crown of France, virtually at all costs, immediately affected the position of this new regime in its external relations not only with the Valois French, but with other powers. We shall examine these in the following chapter.

4

Allies, Mediators and the French Enemy

For a country which lacks extended land frontiers with other continental powers, the sea necessarily serves as its border. Medieval England had other close neighbours, besides France, across the Channel and the North Sea. They could serve as allies, intermediaries or enemies. Thus the seaboard of the Low Countries had never ceased to be of concern to the English. It stood as the second closest cross-Channel neighbour of the English kingdom after northern France. From Gravelines, in the county of Flanders, to Alkmaar, in the county of Holland, the Netherlandish coastline sheltered ports and harbours, protected by sandbanks and shoals, which played vital roles in English trade and commerce. In his *Life and Raigne of King Henry the Eighth* (1649), Edward Herbert, lord of Cherbury, wrote that at the beginning of his reign (1509), the most serious external threat to Henry's security came, as ever, from France, but

> As for the house of Burgundy, and the Low-Countryes ... hee needed not feare anything, unlesse he would willfully provoke them; the causes of love on that part seeming to be perpetuall; as being founded upon the mutuall necessity of those Ports and Havens, which, upon all foule weather the Shipping must resort to, on either side.[1]

There was an essential economic mutuality and reciprocity between the Low Countries and England. Although politically divided among a number of autono-mous – or quasi-autonomous – principalities, the Low Countries provided both markets and sources of supply for English commerce. The multiplicity and plurality of their political structures worked in many respects to England's advantage. Until the early fifteenth century, no one power was supreme over the rest. It was thus very much in England's interests to ensure that French ambitions either to acquire or control any of the principalities of the region were resisted and thwarted. The steady rise of Burgundian power to hegemony over the whole region, however between 1384 and 1430 changed the political climate. If the initially pro-French leanings of the Valois dukes of Burgundy were not to threaten England's security, an alliance had to be constructed with Burgundian power. Any signs of Burgundian disaffection from Valois France were to be encouraged. A pro-French Netherlands – both southern and northern – might, as in 1385–6, lead to a projected invasion of England which could stand some chance of success. If the coastal provinces of northern France and the Low Countries were not to become an armed camp, hostile to England's interests, France and Burgundy had to be kept apart. But, whatever political divisions there were between England and the Low Countries, strong economic and commercial connections were maintained. The export trade in English wool and, later, cloth, flowed through them – via Calais, Bruges, Antwerp and Dordrecht – to much of the rest of Europe, both East and West. English imports of innumerable commodities were either derived from the Low Countries themselves or channelled through them. Hence some of the luxury goods from the East which England imported were often, as we shall see, carried by Italian middlemen and shipped through the ports of the Low Countries. Hanseatic merchants brought timber and furs from the Baltic to England, often via Flanders and Brabant. In c. 1436, the polemical tract known as the *Libel of English Policy* stressed the centrality of the Low Countries to England's import and export trades and roundly condemned the duke of Burgundy for potentially jeopardizing that commerce by his hostile political behaviour.

England possessed no territorial power-base – outside the town, March and Pale of Calais between 1347 and 1558 – in Netherlandish territory, but its economic, diplomatic and (frequently) military presence there was certainly a force to be reckoned with. On the grounds of lack of title, and of sustainable territorial claims, Pope Boniface VIII criticized Edward I of England for his intervention in Flemish affairs against France in 1297. The pope told English envoys in 1300 that

> he [Edward] has done much wrong and has angered us greatly because he has gone to Flanders where neither he nor his ancestors have ever had any rights, and has allied with the Germans and Burgundians to make war on the kingdom of France. If he had gone to Gascony, which is his land, to defend or recover it, that would be quite another thing.[2]

By no stretch of the imagination could a case be constructed for English possession of any part of the Low Countries, but long-standing alliances with the powers of the region were firmly in place from an early date. Some of these powers were represented by princes and lords who were vassals of the German Empire; others by liegemen of the crown of France. There was no fully sovereign prince in the region; each one acknowledged a feudal relationship to some other, theoretically higher, authority. Flanders and Artois were fiefs of the French crown; while Namur and a small part of eastern Flanders were imperial fiefs, as were the much larger and more significant duchy of Brabant, together with the counties of Hainaut, Holland and Zeeland. The English monarchs were therefore concerned to woo, inveigle, or bully these rulers to their side, using all the weapons in their armoury. Between the twelfth and fourteenth centuries, economic and commercial interests dictated and determined much English behaviour towards the Low Countries. As the largest single net importers of English wool, the textile industries of Flanders, Brabant and – at a later date – Holland and Zeeland, were dependent on English sources of supply and their economic fortunes could be adversely affected by disruption, piracy on the high seas, embargo and blockade. Much of the wool crop of English twelfth- and thirteenth-century Cistercian houses, for example, was consumed in Flanders, and the rulers of Netherlandish territories had always to keep a watchful eye on relations with England. In the fifteenth century, the Low Countries also became a market for hard-wearing and high-quality English cloth – worsteds, says, kerseys, serges and so on. The demand for foodstuffs among the growing urban populations of the region before the Black Death also stimulated English corn exports, often channelled through the port of Southampton. The subjects of Netherlandish rulers – and those rulers themselves – could therefore be placed in awkward dilemmas if and when a conflict broke out between England and the sovereign lord – the king of France or the German emperor – of their own immediate lord. Thus the men of Bruges, Ghent and Ypres – dependent on the English wool trade for the supply of their looms – could stand to lose from conflict between England and France. The count of Flanders, as a peer of France and vassal of the French crown, was obliged to serve that crown against its rivals and enemies – of whom one was, increasingly, the crown of England. An internal tension thus reigned within the county of Flanders between loyalty to the count and concern among his subjects for their own economic and commercial interests.

The ports and harbours of the Low Countries could also provide safer crossing-places for the English at times of war with France. The Narrow Seas were often infested with enemy shipping, pirates and privateers. Sluis (Sluys, Escluse) in Flanders was especially important in this respect, because it linked Bruges and its wider hinterland to the ports of London, Yarmouth, King's Lynn and Boston. The sea passage, although longer than that between Dover and Wissant or Calais, was often more secure, and English royal messengers often used the route via Sluis. It gave easy access to the duchy of Brabant and to the principalities of the Rhineland. Bruges was to become, by the later thirteenth century, a commercial and financial centre of such importance to the western European economy that it eclipsed its former rivals – the city of Arras in Artois and the Champagne fairs – completely. The presence of substantial colonies of both Italian and Hanseatic merchants and financiers made Bruges a meeting-point in many respects, and the rise of Italian merchant-banking networks with branches there transformed the credit systems of northern Europe. The English crown formed part of a wider network of clients serviced by the emergent Sienese and Florentine firms of Riccardi, Frescobaldi, Bardi and Peruzzi. They were the precursors of the Medici bank, with its branches in Lyon, Bruges and London, in the fifteenth century. Constant passage of people, goods, merchandise, letters of credit and bills of exchange between England and the Low Countries made their economies mutually dependent. Once again, the sea was acting as a highway rather than as a barrier.

The two areas were also interconnected by means of trade with Italian states, especially with the republic of Venice. Since the early fourteenth century, the Venetians had dispatched the 'Flanders galleys' to sail via the lengthy passage from the lagoon by way of Istria, Corfu, Otranto, Syracuse, Messina, Naples, Majorca and Lisbon to the ports of Calais, Sluis and Middelburg. In 1317 the republic appointed its first captain of the Flanders galleys, Gabriele Dandolo, who was also envoy to England in 1316–17. It was vital for the galleys, each propelled by 180 oarsmen, to gain safe-conducts from the English crown once they had entered the territorial waters of the kingdom, through the Western Approaches and into the Channel, whether or not they put in to English ports. But the practice grew up, in the later fourteenth century, of dividing the galleys between Flanders and England – out of an annual fleet of four or five vessels, at least two would part company with the rest and sail to Southampton or London. Yet they still formed part of the Flanders fleet, under the overall command of its captain, and considerable latitude was allowed to the masters of the galleys to decide upon whether to put in to English, as well as Flemish, ports. By the 1390s, after a hiatus in sailings between 1359 and 1374, an annual visit to England was the norm. But the close interconnection between the English and Flemish trades is evident from the records of the Venetian republic.[3] Under-lading, or a shortfall in sales and purchases in Flanders, could be compensated by cargoes for sale in England – usually off-loaded from one galley to another, or into English or Flemish ships – either in the 'road' off the Downs or, more safely, at the harbour of Camber before Rye. In December 1398 the Venetian Senate also decreed that five galleys should be fitted out, as usual, for the Flanders voyage, three bound for Sluis, the other two for London, and that

> ten days after the arrival of the captain [of the Flanders galleys] at Sluis with the three galleys he is to confer with the masters, and, having carefully considered the state of the country, he is then to decide whether all three … galleys can reasonably expect to obtain full cargoes there – in which case they are all to remain; but otherwise, if it appear, from lack of goods at Sluis, more advantageous that one should go to London, the third galley is to join the other two in that port, the master placing himself under the command of the vice-captain there.[4]

The interconnectedness of the Anglo-Flemish trade was clearly a marked feature of Venetian economic policy at this time. This fundamental fact also carried strong political and diplomatic implications. There was a 'natural' economic alliance between England and, in particular, the county of Flanders, which was replicated in political terms. And that alliance did its best to exclude the French enemy.

In 1101, 1110 and 1163, treaties were concluded between the rulers of England and Flanders, all of which were drawn up and agreed at Dover.[5] In 1101, Henry I of England had promised to pay Count Robert II of Flanders an annual fee of 500 l. st., in return for the military service of 1,000 Flemish knights in England or the duchy of Normandy, and of 500 in the county of Maine. The relationship appears to have been conceived on a basis of equality – the count held his money-fee from his 'friend' the king. The treaty was confirmed in 1110. By 1163, however, the terms had changed: Henry II and his son Henry were the parties on one side, and Count Thierry and his son Philip (of Alsace), on the other. But a subordinate feudal relationship was set out in 1163 for, although Count Thierry had entered into the agreement quite willingly and freely, Henry II was described as his 'lord and friend' (*dominum et amicum*). Homage was to be performed by Philip of Alsace. The treaty alleged that Thierry had already paid homage to Henry I. Although no land changed hands, a personal feudal bond, based on a money-fief, had been created. The evidence suggests that the count of Flanders had become a client and liegeman of the king of England, as king, rather than as duke of Normandy and Aquitaine, or as count of Maine and Anjou. This feudal relationship could only lead to difficulties with the count of Flanders' feudal suzerain the king of France, especially when the revival in Capetian authority associated with Philip Augustus (1180–1224) began to make its impact felt. It was as a result of these treaties of alliance with England that Ferrante, count of Flanders, fought with the Plantagenet host at Bouvines, and was defeated there by Philip Augustus's army in 1214. Yet Flanders remained ambiguously and ambivalently placed between England and France and few, if any, counts of Flanders could afford to forfeit English support and the benefits of English commerce to their Netherlandish subjects. Flanders, as well as England, thus presented a Janus-like aspect.[6]

There were, until the rise of Burgundian power (from 1384 onwards), profound differences in the relations between the various Netherlandish principalities and the kingdom of England. These had an impact upon England's subsequent, and consequent, relations with the kingdom of France. Some principalities of the Low Countries (e.g. Brabant, Hainaut, Holland), as we have seen, were in effect independent of France, as they were imperial fiefs. As potential allies and clients, to be recruited against the French enemy, the principalities in imperial allegiance – Brabant, Hainaut, Holland and Zeeland, Guelders, Luxembourg, Namur and part of Flanders – were sought by the rulers of England throughout our period. Henry I's Flemish alliance continued under his successors. A major means of securing pro-English, or at least neutral, neighbours bordering both the German empire and the kingdom of France was the marriage alliance. As the instructions to the English ambassadors to the congress of Arras (1435) pointed out: 'mariage is alweyes oon [of] the principal thinges that nurisshethe and holdethe togideres rest and pees betwix princes, poeples and cuntrees that han stonde in longe difference'.[7] The negotiation of marriage contracts with Netherlandish rulers intensified especially during periods of tension in Anglo-French relations. The encirclement of France by a coalition of powers under English patronage, financed by English money, was a marked feature of the 1290s, when Edward I was building up his continental defences against the increasingly assertive behaviour of Philip the Fair. Marriages were thus contracted with Brabant (1290), Flanders (abortively, 1293), and Holland (1297), while more easterly and southerly principalities such as Bar and Savoy were also brought into the Plantagenet fold. Edward also made alliances with the German emperors – a precedent to be followed by Edward III in 1336–8. Both Hainaut (1327) and Guelders (1332) were also allied to England by marriage at the beginning of the Hundred Years War – one result of the failure of Edward II's marriage to Isabella of France to heal Anglo-French differences. It was a cardinal feature of French diplomatic and military activity throughout the period to attempt to ensure that the county of Flanders – a French fief – did not fall into the hands of the Plantagenets. An Anglo-Flemish marriage alliance was simply unacceptable to both Capetian and Valois rulers – hence the failure, engineered by a Franco-Papal alliance, of Edward III's proposed marriage of his son Edmund of Langley to Margaret de Male, heiress of Flanders, in 1369. The way to the establishment of (at that time) pro-French Burgundian power in Flanders and Artois was thus paved by the thwarting of English ambitions on this area of the European stage.

But the possibility of a durable Franco-Burgundian alliance was wrecked by the internecine feuding of the higher French nobility. This was always a useful, if indirect, weapon in England's repertoire whereby the authority of the Valois crown could be undermined, or even nullified. The Hundred Years War was also a French civil war. On 10 September 1419, John the Fearless, duke of Burgundy, was assassinated by partisans of the Armagnac/Orléans or 'dauphinist' cause during a diplomatic interview on the bridge at Montereau. The murder by supporters of John the Fearless of Louis, duke of Orléans, on 23 November 1407 was avenged by this act. In 1521, when Francis I of France was being shown the Burgundian mausoleum in the great Charterhouse of Champmol by a Carthusian monk, the consequences of John the Fearless's assassination were spelt out to the king. 'My lord', said the Carthusian, pointing to the duke's skull, 'that's the hole through which the English entered France'. The alliance with England made by John's heir, Philip the Good (1419–67), and its subsequent embodiment in the treaty of Troyes (1420), was to transfer Burgundian allegiance from the Valois to the Lancastrian claimant to the French throne. The ruler of the Low Countries became a liegeman of Henry VI, and Philip was also closely linked to the Regent Bedford by the marriage of his sister. The Anglo-Burgundian alliance was, like so many of its kind, doomed to fail. But its duration (1420–35) allowed Henry V and Bedford to conquer Normandy and consolidate their position in Lancastrian France without fear of a rearguard action from Burgundian supporters. By 1420, the Burgundian ruler of Flanders and Artois had taken an oath of loyalty to the house of Lancaster and, on the death of the insane Charles VI of France, was to enter the direct allegiance of the Lancastrian French crown. A substantial part of the Low Countries was now in effect in English allegiance and, during the next 15 years, war was waged against Valois or 'dauphinist' France by an Anglo-Burgundian coalition. Henry V's aims of territorial gain in France rested, for their realization, upon Burgundian support. As we shall see in a later chapter, the Anglo-Burgundian alliance provided a blueprint for later liaisons and *rapprochements* with the Habsburg successors to the Valois dukes. He (or she) who ruled the Low Countries was a vital constituent in supporting, or hindering, England's evolving role as a land power on the continent of Europe. But there were other powers with vital roles to play in determining England's external relations and in mediating between England and France. One of the most important of these was the papacy.

The story of England's relations with the papacy from the mid-twelfth century onwards has often been told; it is not intended to repeat that story here. Our concern is with England as a continental European power, and the role of its continental dominions in influencing and shaping its external relationships, especially with the kingdom of France. England's continental possessions had been a concern of the popes from an early date. Under the Angevin kings, the popes had regarded the occupants of the English throne very much as French princes, whose powers over such matters as the provision of incumbents to benefices within their various continental territories they sought to limit. All the dioceses within the Angevins' continental lands fell within the jurisdiction of French metropolitans: Canterbury and York had no authority over them. There was no English ecclesiastical imperialism. Yet, in that part of his dominions where he possessed the greatest power – the kingdom of England – Henry II's aggressive behaviour towards the Church was ultimately to rebound to his disadvantage. The murder of Thomas a Becket in 1170 delivered something of a trump card into the hands of the papacy, and the interdict imposed on England under King John compounded this sense of submission to the authority of Rome. Yet the twelfth-century popes needed allies; and they needed them badly. To resist the encroachments and attacks of the Empire, the Angevins, among many others, were recruited to aid the papacy. Angevin help, or at least neutrality, was needed to offset the *démarches* of the Hohenstaufens. There was constant to-ing and fro-ing between England and Rome, and the English Church was represented at the *curia* by a body of well-trained ecclesiastical careerists. Norman monasteries remained anxious to preserve their English lands and rights, and helped to swell the stream of petitions to Rome. There was no perception among the popes that the Angevins were anything other than the legitimate lords of their continental territories. Indeed, the pious bequests and endowments which they gave to churches and religious houses, such as the abbey of Fontevrault, within their French lands served merely to underscore that legitimacy. But the mid-thirteenth century saw changes in European power-relationships that had important consequences for Anglo-papal relations.

The death of the Emperor Frederick II of Hohenstaufen in 1250 and the subsequent elimination, accomplished by an alliance between the popes and the French house of Anjou, of his heirs, opened up a power vacuum. There was an interregnum in the German Empire until the election of Rudolf of Habsburg in 1273. Who would fill the vacuum? England's role as a major European power made its ruler a natural candidate for active participation in the dismantling of the Hohenstaufen inheritance. Henry III (1216–72) adopted a policy of intervention, on the papal side, in Italian affairs and sought to extend the influence of his house through the election of his brother, Richard of Cornwall, as king of the Romans in 1257. To some extent, these ventures diverted English energies and preoccupations away from the existing continental possessions – in Poitou and Aquitaine – and Henry's agreement to what was regarded by many as a very disadvantageous treaty with France (at Paris in 1259) was in part determined by the need for an *entente* with Louis IX. A war with France would have been an expensive and unwelcome distraction from Henry's aim of enhancing the role and status of the Plantagenets on the Italian and imperial stage. His successor adopted a rather different stance. As we have already seen, the reign of Edward I formed a crucial turning-point in English attitudes towards the kingdom of France and towards the feudal status of the English monarchs as dukes of Aquitaine. The papacy was henceforth to play an important role in the Anglo-French relationship. It was committed to the cause of peace between the secular powers of Christendom, predicated upon the need to achieve at least a semblance of Western unity if a viable crusade was to be mounted. The continental possessions of the English crown, however, often stood in the way of that peace-making and peace-keeping mission. In 1294, issues relating to Aquitaine had brought England and France to war. The pontificate of Boniface VIII (1294–1303) witnessed an escalation of both Anglo-French and Franco-papal conflict, in which the question of sovereignty over the duchy was a major source of friction. Boniface exercised his right to intervene in the affairs of secular powers *ratione peccati* (by reason of sin), as formulated by Innocent III. But his arbitration was not accepted, and papal mediation became hopelessly embroiled in a relentless struggle with Philip the Fair of France, ending in Boniface's humiliation and death after the Anagni 'outrage' of 1303. This event – the work of an alliance between his inveterate enemies, the Colonna family, and the crown of France – marked the humiliation of the medieval papacy and the final death of the universalist dream of the Gregorian period. Boniface's palace at Anagni was seized and occupied by his adversaries, he was forced to flee, the papal treasure was looted and the fleurs-de-lis flew above the papal residence. The papacy's authority, and its role as an arbiter between the powers of Western Christendom, had suffered what was to become an irreversible setback.

The post-Bonifacian papacy was in many respects a rather different animal – because it had to be such. The emergence of a third party among the electoral body of cardinals was one of its most striking features. Until that date, the College of Cardinals had been very largely composed of Italian and French members. None of the first three popes of the so-called 'Avignonese' period, when the papacy established itself at Avignon (1309–78), were Italians. Nor were they 'French' in the sense that the term was understood in the fourteenth century. None came from northern or central France, the traditional reservoir of candidates for high office in the French Church and in Capetian royal service. All of them originated from south-west France. The first of them, Clement V (1305–14) was not only a Gascon who had been bishop of St-Bertrand-de-Comminges and archbishop of Bordeaux, but also a king's clerk of Edward I of England. His abiding concern that England and France should not go to war again over his own much-loved homeland of Aquitaine meant that papal vigilance was constantly exercised to that end. Here was a pope with an intimate knowledge of Gascon affairs and his pontificate, if it did nothing else, at least kept England and France on relatively amicable terms. The tumultuous events of 1294–1303 were not to be replicated under Clement V. Edward I and Edward II enjoyed a degree of papal support – and of personal concern – which was unusual. Clement's successors – John XXII (1316–34) and Benedict XII (1334–42) – were also southern Frenchmen but they had never been in Plantagenet allegiance. Nevertheless, both made strenuous efforts to keep the Anglo-French peace, despite the failure of mediation in 1323–4 to prevent another war. A proposal to take the issues before the papal court in 1324 failed. The progressive decline of English confidence in papal arbitration can be traced to the pontificate of Benedict XII, and it was to be resoundingly endorsed during the reign of his successor, the former French curial bishop, Clement VI (1342–52). England and France were at war, and remained at war, for the rest of the fourteenth century. An impasse had already been reached, before the outbreak of the great western Schism in 1378 effectively removed all possibility of Anglo-French reconciliation through papal mediation. In 1374–5, the peace negotiations at Bruges had broken down, partly as a result of English rejection of the French cardinals as mediators. A schismatic papacy condemned all attempts to arbitrate Anglo-French (and all other) disputes to failure. It was only with the rise of conciliar efforts to end the Schism that any hopes of restoring confidence in papal mediation were rekindled. But, as we shall see, the conciliar period brought its own problems with it. The balance of forces in western Europe had changed and the councils – intended to be arenas in which the settlement of contentious issues might be achieved – became in some measure battle-grounds on which those secular power-struggles were played out.

The Church councils of the later Middle Ages had been organized on the basis of 'nations', each of which had a consultative place, voice and vote in the proceedings at Lyon (1274), Vienne (1311) and Pisa (1409). Four nations – French, German, Spanish and Italian – were established, although the representative structure bore little relation to political or territorial notions of nationhood and was riddled with anomalies. Conciliar organization had more in common with the structure of medieval universities, which were also formed into 'nations'. Before the council, which met at Constance (1414–18) to resolve the Great Schism, English delegations to the councils of the Church had formed part of the German nation. The facts of early fifteenth-century political life, however, must have encouraged the notion (at least among the English and their allies) that they ought to be considered as a separate nation, enjoying an importance out of all proportion to their size. The issue was thrown into higher relief by the 'implacable feud' generated between England and France by the Anglo-French war.[8] English proctors at Constance argued that they ought not to be considered as part of the German nation. They claimed that Benedict XII (1334–42), in his bull *Extravagans, Statuimus* which set out the composition of the nations, had placed the provinces of Canterbury and York not with the Germans but between the provinces of Narbonne, Toulouse and Auch on one side, and those of Compostella and Seville on the other.[9] Irish and Scottish provinces 'which are well known to be part and parcel of the English' [or British] 'nation' were similarly treated. If, argued the English, Benedict had intended to define the English nation as part of the German nation, 'he would not have scattered those provinces, together with the province of Gascony and other places well-known to belong to the English nation, among the provinces of other nations, but put them with those of the kingdom of Germany'.[10] The overwhelming English victory achieved over the French at Agincourt (1415), and Henry V's subsequent alliance (1416) with the Emperor Sigismund, as well as Henry's claim to the French throne, enabled the English to assert parity of status, and equivalence of political and diplomatic weight, with the French, German, Spanish and Italian nations. At Constance, by the beginning of the council's first sessions in February 1415, the English had already been meeting separately from the rest.

Henry V's subsequent conquest of Normandy (1416–24), plus the retention of the duchy of Aquitaine, allowed the English, under Cardinal Henry Beaufort, to argue forcefully for English nationhood in a conciliar context. In the course of the argument, recourse was had to the dubious grounds that the English crown exercised control over no less than 110 dioceses in England, Wales, Ireland

and France.[11] Some of these dioceses, especially in Ireland, were very small and miserably poor. The number of Irish dioceses was inflated from an actual 32 to a fictitious 60, and the four 'English' provinces decreed by Benedict XII (Ireland, Canterbury and York, Scotland and Bordeaux) for the purpose of holding chapters of the Benedictine order, were increased to eight by the English apologists. Despite French protests, all counter-arguments were rebutted (on 31 March 1417) by Thomas Polton, Henry V's proctor and ambassador. He argued that the French claim that the English did not constitute a nation at the council was unsustainable on every count. The evidence of linguistic diversity was even introduced into the argument, when he asserted:

> Where the French nation has, for the most part, one vernacular which is wholly or in part understandable in every part of the nation, within the famous English or British nation, however, there are five languages ... one of which does not understand another. These are English, which English and Scots have in common, Welsh, Irish, Gascon and Cornish. It could be claimed with every right that there should be representation of as many nations as there are distinct languages. By even stronger right ought they [the English], as a principal nation, to represent a fourth or fifth part of the papal obedience in a general council and elsewhere.[12]

Quite unlike more recent concepts of nationhood, it was here argued that the conciliar 'nations' should not reflect linguistic uniformity but should be representative of polyglot and multi-lingual communities. Yet the evident linguistic diversity of the kingdom of France was resolutely ignored by Polton, while the inclusion of the Gascon dominions of the English crown as part of the English, rather than French, nation was significant. With the completion of the conquest of Normandy (1424) and the extension of English and Anglo-Burgundian power into Lancastrian France, another language-group – the French – would be added to the list of vernaculars spoken within the territories held by the English crown. The possession of continental dominions was once again thought to enhance the European status of the English kingdom. Their loss or abandonment, according to this line of reasoning, would inevitably diminish the kingdom's standing among the powers of Christendom. It was an argument for continued offensive and defensive war.

The subsequent council at Basle (1431–49) witnessed an important change in conciliar organization which, in turn, both influenced and reflected the standing of European powers; the system of 'nations' was in effect abandoned in favour of one of 'deputations'.[13] These were to number four, 'among which the membership of the council should be equally distributed as far as possible'.[14] This was intended to mitigate, if not eliminate, the tendency for secular influences to become dominant in assemblies, such as those at Constance, organized according to 'national' groupings. It would also allow greater participation by the middle and lower clergy, especially by university academics. An oath of incorporation was also exacted from each deputation as a condition of full membership of the council. Upon their arrival at Basle in 1433, the English refused to accept these conditions, fearing that commitment in advance to abide by collective conciliar decisions, and the scattering of their delegates over the various deputations would gravely reduce the degree of control, unity and influence which they had enjoyed at Constance. English influence was, however, effectively excluded altogether from the deliberations at Basle. The inability (in part self-imposed) of the English delegations to intervene in the debates prevented the negotiation of a mediated peace between England and France, and it has been suggested that 'the failure at Basle' may have been 'an important factor in the depression suffered by the English cause in France'.[15] The English were thus thrown back upon the papacy of Eugenius IV as a source of mediation in their dispute with Valois France, a source against which the council of Basle struggled. Hence, although he remained on good terms with the council, Cardinal Niccolo Albergati acted during his peace-making mission to Arras in 1435 only as a papal, and not a conciliar, legate.[16]

Despite the reverses which the English cause had suffered in France as a result of the raising of the siege of Orléans (1429) and the coronation of Charles VII at Rheims, there was no lack of resolve among them to demonstrate the continued viability of the Lancastrian double monarchy. As early as 1430, ambassadors to England from Aragon and Navarre were told that any treaty of alliance must include not merely Henry VI's English subjects but also those of his realm of France. In August 1434, an English embassy arrived at the council of Basle, claiming to speak for the double monarchy of England and France, and a bitter and unseemly dispute broke out between the English and Valois-French delegates when the Lancastrian-French members appeared.[17] The bishops of Bayeux and Lisieux in Normandy, as well as the bishop of Dax in Gascony, now represented Henry VI, as king of France, and the presence of the two Norman bishops on the English side provoked acrimonious argument. Within two years, however, both English and Lancastrian-French representatives had withdrawn from the council and the dispute petered out. It was to be renewed at the great peace congress convened by the papal legates at Arras in June 1435, when the English assembled 'the strongest Lancastrian-French mission sent by the English government to a peace conference, the whole might of the double monarchy being displayed'.[18] A delegation of 12 members from England and at least five from Lancastrian France journeyed to Arras, including a cardinal, an archbishop, three bishops, two earls and one baron. Instructions were accordingly issued to Henry VI's 'ambaxadeurs borne in his reaume of England ... and also to his ambaxadeurs borne of his reaume of Fraunce'.[19] They were accompanied by an entourage of clerks, secretaries and many laymen, representing the double monarchy at its most impressive. There was clearly no hint of withdrawal from the French possessions, or renunciation of the French title, at this stage. As the son of William Worcester, Fastolf's secretary, pointed out at a much later date, there were many who had urged 'contynuaunce in the righte of the corowne of Fraunce'.[20] It was, as we shall see, to be a theme that continued to influence later English kings and their armigerous subjects, some of whom were always prepared to expound, in Worcester's words:'the reasons and the grounde maters for the juste tytle of enheritaunce and for the avauncemente and may[n]tenyng of the werre ayenste the seid grete adversaries of Fraunce, after the case and the chaunce of werre was thene thoughte beste to be conduyte'.[21]

In the event, Lancastrian France, Normandy and Aquitaine had to be prised from the grip of their defenders by *force majeure*. There was no negotiated settlement, no peace treaty which ended the Hundred Years War. The aims enshrined in the treaty of Troyes (1420) were never to be realized. Neither a dual monarchy of England and France, nor the more limited retention of English possessions within France, were ultimately to prove viable. England's 'most serious external obligation prior to entry to the European Economic Community five hundred and fifty years later'[22] was brought to an end by military defeat. Neither popes, nor councils nor diplomatic congresses had succeeded, by way of arbitration or mediation, in the intractable task of ending the Anglo-French war. Despite the subsequent efforts of English cardinals, papal intervention in Anglo-French and Anglo-imperial relations was to remain very largely a dead letter until the final breach with Rome under Henry VIII. After that event, it was completely annihilated.

5

English Identity: Language and Culture

We have seen how, for much of the Middle Ages, England maintained very close links with continental Europe, partly as a direct result of its retention of its French continental dominions. Yet a major theme of British historical writing has been the emergence, or re-emergence, of a distinct English identity after the trauma of the Norman Conquest. Bishop Stubbs, founder of the Oxford School of Modern History, could write in his 'Sketch of the Constitutional History of the English Nation' appended to his *Select Charters* (1870):

> Every infusion of new blood since the first migration [to England] has been Teutonic: the Dane, the Norseman, and even the French-speaking Norman of the Conquest, serve to add intensity to the distinctiveness of the national identity ... The Teutonic element is the paternal element in our system.[1]

Stubbs's racial interpretation of national identity did not meet with universal approval. By 1920, perhaps in reaction to the events of 1914–18, English historians challenged the primacy of Germanic influence on English constitutional history. T. F. Tout wrote in 1922 of:

> the tendency of English political and constitutional historians not to give due recognition to the French element in English history. One cause of this refusal ... is that excessive following of the Germans which, blatantly expressed by Freeman, is found in more cautious and judicious form in even so eminent a scholar as Stubbs.[2]

What Tout called the 'close interconnection of the French and English peoples'[3] was, he argued, an essential element in England's evolution, politically, socially, institutionally and culturally. It would be to Stubbs, rather than Tout, that modern apologists and propagandists for 'Euroscepticism' might go, emphasizing less the racial element in his thinking than the notion of a distinct, separate, fundamentally Anglo-Saxon identity which has survived 1,000 years of admixture and immigration. It was a notion shared by other eminent scholars (and influential public figures) such as J. R. R. Tolkien. The origins of the popular myth of 'a thousand years of British sovereignty' lie in a confused misapplication of pseudo-historical arguments of this kind. 'Our island's story' is, it is claimed, to be told as one of insular withdrawal from continental Europe, in which the decline of England as a European land power is mistaken for a decline in England's active and inextricable participation in European affairs.

Yet there can be no denial of England's special and particular place in the history of European state formation. In that process, medieval England is often accorded a prominent and precocious role. As we have seen, one authority has uncompromisingly declared that, by 1066, England was already a 'nation-state' – a view apparently now shared by many historians of the Anglo-Saxon period.[4] The Norman Conquest, it is argued, may have temporarily set back the onward march towards nationhood, but the tide (to change the metaphor) was too strong and, it is claimed, foreign rule and occupation could not hold back the inexorable process. It is hardly surprising that this revisionist (or perhaps reversionary) view – which undoubtedly owes something to Stubbs and the so-called 'Germanists' – should have influenced historians working on other periods. A recent work on European culture from 1660 to 1789, for example, sees some degree of continuity between the nationalism which characterized Britain during that period and its alleged origins in the medieval past. Tim Blanning can thus write in his *The Culture of Power and the Power of Culture*, that already, during the Middle Ages, 'a sense of English identity was many centuries old'.[5] He adopts the views expressed recently by Thorlac Turville-Petre, whose very name seems to represent an amalgam of the Anglo-Saxon and the Anglo-Norman, that 'by the middle of the thirteenth century ... a sense of English national identity expressed itself through a consciousness of having a distinct and charted territory, a common history, common cultural traditions, common law, a single economy with a common coinage and taxation, and finally some concept of shared rights'.[6] But there was as yet no common, indigenous, vernacular language. We might agree with all of this, but prefer to speak in terms of 'regnal' rather than 'national' identity. It is an English kingdom, as much as an English 'nation', 'people' or 'state', which is here being celebrated. And that kingdom's relations with other powers and peoples, not only with its Celtic neighbours, but with France, became an essential part of its own self-definition.

Two related questions present themselves in this context: on the one hand, the rise of sentiments of national identity and, on the other, their apparent co-existence with notions of a common or supra-national culture. We know that there was Anglo-French conflict in the later Middle Ages; but was there an Anglo-French culture? If there was, then it would follow that ideas certainly crossed the English Channel – in both directions, perhaps, in times of both war and peace (or rather, truce). One crucial period in Anglo-French relations ran from the mid-thirteenth to the mid-fourteenth century. As we have seen, this saw the origins, preliminaries and outbreak of the conflict which we call the *Hundred* Years War, conventionally dated 1337–1453. Historians of later periods now refer to this as the *first* Hundred Years War: a second was to follow, ending, apparently, only in 1815. Some might argue that these conflicts were merely phases in a *six* hundred years war, punctuated by truces, between England and France. Whatever the case, the thirteenth and fourteenth centuries witnessed some of the origins of that long period of mistrust and estrangement that marked Anglo-French relations until the twentieth century. Old animosities run deep, and the common French view, for example, that it was the English alone, rather than the collaborating French themselves, who unilaterally and exclusively condemned Jeanne d'Arc is alive and well and living in many French, and indeed some British, textbooks.[7]

Yet at an earlier period of Anglo-French relations – that is, the prelude to the Hundred Years War, running from the fateful peace treaty made at Paris in 1259 to the outbreak of the Anglo-French war in 1337 and Edward III's assumption of his claim to the throne of France in 1340 – the issue of identity was already apparent. There can be no doubt that at that time there *was* a sense of English identity, of 'Englishness' and of awareness that the English had their own ethnic origins. Much of this sentiment was beginning to be bound up with language. In 1295, for example, Edward I could make play in a writ of summons to the English clergy – during an Anglo-French war – with the suggestion that the French intended to 'destroy the English language' (*linguam anglicam*).[8] Exactly the same allegation was made by Edward III, somewhat ironically in French, in writs of 1344 and 1346 in very similar circumstances. Now a common language can certainly express feelings of national identity, but we have to ask how common was the English language at this time? Regional dialects and their variants meant that there was in fact no common or standard English at all, and that a man (or woman) from Northumberland or even Lancashire would find it very difficult, if not impossible, to understand someone from Sussex or Devon. The collapse and fragmentation of Old English – the pre-Norman Conquest language – during the later eleventh and twelfth century had made French, in its Anglo-Norman forms, the literal lingua franca of English society. It was only in the second half of the fourteenth century that, as a result of the rise of London English and the language of Chaucer and Gower, with its large number of French loan-words and Gallicisms, Middle English became anything like a common literary vernacular. Most of those whom we could describe as the English middle- and upper-classes spoke French, or its Anglo-Norman variant, as well as a type of English, usually heavily regional in form.

The evidence of an early rhyming chronicle composed in Middle English between about 1294 and 1300, by a monk at the abbey of St Peter's, Gloucester, is interesting in this respect. As we have seen, the monk, whose name was Robert, had a certain sense of pride in his native land.[9] But he did not equate a strong sense of English identity with the use of the English language. He declared:

> The Normans spoke nought but their own speech,
> And spoke French, as they did at home, and did their children teach;
> So that high men of this land [England], that of their blood came,

Holdeth all such speech, that they took from the same,
For unless he speaks French, a man's worth is less,
As low men holden to English, and their own speech confess;
I think there be in all the world countries none
That hold not to their own speech, but England is one;
For I think to know both, well it is,
As the more a man knows, the more worth he is ...'[10]

The monk seems to be saying that in order to attain status and what he would
have called 'worthiness' in English society at the end of the thirteenth century,
you had to speak French. The closest parallel might be with the situation of
Belgium in the nineteenth century, when every Fleming who wished to rise
in society had to speak the French of the upper classes as well as his native
Netherlandish. Of course, the kind of French spoken in England during our
period was not that of Paris and the Île-de-France. Anglo-Norman evolved many
of its own structures and forms, but it was apparently quite comprehensible to
the French themselves, despite the attempts made in French courtly literature to
mock and parody it. Similarly, to judge by some of their letters and the books in
their library collections, the best Parisian French was perfectly well understood
by the English upper classes.

How then did a sense of English national identity emerge? In one shape, it
came from the exploitation of xenophobia (that is, the hatred of foreigners, and
of the 'other', including Jews, Italian merchants and, above all, the French) by
governments, especially at times of crisis. Edward I did this in 1295, as we have
seen, and Edward III was to do likewise after the Hundred Years War began. It
had always been difficult to squeeze money and supplies, through taxation and
purveyance, out of reluctant subjects. The English crown was to some extent in
a more favourable position than some of its European neighbours by this period.
The existence of one central representative assembly – Parliament – certainly
helped it to raise subsidies for war, whether against the French, the Scots, the
Welsh, the Irish or any other enemy. But subjects and their representatives had
to be convinced and cajoled, and one way of doing this was to play upon fears
of the foreigner, his intentions and ambitions. To give the 'English' some sense
of their own identity, the call for aid – whether military or financial – against a
common enemy was best expressed in terms of perceived (or imagined) threats:
to their language, their culture, their livelihoods.

Yet the very fact that some of these exhortations were expressed not in English,
but in French, seems paradoxical. There was apparently nothing to preclude
the most patriotic of sentiments from being presented in a language shared
with the king's enemies. Indeed the first occurrence of the term 'the English
nation' in English administrative, financial and diplomatic sources, round about
1330, is found in French as 'la nacion Dengleterre'.[11] The Latin *natio anglicana*

appears slightly earlier (*c.* 1310–20) in documents emanating from the royal administration. We may also have to be rather careful about how we define 'nacion' or *natio* at this time. 'Nation' in the modern sense will probably not do, as the medieval *natio* could mean a 'people' rather than the inhabitants of a sovereign nation-state. It also served to describe bodies of masters and students at medieval universities, grouped under vaguely geographical categories; so French threats to the English 'people' rather than 'nation', let alone 'nation-state', on the eve of the Hundred Years War might fit the bill better.

This brings us straight to the problem of what kind of conflict the Hundred Years War, in origin, really was: a national war, a feudal quarrel or a dynastic struggle? There were elements of the last two of these in its origins but little, if any, of the first – that is, of the war between nations. We are still in a period when the ruling dynasties were closely linked by both kinship and feudal ties to each other. The Plantagenet monarchy's position after 1259 as a vassal of the crown of France for its remaining French possessions is very well known. So are the dynastic bonds of marriage and their accompanying claims to the throne of France which the English monarchy could assert, for the first time, after the death of the last Capetian, Charles IV, in 1328. But the very concept of 'national' wars, or wars of nations, was distinctly under-developed at this time. It was the *king's* cause that was at issue, supported (or not supported, as the case may be) by the king's subjects as part of their obligation of loyalty to the ruling house. What is remarkable about the reign of Edward III (1327–77) is that the crown was able, by and large, to gather the support of its people for an active, aggressive foreign war, something which many of its greater and middling subjects had resisted in earlier reigns. The unwillingness of the English baronage to fight abroad was overcome by Edward III's conduct of his war aims against France. How this came about is another story – and cannot detain us here.

Was there, then, any kind of English cultural identity before the Hundred Years War, or was England largely a cultural annexe of France in the two or so centuries after the Norman Conquest?

When, if at all, was there a 'triumph of the vernacular' in England? And what is the evidence for an identification of 'national' sentiment with the use of the English language? What part was played by language in the process of the nation's self-definition? It is instructive to note, in this respect, that the first vernacular language to be used, alongside Latin, in the formal documents of English royal administration was Anglo-Norman French, not Middle English, from *c.* 1250 onwards. Letters under the privy seal were drawn up in French from the 1290s until the reign of Henry VI (1422–61). Letters under the secret seal and signet appeared in English for the first time under Henry V (1413–22).[12] By the 1440s some Exchequer documents, such as warrants for issues, appeared in English, as well as bills and petitions presented in Parliament. But one effect of the continued English presence in fifteenth-century France was the continuance of French as a language of government, diplomacy, administration, correspondence and discourse. In October 1404, for example, English envoys to the duchess of Burgundy could refer to the fact that great secular lords, both English and French, such as the dukes of Lancaster, York, Berry and Burgundy, all understood French far better than they did Latin, and thus the 'general truces' between England and France had been drawn up in French rather than Latin.[13] The envoys drew an analogy with St Jerome's Vulgate translation of the Hebrew books of the Old Testament. The realization of a Lancastrian kingdom of France between 1419 and 1424 meant that a new Anglo-French nobility and gentry, holding land and office in the French kingdom and duchy of Normandy, was also born. The use of the French language by them was both natural and imperative. If there was an English 'ascendancy' in Lancastrian France, its native tongue was French, not English. Hence the records of the Paris Parlement and other courts under the Lancastrian regime continued to be kept in Latin or French. As with law and custom, so with language: the kingdoms of England and France, although conjoined in the person of one sovereign, remained independent and separate linguistic and administrative entities.

Yet the war with France, and the consequent growth in more markedly generalized anti-French sentiments among the English, had some influence upon the political and diplomatic use of language. Under Henry V (1413–22) evidence begins to emerge for a greater use of English in correspondence. In June 1422, for instance, Pope Martin V referred to a letter which he had received from Henry 'in the English tongue, explained to us through an interpreter' [in idiomate anglicano].[14] This had been written in Henry's own hand – in a language in which, perhaps, he felt most comfortable to write unaided. It is arguable whether or not Henry's French was imperfect: on occasion he may have used the argument as a diplomatic ploy. In December 1418, he demanded the use of Latin, not French, in diplomatic exchanges with France, ostensibly because 'he says that he did not perfectly understand it [French], nor did his council' so that if any controversy should arise 'from French usage … then one should revert to the Latin meaning and written record … and he said this on account of the equivocations and synonyms of French words'.[15] Latin should be advocated as the language of diplomacy because it was 'impartial to every nation' [indifferens omni nationi].[16] The primacy of Latin and French in international dealings meant that other vernacular languages were not often widely known or understood outside their countries of origin. Despite the evident 'imperialism' of the English crown during the fifteenth century – expressed on the international stage through, for example, the general councils of the Church – the English language was well known only in the British Isles (including Scotland, where it was used for

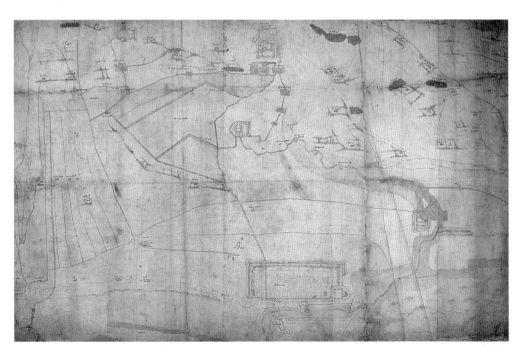

1. Henry I of England, Duke of Normandy, crossing the Channel in a hulk. The regularity of cross-Channel journeys by the Anglo-Norman and Angevin kings was a common feature of the period up to 1204 (*Chronicle of John of Worcester, c.1118–40*). *The Bridgeman Art Library.*

2. Map of Calais and the English Pale in the reign of Henry VIII. The map shows the town of Calais and the outlying fortresses at Guînes, Ardres, Fiennes, Sangatte and Hamme. The strategically vital strongpoint at Newneham Bridge ('*ne non bruge*' on the map) can be seen just to the north-east of the town (*Chronicle of Calais*). *The British Library.*

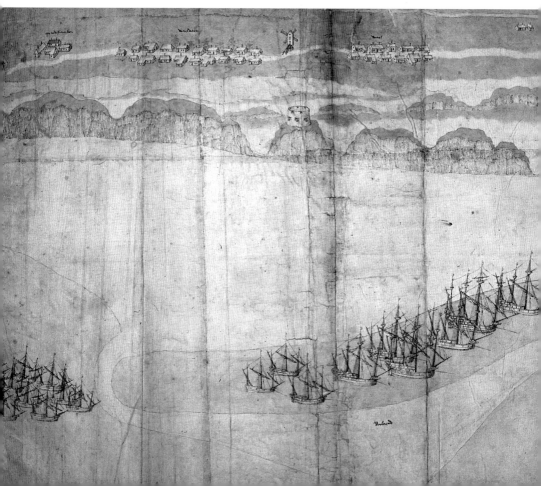

5. Town seal of Winchelsea, one of the Cinque Ports, early fourteenth century. The seal depicts a typical vessel of the period, with 'castles' at bow and stern, and bears the legend: 'The seal of the barons of the lord king of England of Winchelsea' (National Maritime Museum, Greenwich). *The Bridgeman Art Library.*

3. (*previous page – top*) Computer-generated reconstruction of the former Plantagenet castle of the Ombrière at Bordeaux, now totally destroyed, set beside the modern adjoining buildings on the site today. It was from the Ombrière that the duchy of Aquitaine was governed during the Plantagenet and Lancastrian periods. *AXYZ Images. With the kind permission of the municipality of Bordeaux.*

4. (*previous page – bottom*) View of Calais in the reign of Henry VIII. The town was heavily fortified and its harbour defended by the 'Rysbank' fort which acted as a barbican (*Chronicle of Calais*). *The British Library.*

diplomatic correspondence beside Latin and French). This was to remain so until the eighteenth century. Some foreign rulers and their nobles, however, had more than a passing acquaintance with it.

As a result of his capture and imprisonment in England between 1415 and 1440, Charles, duke of Orléans, composed lyric and narrative poetry in English as well as French. His brother, Jean, count of Angouleme, also a prisoner in England, is known to have owned a manuscript of Chaucer's *Canterbury Tales* (BN, MS angl. 39). But these were exceptional cases: it has been observed that 'a reading knowledge of French among the [fifteenth-century] English nobility could usually be taken for granted; the reverse could not'.[17] Strong family ties, as well as extended periods of residence in England, could also encourage knowledge of English at this time. In August 1475, for example, Charles the Bold of Burgundy, who had married Margaret of York seven years previously, spoke angrily to her brother Edward IV of England in English about his duplicitous behaviour in negotiations with France. Commynes tells us that 'ledict duc se courroussa et parla angloys (car il scavoit le langaige)' ['the said duke became angry and spoke English (for he knew the language)'].[18] There was, however, no question of Edward's competence in French: a few days later, Commynes tells us, Edward had met Louis XI of France at Picquigny and conversed with him 'en assez bon francois' ['in quite good French'].[19] Some Burgundian nobles, such as Louis de Bruges, lord of Gruuthuse, as well as some commercial and mercantile intermediaries between England and the Burgundian dominions, may also have spoken English at this time. But they were in a small minority. At lower social levels, monoglotism seems to have prevailed. In October 1442, English soldiers serving at La Réole in Aquitaine had to be provided with an English-speaking Dominican confessor because 'they neither spoke nor understood French nor Gascon'.[20] This must no doubt also have been the case in many of the Norman garrisons, manned largely by English soldiery, at that time. Among those who could both read and write, use of the vernacular was relatively widespread by that date. Yet, although Middle English became an acceptable language of literary production and discourse among the higher echelons of English society between 1380 and 1420, it remained an essentially insular tongue. There is no evidence that Chaucer, Langland or Lydgate were known outside the British Isles and the March of Calais. Spoken and written English remained beyond the boundaries of a European audience.[21] Yet this very insularity pointed to an important feature of English culture: while continuing to share much with their continental neighbours, the English now had a common written language. However artificial and contrived it was, the emergence of literacy in Middle English – whereby the vernacular language assumed many of the functions performed by Latin and Anglo-Norman – marked a significant stage in the process whereby England acquired a 'native' tongue equivalent to the *volgare illustre* of Italy and France.

It could be claimed that a number of received impressions about later medieval culture – and medieval culture in general – tend to influence our views of England's place in that cultural world, and of its relations with its French neighbour.[22] England's position as part of a predominantly francophone world, between the late eleventh and late fourteenth centuries, inevitably raises questions of cultural 'superiority' and its implications.

The first of these impressions is that the pre-eminent culture of Western Europe during the twelfth, thirteenth and fourteenth centuries was French, and that all others were overshadowed – or even eclipsed – by that of France.[23] For example, the very existence of an English court before the Tudors has been questioned. The material and ceremonial environment in which the later medieval English monarchy lived and performed its ceremonial functions is thought to have been relatively modest when compared with that of the French crown. But the English monarchy, as did the French, possessed what one might call Great Power status, with a degree of imagery, pomp and grandeur to match that role. One suspects, moreover, that later Capetian propaganda, including the eulogization of Louis IX, plus later historians' quite justified admiration for the cultural and intellectual achievements of Paris in the thirteenth century, have set the tone of much subsequent scholarship. Something called a 'court style' is said to have been born (at least in architecture and possibly manuscript illumination) under St Louis and his successors; European courtly literature is considered to be either exclusively French, or heavily influenced by French models; and the political and social functions of a court are normally traced to essentially French prototypes.

Now this picture is, superficially, an attractive one: French, since the mid- to late twelfth century, had been the language of many vernacular literatures and of much aristocratic discourse and everyday speech. Due weight must be given to the fact that the royal and princely households of, among others, England, Flanders, Artois and Hainaut between *c.* 1270 and 1350 were largely, if not exclusively, francophone.[24] But to see *francophonie* (in its more modern sense) as both a symptom and instrument of French cultural hegemony would be to distort and misread the evidence. It has been argued (by John Gillingham and Rees Davies among others) that a strong sense of 'regnal solidarity', or of national or regional identity, was in no way incompatible with the use of French, or of one of its dialects or variants, by people for whom the Capetian or Valois crown meant little or nothing – including, of course, the English. Nor do the mixed, bilingual court cultures of the Low Countries, especially of Brabant and Holland, fit easily into this monoglot pattern. A Middle Dutch courtly literature emerges in the second half of the thirteenth century. Even at the court of Flanders, usually regarded as one of the more thoroughgoingly 'French' establishments in the fourteenth century, the use of Netherlandish by both Flemish nobles, and by the evidently bilingual clerks who wrote the household accounts of Louis de Male in the 1370s and 1380s, is striking. Moreover, the uses and adaptations of French themes in the vernacular literature of the period – Middle Dutch, Middle High German and Middle English poems and prose romances – also suggest that these literatures began to assume lives of their own. Court culture is thus seen as being much more diverse and multi-faceted than before, while recent work on, for instance, the visual arts in medieval England also seems directed towards that view.

There is a danger of over-reaction – and therefore of over-statement – in this line of argument. Rival chauvinisms tend to introduce more heat than light into the debate. The point was well put by Paul Binski, from an art-historical perspective, that 'we must be wary of the deeper chauvinisms of art history, the resistant beliefs in the supremacy of Parisian art over French, of French art over English, or of Italian art over both'.[25] It remains a truism that a degree of common, francophone culture prevailed among western European aristocracies. One (but only one) expression of this sense of cultural community lay in the cult and practice of chivalry. But there were other manifestations of 'internationalism' or 'supra-nationalism' which deserve a hearing. The princely court, because it provided a focus for diplomatic exchanges and dynastic marriages; for the patronage of artists and performers drawn from a very wide geographical area; and (not least) for tournaments and other events which overrode national or regional boundaries, inevitably tended to be cosmopolitan in nature. I have tried to set out some of the main traits of this common culture of the courts elsewhere, arguing for the vital role played by well-placed intermediaries – both clerical and lay – between the higher levels of English and French society in the century before the Hundred Years War.[26] These were men and women who shared certain cultural norms and expectations of courtly behaviour, to whom concepts such as *debonaireté* or *courtoisie* had real and significant meaning. The 'courtly' quality of *debonaireté* was especially prized, with its connotations of affability, good nature, moderation and slowness to anger. Among the English nobility and knighthood, at their higher levels and among those retained in the king's, queen's and their kinsmen's and kinswomen's households, there was clearly a broad familiarity with their continental neighbours. Plantagenet retention of territories within France – that is, Aquitaine and Ponthieu – and very strong dynastic links with both France and the Low Countries, could only further such tendencies. As a result, one is constantly confronted with paradoxes and apparent anomalies in this world of high politics and ambiguous relationships.

The enormous popularity of the tournament can also play havoc with mono-lithic notions of knightly dedication to 'national' or even 'regnal' causes at this time. Take the case of Sir Giles Argentine, who in 1302 and 1306 in effect deserted Edward I's army in Scotland in order to participate in tournaments, one of them abroad.[27] He was not alone, for the names of 21 other household knights, including a Basset, two Beauchamps, two Bohuns, Chandos, Gaveston, Leyburn and Mortimer were also recorded as being absent without leave. Conversely, French knights, including Jean de Prie in 1279 and Jean de Nesle in 1290, attended tournaments in England, despite the tournament bans imposed by the French crown.[28] It seems, moreover, that the increasingly prevalent idea that the English aristocracy had ceased to be international by the thirteenth century (if not before) has to be qualified by evidence of this kind. If, as seems plausible, attachment of some kind to the royal household and its dependent offshoots was not uncommon among the knighthood (especially among the *milites strenui*), then it could be argued that an entrée into the more cosmopolitan world of the court served to preserve some degree of internationalism among this elite.

There are also historiographical issues which come into play in this context. British historians tend, perhaps, to be unduly influenced by opposing tendencies within British and French historical writing: on the British side of the Channel historians have tended to cut their medieval kings down to size (a tendency well illustrated by K. B. McFarlane's critical examination of Edward I);[29] whereas among French historians the monarchy tends to be elevated above the rest of aristocratic society, representing the majestic continuity of the State. It was, until quite recently, doubtful whether any contemporary English medieval historian would, or could, ever write in such terms. Recent developments have, however, given rise to the advocacy of a more 'statist' or 'centralist' view among historians of medieval England and its dependencies.[30] Yet later medieval English kings, it is argued, were all too human; from 1327 onwards they tended to be killed by their own subjects; their alleged extravagances and financial embarrassments are recounted by English historians with evident relish; and their supposedly ramshackle and penurious households are declared not to be true courts until Richard II attempted to create a court on the French pattern and got his just deserts. British historical writing may have been much influenced, perhaps unconsciously, by the nation's traumatic experience of Stuart monarchy in the seventeenth century. Attitudes towards the Crown, its court and household, came to be determined by the overriding objective of preventing the emergence in Britain of anything approaching what were deemed to be the absolutist regimes of continental Europe. After 1688, there could be no British Versailles, no representational court culture of the kind promoted there, or at Potsdam or the minor courts of Europe.[31] The Crown was literally cut down to size by parsimonious Parliamentary grants to its court and household, while cultural patronage found its best representatives among the aristocracy and the affluent middle-class public, especially in London. It is hardly surprising that British historians should, until relatively recently, have adopted similar attitudes towards the pre-Stuart monarchy.

Recent work has, however, gradually begun to move in a contrary direction. To argue, for example, that because the Plantagenet monarchy was constantly itinerant it did not establish a firm political, ideological and cultural base is to misread the evidence. Plantagenet mobility did not preclude the holding of courts of considerable splendour – not least at events such as the Feast of the Swans at Pentecost 1306 – and recent work, for example, on material culture and the distribution of liveries in Edward I's and Edward III's households suggests a much more lavish provision for 'courtly' activities than had previously been suspected.[32]

This meant that the English court was in no way out of line with developments elsewhere in Europe. There was, at this level, something approaching a common, shared culture, which extended over high-status patrons in both Church and State. A good example of the close cultural connections between France and England in the later thirteenth century is to be found in the history of the Norman Benedictine abbey of Fécamp. Now Fécamp was the first Norman monastery to receive an English endowment, and that endowment pre-dated the Norman Conquest.[33] After 1066, the abbey held extensive and valuable English lands, including the priories of Coggs (Oxfordshire) and Warminghurst (Sussex), from which its steward in England sent an estimated 400 marks to the abbot in 1294.[34] With the outbreak of Anglo-French war in June 1294, however, Edward I regarded all French monks in England as threats and potential enemies and confiscated their property. Yet, as Donald Matthew has shown, Fécamp was relatively well treated by the English crown and its agents at this time. Within weeks of the outbreak of war, custody of Fécamp's English lands was restored to the abbey and, as was the custom with other alien priories, royal protection was secured on payment of fines and an agreement to account for all revenues at the Exchequer. Further sanctions were taken by Edward in 1297, but in April 1298 the abbot of Fécamp – after petitioning the king – recovered his English estates and was then excused payment of fines because of certain 'special services' he had performed for the king. What these were remains unknown, but the abbot and convent's awareness of the value and significance of its English connections and holdings may also have received expression in a somewhat unexpected manner.

At this time of Anglo-French conflict, building work was in progress at Fécamp itself, namely on the construction of the Lady Chapel at the east end of the abbey church of La Trinité. The building programme was completed by 1307, and the chapel was adorned with a series of stained-glass windows representing the lives of two saintly kings, one English and one French: Edward the Confessor and the very recently-canonized (1297) Louis IX, whose cult was authorized in 1305.[35] Their date suggests the possibility of connection with political events: perhaps with a desire of the abbots and convent to retain the goodwill of English kings, who often conspicuously lacked that quality, or to celebrate the marriages to French brides of Edward I (1299) and Edward II

(1308).[36] There was no other representation of the Confessor's life in French art, with one exception, before this date, although his name appeared in the Litany and Sanctoral of some French churches, especially in Normandy. Now the Confessor had been in exile at Fécamp until 1041, and his anniversary had been commemorated there ever since. The Fécamp Lady Chapel, with its series of 11 surviving glass panels depicting scenes from his life, dates from the abbacies of Guillaume de Putot (1285–97) and Thomas de St-Benoît (1297–1307). There were originally probably 20 scenes from the Confessor's life and 20 from St Louis', set under architectural canopies very similar to those in the north aisle glass at York minster (also dating from c. 1306). A date of c. 1310 for the Fécamp series has been proposed by the compilers of the most recent volume (for Haute-Normandie) in the *Corpus Vitrearum medii aevi* (2001).[37] But the source for the life of St Edward seems not, as once argued and accepted by the compilers of the *Corpus*, to have been an Anglo-Norman verse *Estoire de Saint Aedward le rei* attributed to Matthew Paris, now in the University Library, Cambridge, dating from c. 1240–50.[38] There are substantial differences in the iconography and representation of the scenes from the Confessor's life between the glass and the manuscript. It seems that the glaziers, working at Rouen – or whoever drew up a programme for them – may have worked from a version of the earlier *Life* of the Confessor by Ailred of Rievaulx, probably written to mark the first translation of the saint's relics in 1165. An Anglo-Norman verse translation of a version of this work certainly existed by 1200.

Among the scenes from St Edward's life which were illustrated in the glass at Fécamp were: (a) Edward and his wife Edith taking a vow of chastity; (b) Edward attending mass and witnessing a miracle during its celebration; (c) Edward directing the reconstruction of Westminster abbey (consecrated in December 1065). They are paralleled by scenes from the life of St Louis, including: (a) St Louis returning from the Seventh Crusade; (b) St Louis feeding a leper at Royaumont; and (c) St Louis delivering the crown of thorns to the bishop of Paris. Appropriately, the ground colour for the scenes from the Confessor's life is red; that for St Louis is blue, sown with fleurs-de-lis, making the two series heraldically consistent. The St Edward series was prefigured at a slightly earlier date (c. 1280) by the windows representing saints with English connections in the west aisle of the north transept of Amiens cathedral.[39] These showed St Edward the Confessor, St Edmund and St Augustine of Canterbury and have been associated with the *Mise* of Amiens in 1264 when Henry III met St Louis to receive his arbitration of his dispute with the English baronage. The fact that images and representations of the lives of both St Edward and St Louis are known to have been made in France before the Anglo-French marriage of 1308 means that we need not necessarily link the Fécamp glass to that single event. At Fécamp the references to the Confessor were especially relevant and, as we have seen, the programme may have been drawn up during, or shortly after, the Anglo-French hostilities of 1294–1303. The abbey stood to lose very substantially from war between England and France as a result of confiscation of its English holdings.[40] There were therefore pressures within France for the two rulers to keep the peace. To commission representations of the life of a French, as well as an English, saintly king also enabled the house at Fécamp to keep a foot firmly in both camps, Capetian and Plantagenet.

It has been pointed out that the Fécamp cycle of the *Life* of the Confessor 'must be regarded as French in style, though with close English affinities; its iconography is entirely English'.[41] The compilers of the *Corpus vitrearum*, while emphasizing the links to Paris and Rouen, also admit to the presence of English influences on the style of the glass, with its elongated figures, delicate depiction of faces, and architectural framing.[42] The cycle at Fécamp also stresses the significance of Westminster as the centre of his cult.[43] Now the creation of Westminster abbey as we know it today was of course largely a product of the reign of Henry III (1216–72). It became the focus of a thriving cult of St Edward: the king adopted the saint as his patron, beautified his shrine in 1267–8, named his eldest son after him, had a fictitious coat of arms invented for the Confessor and commissioned wall-paintings, stained glass and sculptures of his life. The great building programmes and decorative schemes begun at Westminster under Henry III were continued by his successors, especially by Edward I and Edward III. But what has this to do with Anglo-French relations? First, it is clear that the closely inter-related courts of England and France at this time strove to imitate and emulate each other. The campaigns of building initiated by Henry III and Edward I, and the near-contemporary developments on the Île-de-la-Cite, at the Louvre and at the abbey church of St Denis under Louis IX and Philip the Fair were similar in intention. Sir Howard Colvin has remarked that 'what Rheims and St Denis were to the house of Capet, Westminster should be to the house of Plantagenet'.[44] The sacral kingship of the Capetians was now to be paralleled by the growth of what might be termed a Plantagenet ideology resting upon the cults of English king-saints, while the Angevin inheritance of the English crown now began to play a secondary role, though it was still remembered by close ties with and gifts to the abbey of Fontevrault, that ancestral burial-place of the house of Anjou. But the burial-place of the Plantagenets came, in time, to be fixed at Westminster, just as St Denis became that of the Capetians from Louis IX onwards.[45] The direction of the works at Westminster was in the hands of Master Henri de Reyns (Rheims) between 1245 and 1253, and architectural affinities between the abbey church and the cathedrals at both Rheims and Amiens were strong. It is perhaps paradoxical that the close dynastic and cultural connections between England and France at this time in fact led to a promotion of a more anglocentric Plantagenet kingship and its supporting cults. But this was a highly significant development.

It has been suggested (by Professor Sir James Holt) that one reason for the Plantagenet loss of Normandy to the French in 1204, and of Poitou in 1242, lay in the fact that the English royal house did not at that time possess a distinctive ideology.[46] That omission was, however, soon to be rectified, and a cult of Plantagenet kingship, with a clear historical focus, emerged under Henry III and Edward I. In time this became a source to be drawn upon in rivalry and conflict with the French. But another unrelated saint became associated with the English crown and, indeed, people at this time. This was the crusaders' patron saint, the legendary but distinctly non-English George of Cappadocia. There is, however, some evidence of his cult in England at a much earlier date. In English *laudes regiae* (hymns of praise to the king) of the late eleventh century, the soldier-saints Maurice, Sebastian and George were said to ensure 'safety and victory to all English princes and armies'. His emblem – the red cross on a white or argent ground – did not, however, become part of the insignia of English royal armies until the reigns of Henry III and Edward I. By then a much keener and distinct sense of dynastic, regnal and, subsequently, national identity was beginning to develop. The creation of the Collegiate chapel of St George at Windsor in August 1348, and the dedication of the Order of the Garter to him as patron, represented the culmination of this tendency and we can begin to speak of a kind of 'national' chivalry under Edward III, but pledged to support the king's great cause in France.[47]

Second, the tombs and chapels at the east end of Westminster Abbey proved highly influential in determining the future development of commemorative monuments in England. A burial-place at Westminster was sought not only by the Plantagenet kings themselves but by some of their closest kinsmen and kinswomen.[48] Clustering around the shrine of St Edward, in the so-called 'royal chapels', the tombs of Henry III's French (that is, Lusignan) relatives – William and Aymer de Valence – of Edward I's wife Eleanor of Castile and his brother Edmund, earl of Lancaster (Crouchback), and of Edward III's brother John of Eltham are found. All these tombs display very pronounced French influences, stemming from those in St Denis constructed during (and after) Louis IX's re-ordering of the royal tombs in the abbey church. Edward I modelled Queen Eleanor of Castile's tomb upon those in St Denis, and French examples, beginning 30 or so years before, provided a source for the so-called 'weepers' on the side of English tomb-chests. The introduction of the canopied tomb, moreover, set either between columns or in a wall-niche, was a direct importation from France into England. English masons and sculptors were extremely receptive to such influences throughout this period. Many – but not all – of their works possessed a strong family likeness to their French counterparts and prototypes. The integration of French-inspired architectural motifs into English wall-paintings, stained glass, monumental sculpture and illuminated books was increasingly common after about 1260 and may in part reflect the *détente* established between the courts of England and France under Henry III and Edward I. Dr Binski has pointed to a 'common reservoir of styles' and a shared 'court style' in manuscript illumination during the decades around 1300.[49] English scribes and illuminators are found working in Paris, and influences deriving from English styles, with their own particular features, have been detected in French manuscripts. A stock of imagery that was French, rather than English, also informed the decorative scheme chosen under Edward I for the king's Painted Chamber in the palace of Westminster. The Old Testament book of Maccabees, and the personifications of Vices and Virtues found in French illuminated manuscripts such as those of the *Somme le Roi*, probably written by Philip III of France's confessor in the later 1270s, provided both Henry III and Edward I with material of a didactic kind with which to adorn the walls of their chamber.[50] In sum, there can be no doubt of the very close connections between English and northern French painting at this time.

This period of relative political and diplomatic *détente*, however, came to an end in 1294. Although there is evidence of some deterioration in relations between England and France before that date, the outbreak of Anglo-French war over Aquitaine in that year was, as we have seen, in some ways the most important turning-point in the sequence of events which led to the Hundred Years War. Yet the cultural influences and exchanges continued through the War of St Sardos (again over Aquitaine) in 1324–6. It was only after the renewed outbreak of war in 1337 that one can begin to speak of a deeper rift between the courts of England and France, now increasingly bereft of effective intermediaries (including the papacy) who had previously striven hard to keep the peace. This had cultural consequences. The betrothal of Edward III to Philippa of Hainaut – a principality independent of France – in 1326; the accession of Philip VI – as the foremost representative of the house of Valois, which had traditionally been anti-Plantagenet – to the French throne in 1328; and the severing of the feudal bond between the two monarchies when Edward III assumed the title of king of France in 1340: all these events created a climate in which Anglo-French relations could never be quite the same in future. The war of the Capetian succession, as one might be tempted to call the 'first' Hundred Years War, had begun. Plantagenet emulation of the Capetians under Henry III and Edward I, at Westminster and elsewhere, had – paradoxically – produced an image of a more anglocentric monarchy, which reflected political realities. The notion and, in the fifteenth century, the reality of an Anglo-French dual monarchy similarly served to heighten an awareness of English identity. Anglo-French culture was to become more Anglo-Burgundian, but both Henry VII and Henry VIII of England, as we shall see, still had much in common with their French contemporaries. Mutual antagonism was offset by mutual attraction. The two kingdoms, together with their peoples, continued to re-define and re-invent themselves in relation to each other. The English Channel, in cultural terms, remained a highway for, rather than a barrier to, the movement of people and the transmission of ideas.

6

The Legend of Joan of Arc

Charles de Gaulle's views of England's role as France's 'hereditary enemy' reflected a traditional and long-standing French attitude, which had experienced a significant revival in the course of the nineteenth century.[1] De Gaulle dated the origins of that hostility to the Hundred Years War, a period which saw the brief life, martyrdom and subsequent rehabilitation of Joan of Arc (*c.* 1412–31), the Maid of Orléans, as represented in historical writing, popular journalism, pietist hagiography and republican polemic since the 1840s.[2] It had become a widespread belief that Joan had been a victim of the English occupation of northern France in the fifteenth century and that she had been charged, tried, condemned and executed solely by the English. The tenacious survival of this belief can be illustrated by an anecdote. During the Parisian troubles of 1968, a young British student found himself caught up in a violent demonstration. Innocent soul that he was, he thought he might escape arrest, or at least assault, by displaying his British passport. This proved counter-productive. A charging member of the Compagnies Républicaines de Securité promptly hit him with a bâton saying 'that's for Joan of Arc' ['Ça, c'est pour Jeanne d'Arc!']. An episode in the medieval history of France and England still exercised its baleful influence on the popular imagination. But the Joan of Arc story has become a legend and saint's cult of worldwide appeal unparalleled, perhaps, by any other myth which – unlike, for example, the Arthurian legend – rests on historical rather than fictitious foundations. To explain that phenomenon we must discover how the episode has been represented in national histories and how history has been transformed into myth in the consciousness of both nations. A potent constituent in the brew which perpetuates the notion of an 'ancient enmity' between England and France had been added to the mixture.

The phase of the Anglo-French war in which our heroine is deemed to have played such a significant part was essentially Henry V of England's (1413–22) war. As we have already seen, by 1420, the more limited conflict begun in the fourteenth century under Edward III had become a war of full-scale conquest and occupation in northern France. The founder of the Oxford School of Modern History, whose historical interpretations were to prove formative for generations of English scholars and students, devoted some consideration to the subject. William Stubbs, in his *Constitutional History of England in its Origin and Development* (1878) delivered a damning verdict on that war:

> The war of Henry V in France must be condemned by the judgement of modern opinion; it was a bold, a desperate undertaking, fraught with suffering to all concerned in it; but it is as a great national enterprise, too great for the nation which undertook it to maintain, that it chiefly presents itself among the prominent features of the time.[3]

The war, Stubbs continued, 'was to a certain extent felt to be a national glory, and the peace that ended it a national disgrace'.[4] There was no question here that the Anglo-French conflict was anything but a war which pitted nation against nation, and in which the unitary nation-state provided the sole point of reference for historical analysis and enquiry. It is worth comparing Stubbs's view with that of the author of a recent volume in the *New Oxford History of England* (2005). Gerald Harriss, in his excellent *Shaping the Nation: England, 1360–1461* sums up Henry V's war:

> The myth of Agincourt was never forgotten, nor was Henry V's vision ever condemned. That has been left to historians, who have judged the whole enterprise flawed and to have left a *damnosa hereditas* for his successor ... Henry [however] envisaged England and France brought to a mutual peace through a common kingship and promoting internal order and justice through their own institutions and laws. Multiple kingdoms of this kind were both conceivable and feasible in this and the following century, and though it aroused some mistrust many English and French accepted it in 1420 ... But with [Henry's] death ... the peace that was meant to knit English and French together became a war that inflamed their old enmity and reinforced their separate identities.[5]

Clearly the frame of reference has here shifted away somewhat from national glory and national disgrace towards a rather different optic: the more pluralistic, multiple, composite political formations of early modern Europe, in which England and France perhaps provided the exceptions, not the norms. The death of Henry V's vision and achievement was not sudden – his war continued for 31 years after his death (which *was* sudden). Joan of Arc certainly contributed to its demise. But if, as she told her interrogators, her higher aim was to bring the warring powers of Christendom together in a joint venture against the infidel then, ironically, she shared that aim with Henry V.[6] Yet both of them succeeded only in inflaming and protracting the conflict between the two kingdoms. Such is often the fate of charismatic visionaries who have engaged in military activity.

To establish the place of the Joan of Arc story in the national histories of both France and England is not a particularly enviable task. It condemns the hapless historian to exposure to a veritable torrent of secondary literature about her. This has been written from every conceivable standpoint and vastly outweighs the historical sources for her brief, if action-packed, life and its abrupt end.

Even the dossier of evidence presented to the Vatican for her canonization process between its inception in 1894 and its successful conclusion in 1920 ran to 1,740 pages, far in excess of the total volume of records upon which it rested.[7] Much of this subsequent writing is concerned with advocating and furthering a particular cause – and much of it, as history, is nonsense. In national histories, it has contributed a minor share to what Patrick Geary has, perhaps over-dramatically, described as that 'toxic waste dump, filled with the poison of ethnic nationalism'.[8] Its interest lies solely in what it can tell us about the subsequent changing political, religious and intellectual climates in which Joan's story and its aftermath was debated, often passionately, far less often rationally. It could, for example, be argued that the Joan of Arc received by us in the twenty-first century, is still essentially a creation of the French Third Republic; or, if not a creation of that period, at least a product of the bitter and unrelenting controversies which erupted during its course, notably between 1870 and 1914. The First World War and its aftermath demanded a symbol of national unity and a patron saint for the immense sacrifice offered by the French people: this hastened her canonization by both Church and State in 1920, when she received both a liturgical and secular feast day. This was soon to be followed by her appropriation by another set of rival and, in the event, diametrically opposed interests – Vichy and France Libre – between 1940 and 1945.[9] Since then, the battle for possession of Joan of Arc has raged on unabated between the French political Left, Centre and Right, recently inflamed by a re-kindling of ethnic and racial tensions and expressed, for example, by the Front National in the words:

> She [Joan] is there to tell us that we belong to a community [that is, a nation] which is ours, which is different from that of others, and of which we should be proud, because it is our own and that of our ancestors.[10]

As an icon of national identity, national consciousness, national exceptionalism and exclusivity, and of political and cultural nationalism, Joan of Arc seems to meet all the criteria for inclusion among those who have played a fundamental – if unwitting – part in the construction and reconstruction of national histories in Europe.

Much of this is, of course, common knowledge, and it is not necessary to dwell in detail on the political and intellectual debates which lie behind much of the writing about Joan of Arc. Yet to make her into an icon of nationalism, she has in effect to be emptied of much historical content and removed from her historical context. Or, alternatively, that context has to be represented and interpreted in a particular, often partisan, light and from a standpoint compatible with assumptions about the nation prevailing at a given time. We are presented with a national icon *avant la lettre*. Now historians of French national identity or, as some would prefer it, of French national consciousness, simply cannot agree

whether or not such notions existed at all before 1789.[11] There is no consensus on
the issue and the jury is still out on that question. Twenty-first century concepts
and features of the nation may not be applicable to later medieval France which
(like early modern France) 'was still heavily illiterate, multilingual, riven by
myriad internal boundaries, and hampered by poor communications'.[12] How
could any widespread sense of being part of a distinct national community,
real or imagined, have evolved in such conditions? Even among the political
and intellectual elite, where one might expect to find an articulate expression
of national consciousness, there is very little to suggest its existence. The
propaganda emanating from the Valois house of France in the fifteenth century
saw the *monarchy* as the incarnation and embodiment of the French people
– as did Joan of Arc herself. Much of the argument against the Lancastrians was
couched in essentially dynastic – not nationalistic – terms, in which the ideology,
attributes and symbolic insignia of the French crown were set out in a language
of legitimacy rather than of cultural, linguistic, ethnic or racial exclusivity.[13] After
all, there were a number of different peoples, many of whom did not have French
as their mother tongue, in fifteenth-century France. Aside from the propaganda,
political reality and political behaviour did not accord easily with sentiments of
national identity or currents of national feeling. Take the case of Joan's judges
and assessors at Rouen in 1431.

   The career of one of those judges well illustrates the prevailing climate in
which her trial, condemnation, execution and subsequent rehabilitation took
place. He makes little appearance in the standard national histories – except as a
villain 'of blackest infamy' as Andrew Lang called him – and it is easy to see why.[14]
He provided Anatole France, in his *Vie de Jeanne d'Arc* of 1908, with excellent
illustrative material to support his case against the clergy and all their works.[15]
He even provided Père Jean-Baptiste Ayroles, SJ, in his five-volume, 3,500-page
exercise in hagiography *La Vraie Jeanne d'Arc* (1890) with an example of 'one
of the … precursors of Luther and Calvin'.[16] Master Thomas de Courcelles was
not an Englishmen, not even a Burgundian.[17] He had been a bright boy from
Normandy at the Sorbonne, rising through a doctorate to a professorship in
theology and the rectorship of the University of Paris. He was destined for
a good benefice in the Church and became a canon of Notre-Dame, eagerly
embracing the Anglo-Burgundian regime at Paris after 1420 and becoming a
convinced Gallican and conciliarist. As a willing supporter of Anglo-Burgundian
power, he served as an assessor on the tribunal which tried Joan, having also
been active in laying the charges against her in the first place. He was one of the
minority of three out of her 13 judges and assessors who recommended that she
be tortured on 12 May 1431.[18] She was not, in part because it was thought that
to do so would only cast aspersions and 'bring slander' upon the trial. Most of
the tribunal thought it would in any case serve no useful purpose. It is also to

Courcelles – who was on the whole scrupulous and painstaking – that we owe the definitive Latin version of the trial record. But, 20 years after Joan's death, political circumstances had radically changed – and Thomas de Courcelles had changed with them. 'Joan's' dauphin – the exiled and beleaguered Charles VII of the 1420s – was back in power and the English, having lost their Burgundian allies in 1435, were holding only Calais. Nothing happened to Courcelles. He retained his canonry, and subsequent deanship, of Notre-Dame and his professorship at Paris. He went on, as a supreme irony, to preach the funeral sermon for 'Joan's' dauphin in his cathedral in 1461.[19] He had been interrogated by the commission for Joan's rehabilitation in 1456 about his role in her trial. He claimed to be suffering from complete loss of memory and remembered nothing. When confronted with the record of his recommendation that she be tortured, he had no memory of it.[20] No charges were levelled against him, nor were they against any of the surviving judges, assessors and other participants in the trial of condemnation. Clearly the kind of betrayal of the French state and nation for which collaborators were tried, imprisoned and executed in and after 1945 simply did not apply in the mid-fifteenth century. It was not the aim of the newly-restored Valois regime of Charles VII to exact retribution from those who had aided and supported the previous government of Lancastrian France and Normandy. Many of them were far too useful to the new regime to be dispensed with. We will never understand later medieval politics and political ideas if assumptions derived from more recent political and moral climates are brought into play. Trafficking with the English and their Burgundian allies had been a fact of life, and a means of survival, for many 'true, good and complete Frenchmen' as Philip the Good of Burgundy – no friend of the Maid of Orléans – was described in 1435.

Nor, it can be argued, are nineteenth-century concepts any more appropriate to the fifteenth-century environment in which the historical Joan of Arc lived. So St Joan, or the Maid of Orléans, has had to be re-invented to accord with prevailing notions of the nation both over time and at any given time. The problem here lies in the fact that a number of different notions of the nation might co-exist at the same time, as they evidently did during the Third Republic. These concepts tend to be reflected in the historiography of the Hundred Years War. In particular, the roles attributed to the English, the Burgundians and the French themselves in the story of Joan of Arc's emergence, active life, capture, trial, condemnation, death and subsequent rehabilitation reflect and embody essentially time-bound and context-dependent assumptions about national identity. As so often in the study of French historical writing about the state and the nation, one has to begin with Jules Michelet in 1841. One important strand in the Third Republic's subsequent presentation of Joan derived from volume 5 of Michelet's *Histoire de France*, supported by the first scholarly edition of the documentation of her trials of condemnation and rehabilitation by his pupil, Jules Quicherat, published between 1841 and 1849.[21]

It is well known that, for Michelet, the populist democrat, Joan of Arc had all the characteristics of a lay saint – a daughter of the people, of peasant stock, who incarnated the nation, gave her life for it, defying the institutional Church and refusing to submit to its pernicious authority. Michelet saw Joan as the first to express what she herself described as 'the pity' (*pitié*) or 'pitiful nature', 'sorrow' or even 'tragedy' of the kingdom of France, in which 'French blood' was being spilt in a war between both internal and external foes.[22] It is worth quoting him at some length, as one root from which the patriotic, nationalist plant was to grow:

> For the first time, we feel it, France is loved as a person. And she [note the feminine] became such, from the day when she was first loved. Until then, there was just an assemblage of provinces, a vast chaos of fiefs, a huge country, of uncertain identity.
>
> But, from that day, she became a Fatherland (*Patrie*). What a fine mystery! Moving, sublime! See how the immense and pure love of such a young heart [Joan's] would embrace a whole world, give it this second life, the true life which love alone can bring … How much she loved France! … And France, moved, began to love herself. You see it from the very first day that she [Joan] appeared before Orléans … Let us always remember that our Fatherland was born from the heart of a woman, from her tenderness and her tears, and from the blood which she gave for us.[23]

There is, of course, something of the Christ-like sacrifice about all this – and Michelet, in 1853, although he retained this passage, was to remove what he considered other over-pious sections from his first edition, as a result of his 'philosophical and political development, and … his conflicts with the clerical party'.[24] But the Maid had begun her sacrificial and redemptive journey through French (and other) historical writing.

By 1849, the existence of Quicherat's edition, with its copious commentary on the sources, had meant that there was now a publicly available arsenal from which ammunition could be drawn.[25] Quicherat drew down some clerical opprobrium on himself for his relatively favourable assessment of the trial of condemnation's records and procedures as against what he called the 'diffuse and confused' nature of the rehabilitation trial. Père Ayroles, SJ, in 1890, while acknowledging the debt owed to Quicherat for his edition, could sound off with the exhortation:

> Because the glory of Joan demands it, one should not extend Quicherat's authority beyond the limits of … his competence, that is, palaeography alone … Trained by the Caesarean University [i.e. the secularized Sorbonne] a man of the generation of 1830, he shared the hateful and loathsome prejudices towards the Church of an epoch when the bourgeoisie, that daughter of the [faithless] Voltaire, promised itself an endless reign.[26]

Increasingly identified with the views of free-thinkers and freemasons, secular representations of the Maid were perceived as a frontal attack on the Church by Monsignor Félix Dupanloup, bishop of Orléans. After some preliminary skirmishes in 1855, the battle for possession of Joan of Arc began, with Dupanloup's eulogy of Joan in 1869. On the other side, Michelet and his followers were to some extent drawing upon a pre-existing tradition of secular historiography, influenced by the Enlightenment. This tapped a vein common in the work of Gibbon and Hume, in which the Middle Ages were depicted as an essentially unenlightened age. Joan of Arc was a victim of ecclesiastical persecution, and David Hume could write of her:

> This admirable heroine, to whom *the more generous superstition of the ancients* would have erected altars, was, on pretence of heresy and magic, delivered over alive to the flames, and expiated, by that dreadful punishment, the signal service which she had rendered to her prince and to her native country.[27]

The spirit of Michelet, and of the conflict between clerical and secular parties, lived on in French historical writing well into the twentieth century. In 1945, Edouard Perroy – to whom we shall return – published his *Hundred Years War*, much of it written, as he confirmed, while on the run from the Gestapo. The account which he gave of Joan of Arc is striking in many ways, not least for its cool, relatively detached view of what he saw as her limited contribution to France's fifteenth-century recovery. But it is in his treatment of the clergy who formed her judges and assessors that real depth of feeling shows itself. 'These men', he wrote

> felt only horror and hatred of the accused. Everything about her infuriated and scandalized them, even the dignified simplicity of her life [the noble peasant], the vivacious readiness of her replies [the French spirit at its best], the obvious modesty of her bearing [clearly a Micaëla, not a Carmen]. The cruelty of the procedure shocks our consciences as modern men. But it was simply that of the Inquisition, which was daily applied, without offending anyone, to any number of poor wretches, whom public malignity, the stupid self-sufficiency of their accusers, and the suspicious fanaticism of their judges led to the stake.[28]

This might be described as one version of that robustly secular point of view cultivated by the École Normale Supérieure under the Third Republic, in part as a reaction against the promotion of a Joan of Arc cult by the Church. What made Joan's case so compelling yet so difficult to integrate satisfactorily into national history was the fact that her judges and assessors were Frenchmen. There was no irregularity in the constitution of the tribunal which tried her at Rouen in 1431: the presiding judge, Pierre Cauchon, bishop of Beauvais, had been careful to recruit a distinguished body of 131 assessors, counsellors, advocates, proctors and investigating officials, drawn from the abbots of the great Norman monasteries, the Dominican order, the upper ranks of the Norman clergy and the professors, doctors and masters of the University of Paris. The France of 1431 was a France at war with itself, as well as with the English.

The historical facts, as far as we can establish them, were these: Joan of Arc was captured by Frenchmen (by Burgundian troops in the service of the Lancastrian dual monarchy of England and France); abandoned by Frenchmen (the regime of 'her' dauphin, Charles VII); sold by Frenchmen (Philip the Good, duke of Burgundy) to the Lancastrian government; charged with heresy by Frenchmen (the University of Paris); tried by Frenchmen (the judges, assessors and proctors at Rouen in 1431); and executed by Frenchmen (the *bailli* of Rouen and his deputies). A sorry story – on all sides, French, English and Burgundian – from which, it could be claimed, no one (except the victim) emerges with any credit. It is not the function of the historian to apportion blame and administer censure: but this has not prevented many from doing so. Perroy can speak of the condemnation trial as a 'tissue of vile calumnies and odious nonsense', while (interestingly) warning us that 'we should not suppose that all these judges had sold their consciences or cravenly let themselves be influenced by the holders of power ... There was no need for Bedford [the regent of France for Henry VI of England] to exert pressure on the judges. They went more than halfway to meet him.'[29] Clearly, these were archetypical collaborators, the willing instruments of a regime which, it was claimed, did not represent the 'true' crown of France. Perroy's British contemporary Ernest Jacob went much further towards condemning Joan's judges and assessors when he wrote, in his volume of the *Oxford History of England* (1961) of 'the atmosphere of hatred surrounding her and the hypocrisy of the trial' in which a pre-determined verdict was reached, 'under threats and pressure brought to bear by the English'.[30] The historical evidence actually suggests a rather different interpretation of events: the allegations of direct English pressure come from the carefully staged rehabilitation trial of 1456, in which many witnesses were anxious either to clear their own names or ingratiate themselves with the prevailing (and victorious) French regime.[31] And it was precisely on the grounds that such damaging allegations might be made that the Lancastrian administration had resolved to keep its distance from the trial proceedings at Rouen 25 years earlier. No one publicly played the role of Pontius Pilate in the Passion of Joan of Arc.

British national histories – not normally discussed in this context – have tended to be remarkably accepting of the view that it was as a result of English coercion, pressure and threat that Joan was condemned and put to death. Andrew Lang, admittedly taking a somewhat self-righteous, blameless Scots view, claimed in 1908 that 'there is no Englishman alive who, from obsolete national prejudice, would try to diminish her greatness, or to palliate the shameful iniquity of his ancestors in all their relations with her'.[32] Rudyard Kipling – no historian but a representative of, and commentator on, public opinion in Edwardian England – could reflect the prevailing mood when he wrote of the 'undying sin we shared in Rouen market place'.[33] From a fundamentally hostile stance, as taken up from the sixteenth century onwards, English opinion began to change dramatically at the end of the eighteenth century. Shakespeare's and Fuller's denigration of the Maid was now offset by a chorus of eulogy. With the appearance of an English translation of Quicherat's edition of the trial records in 1903,[34] Joan of Arc became public property, as it were, in the English-speaking world, attracting a rash of biographies, more often by popular writers – some of them Scots – than by professional historians. Unlike their French contemporaries, these writers achieved a striking degree of unanimity in their presentation and interpretation of Joan as the victim of an essentially unjust regime, waging an unjust war, but a regime and a war in which many Frenchmen were apparently willing, active collaborators. Historiographically a comparison between Jacob's account of Joan's career and achievement in the *Oxford History* of 1961 and Harriss's in 2005 is revealing. Where Jacob is condemnatory of her judges and accusers, Harriss says virtually nothing about them and simply reports the facts laconically:

> She was publicly burnt in the Old Market on 30 June [1431]. Neither Pope Eugenius IV nor Charles VII attempted to intervene. The trial had portrayed her as a woman of loose morals and an envoy of the devil whose victories had been gained by sorcery, a view acceptable for different reasons to Charles VII, his military commanders, and the English.[35]

The abandonment of the Maid to her predictable fate, after her predictable relapse, by those who might conceivably have intervened to save her, provides the only note of implied censure in this account. In any case, the emphases of academic history have shifted away from the political dimension of the story: recent work has sought to place Joan in a contemporary context of religious belief, in which her Christ-like aspects and attributes were noted and stressed. The most recent scholarly contribution – Colette Beaune's *Jeanne d'Arc* (2004) – is at pains to stress this identification and imitation, whereby the Son of God became the Daughter of God ('Fille de Dieu'), as Joan was called by her Voices. As Beaune concludes: 'the disciples of St Francis had seen in him another Christ (*alter Christus*). The novelty here lay in the fact that a woman dared to appropriate to herself the role of the Saviour'.[36] This means, of course, that she has received attention from historians of gender. Her assumption of a male role, and of male dress with all its controversial implications were, of course, of great concern to her contemporaries, just as recent historical scholarship tends to interpret these issues in the light of changing concepts and constructions of masculinity and femininity.

In the final analysis, the spiritual and secular canonization which Joan of Arc has undergone over the past 200 years has made the 'real' historical figure less and less accessible. The sheer volume of pious cant and humbug, on both the spiritual and secular sides, compounded by varying degrees of nationalist eulogy, ultimately enshrining her as a symbol of national unity, reached its height under the Third Republic. But she poses grave problems for those in power, spiritual or temporal, and of whatever political or religious persuasion. Her refusal to submit to authority can only be justified and, in effect, purged if her accusers, who represented that authority, can be depicted as essentially prejudiced, corrupt, self-serving, acting under pressure from a foreign power and determined to eliminate her. It became a historical and historiographical necessity to create that image. This enables France's national saint, beloved of right-wing nationalists, Catholic monarchists and fascist extremists, to be taken up and adored by those exercising power from the Right, the Centre or the Left. That is perhaps what has made her cult so potent. But in terms of what actually happened in the fifteenth century, most of this is not only irrelevant but misleading. Joan of Arc did not need to die in 1431. The recantation and abjuration which she made on 24 May was quite enough to achieve what the Lancastrian administration desired: an admission that 'her' dauphin owed his coronation and his crown to a heretic and sorceress. Even if she had been spared and had escaped from the captivity which would have been her lot, there was little likelihood that her own side would have sought to use her again. She had outlived her usefulness and the fragile, unstable regime of Charles VII was in any case wracked with faction and rivalry. She had become a political and diplomatic liability, not an asset, to her own side as a reconciliation and alliance with the duke of Burgundy – whom she had insulted and castigated in her letters of defiance, and whose troops she had fought – was now being actively sought. So the account of her subsequent relapse in the trial record itself, at the point where the notary inserts the famous marginal *nota*: 'the fatal reply' (*responsio mortifera*) into the record, has a ring of true authenticity about it. She told her interrogators:

> That God warned her through St Catherine and St Margaret of the great ... treason to which she had agreed by making her abjuration and revocation to save her life; and that she had damned herself to save her life ... Item, she said that if she should say that God had not sent her, she would damn herself; for it was true that she had been sent by God.[37]

This seems quite consistent with everything we know about her and her faith in her Voices which, she said, she had disobeyed and betrayed by her abjuration.

Where then does this leave her in the Pantheon of what used to be called 'heroes of the nations' and in the ranks of those figures – Louis XIV, Napoleon, De Gaulle – who have contributed substantially to the process whereby the

French have defined themselves in relation to their ancient, hereditary enemy – the English? It could be claimed, first, that Joan's exceptional personality hardly conforms to stock nationalist constructs, such as those of the people's liberator, or the freedom-fighter against tyranny and oppression. If half of the kingdom of France acknowledged, and continued to acknowledge, with varying degrees of willingness or reluctance, the regime against which she fought, she can hardly be classed as a bringer of national unity or a deliverer of a whole people from an oppressive foreign yoke. In the history of French national consciousness and its evolution, her role has been as divisive as it has been unifying. If she was a martyr at all, she was a martyr not for some anachronistic, abstract concept of 'France' but to the cause of her own conscience, prompted by the Voices which she claimed to hear and the apparitions she claimed to see. Nationalizing Joan of Arc merely tends to belittle and diminish her in the eyes of the world outside France. For despite teleological accounts of the onward march of the nation-state – in which she has certainly played her part – there was nothing pre-ordained, let alone God-given, about the manner in which the separate national identities of England and France emerged and evolved.

7

The Fall of Lancastrian France[1]

They would lose by their treaties what they had gained by their weapons.

Montesquieu, *L'Esprit des lois*, Part 2, Book 10, Chapter 9

The mid-fifteenth century witnessed the fall to the French monarchy of the continental territories of the English crown, with the sole exception of the town, March and Pale of Calais. Gascony (Aquitaine, Guyenne), England's oldest surviving continental possession, surrendered twice to the French – in 1451 and 1453 – as did the more recently re-acquired duchy of Normandy (once, in 1450).[2] But the Gascons did not yield without a fierce though ultimately hopeless struggle, unlike their Norman counterparts who quickly surrendered.

The battle at Castillon on 17 July 1453 effectively brought that phase of the conflict which we have decided, with hindsight, to call the Hundred Years War to an end. But 300 years of English administration in south-west France was not easily forgotten by the Gascons. Many inhabitants of the duchy of Aquitaine, or Guyenne as it had then come to be called, had fought side by side with the English against the French, supporting their 'natural and sovereign lord' – Henry VI – against Charles VII of France. The Anglo-Gascon union, but not the Anglo-French war, was finally to be terminated – by force rather than by any kind of voluntary or negotiated agreement – in 1453. But for some long time afterwards no one could confidently say that the war had ended. There was no treaty of peace; as we have seen, the English crown did not renounce its claims to hold titles and lands in France; and a state of both overt and latent hostility, punctuated by truces, characterized Anglo-French relations for centuries to come.

National traditions – British and French – of historical writing have produced interpretations of the consequences of the defeat inflicted upon Anglo-Gascon forces by the French in 1453 which owe much to the nationalisms, and to the national myths, of the nineteenth century. But these have been challenged, especially by those who do not see the unitary nation-state as an organic growth. It has recently been argued that nineteenth-century concepts of ethnicity have 'turned our understanding of the past into a toxic waste dump, filled with the poison of ethnic nationalism'.[3] Though exaggerated, this view deserves a hearing because in both Britain and France historians of the nation-state have tended to identify state formation with cultural identity and sometimes with cultural homogeneity.

For them, the territorial integrity of the nation-state becomes a pre-requisite for the creation of cultural and linguistic communities. To British historians, the loss of England's French possessions was thought to be beneficial to the evolution of an island nation: not only did it bring to an end the chronic problem of paying for a long-standing and allegedly unpopular foreign war, but it enabled English rulers fully to concentrate on the serious, if not pre-ordained, task of creating a unitary nation-state in their island kingdom and its Celtic dependencies. With the loss of most of the French possessions of the English crown, Scotland, Wales and Ireland – it is argued – consequently became the object of English attentions on a scale that had not been evident since the reign of Edward I.

For French historians, the expulsion of the English represented a turning point in the onward march of the French nation-state towards that Paris-centred hexagon which was to enshrine the nation's destiny and identity. In a relatively brief space of time, between 1449 and 1453, the French possessions of the English crown were lost.[4] With the sole exception of the Calais Pale, all English-held territories in France, whether inherited or conquered and occupied, fell to French forces. An Englishman, James Gresham, writing on 19 August 1450, could tell his 'master' John Paston that 'this very Wednesday it was reported that Cherbourg has fallen, and we have not now a foot of land in Normandy, and everyone fears that Calais will very soon be besieged'.[5] The dramatic events which led to the rapid collapse of English forces in Normandy, Maine and the duchy of Guienne delivered a profound psychological shock to the Lancastrian government in England and dealt a grievous blow to those Englishmen who had invested their energies and fortunes in Lancastrian France. Normandy fell to the French with comparative ease; Guyenne also fell, but posed rather more difficult problems to them, for it was England's longest-held continental inheritance. Calais alone, conquered and settled with Englishmen by Edward III in 1347, held out and did not succumb to French power until 1558.[6] The reasons for this apparently anomalous survival of English continental dominion will be discussed later. Why, on the other hand, did the Norman and Gascon possessions of the English monarchy fall so relatively quickly to the French, and what effects did their loss have on English politics, trade and society? How did the English react and respond to that loss?

The collapse of the Lancastrian regime, or double monarchy, in France (which had been created by the treaty of Troyes) was preceded as much by diplomatic as by military setbacks in the late 1430s and early to mid-1440s.[7] Montesquieu, writing in 1748, could characterize contemporary Englishmen as impatient with the diplomatic process – obstinate, intolerant of delays, but courageous – and their fifteenth-century forebears may have shared some of those qualities.[8] Joan of Arc (d. 1431) had certainly helped to have the dauphin Charles crowned at Rheims as 'rightful' king of France in 1429. A certain inevitability, whether divinely ordained or not, has been credited to the process whereby the Maid of Orléans' mission led to the expulsion of the English from France. But the first signs of real and sustained French military and diplomatic recovery were visible only after 1435. The defection of Philip the Good, most powerful of the dukes of Burgundy, from the house of Lancaster to that of Valois in that year greatly assisted this development. Some Englishmen, such as the veteran soldier Sir John Fastolf (Shakespeare's Falstaff), considered Philip the Good's 'treason' to mark the beginning of the end for Lancastrian France.[9] But the immediate effects of his volte-face were *not* disastrous for English war aims: Humphrey, duke of Gloucester, routed a Burgundian besieging force outside Calais in 1436, and Philip the Good of Burgundy never again contributed substantially to the Valois war effort against the English. His resources were increasingly absorbed by the suppression of Flemish revolts and by the expansion of his Burgundian dominions further into the Netherlands.[10] The close economic relationship between England and Flanders, mediated through Calais, was too valuable to be thrown away and mercantile truces to protect the wool and cloth trades were soon established after 1437. Yet the withdrawal of Burgundian support within Lancastrian France, where so much depended upon the loyalty of Burgundian partisans, gradually undermined the regime. Paris, an Anglo-Burgundian city since 1420, fell to Charles VII's troops in 1436 and this symbolic act carried great significance. The Lancastrian regime in France became increasingly confined in the north to the duchy of Normandy, with Rouen, not Paris, as its capital. In the south-west, the citizens of Bordeaux, Bayonne and some members of the Gascon nobility and clergy formed the principal supports of the English regime. This position was tenable, especially in the south-west; but, in the north, it would last only as long as the Lancastrian regime commanded local support. It also depended upon the extent to which English garrisons in occupied Normandy were properly paid, victualled and disciplined. If they were not, they would prey upon the local French population and arouse deep popular animosity. English military organization in Normandy had on the whole been effective, and was one of the most durable legacies to their successors of Henry V and his brother John, duke of Bedford, regent of France until his death in 1435.[11] Lancastrian Normandy was a viable concern, as long as these conditions were fulfilled.

The first symptoms of an impending crisis in Normandy were apparent soon after 1435. The death of Bedford removed an able and respected governor, peasant revolts broke out in parts of the duchy, the Lancastrian regime failed to deal effectively with the problems of disorder and brigandage (which Henry V and Bedford had contained) and violent disputes among English commanders about the direction to be taken by the war effort took their toll.[12] Although Henry VI's (1422–61) government in both England and Normandy during the early years of his minority (1422–8) was surprisingly solvent, by the 1430s

financial problems pressed hard upon available resources.[13] When Ralph, Lord
Cromwell, was appointed Treasurer of England in 1433, he produced estimates
of income and expenditure which revealed a chronic state of deficit in the public
revenues of the English crown.[14] This was not because England was in any
sense a poor or 'under-developed' land in the fifteenth century. The surviving
cathedral, collegiate and parish churches, with their elaborate chantry chapels
and the well-appointed castles and manor houses of the nobility and gentry
do not suggest an impoverished nation in the throes of financial bankruptcy.
Foreign observers commented favourably upon the quantity of meat (and beer)
consumed by the lower orders, in contrast to the largely bread-based diet of
their continental, especially French, counterparts. The lawyer Sir John Fortescue
wrote in the 1470s of the greater material prosperity to be found among the
English rural population.[15] But the foreign war of conquest and occupation
begun under Henry V, unlike the raids and plundering expeditions of Edward III
and the Black Prince in the fourteenth century, made unprecedented demands
on English resources. It became clear, albeit gradually, that the war could not
pay for itself. Not since the later twelfth and early thirteenth centuries, when the
Angevin kings of England were forced to defend their French lands against the
incursions of Philip Augustus, had the English crown's revenues been under such
continuous strain.

Public penury had parted company with private affluence in fifteenth-century
England. The consequences of this tendency contributed significantly to the
deteriorating position in Lancastrian France. Many Englishmen were much
wealthier than their fathers and grandfathers had been, but the crown's ability
to tap that wealth was very limited.[16] The English upper classes were relatively
lightly taxed: the burden of the Parliamentary subsidy fell upon the rural
population of the rank of 'yeoman' and below. It had been fixed at one-tenth
and one-fifteenth of the value of movable goods in town and countryside in
1336, but manor houses and their contents were exempt from it. The machinery
whereby taxes were raised and collected was also complicated and cumbersome.
War did not wait for Parliamentary taxation to be voted, assessed and gathered.
Nor was the system whereby the customs duties on wool, cloth, leather and other
commodities were levied conducive to the rapid and effective mobilization of
capital. The customs were increasingly employed as securities upon which loans
were raised, and this tendency ultimately destroyed the financial credibility of the
Lancastrian regime. Creditors found that their loans were assigned for repayment
upon sources of revenue which had already been pledged to others, and there is
evidence of attempts by the government to force loans from reluctant subjects
during the crises in the French possessions of the 1440s and 1450s.[17] There was
thus very little incentive for men to lend money to the crown unless cripplingly
high rates of interest were offered to them by the Exchequer. While individuals in

both town and country made their fortunes – witness the clothiers, wool growers and wool merchants of East Anglia and the West Country – the crown fell deeper and deeper into debt. The end of the house of Lancaster in 1461, when Henry VI was deposed, was in some respects a form of foreclosure upon a dynasty which was both financially and politically bankrupt.

The Lancastrian war effort in both northern and south-west France had for some time been underwritten by a few great creditors, such as Cardinal Henry Beaufort.[18] His death in 1447 removed one of the major financial props of the government. It became increasingly difficult to harness and channel English resources to the French war. From March 1449 onwards, military defeat was added to financial exhaustion. The taking of the Breton frontier fortress of Fougères by the Aragonese mercenary captain François de Suriennes, who was in English pay, broke the truce which had been made by the duke of Suffolk with the French at Tours in 1444.[19] The short respite from hostilities granted by that truce was now at an end. Spurred on by a powerful Breton faction at his court, Charles VII resolved to punish this act of truce-breaking and re-opened the war with the English on 31 July 1449. In the short space of 15 months, all Henry V's and Bedford's conquests in Normandy fell to the French. Maine and Anjou had already been ceded to Charles VII by Suffolk in accordance with the terms of the agreement whereby Henry VI married Charles's niece Margaret of Anjou in 1445. A combination of effective siegecraft, well-deployed artillery, ruse, bribery, incitement of the local population and negotiation of agreements to surrender with English garrisons reduced the duchy of Normandy to obedience by August 1450. Some English captains and their companies did not, however, give up without a fight and Sir John Fastolf's secretary William Worcester proudly recorded the deeds of many of them even in these dark days. But the majority of beleaguered garrisons negotiated surrenders with the French and were in effect paid to go away. What had taken over seven years to achieve was destroyed in less than 18 months.

In the duchy of Guyenne, however, very different conditions prevailed.[20] Largely released from involvement in Normandy by 1451, Charles VII's companies of *ordonnance*, the core of his standing army, were then deployed against Henry VI's most ancient surviving inheritance in south-west France. The seizure of the possessions of his chief creditor, the *argentier* Jacques Couer, and substantial grants of taxation from the French provincial Estates enabled Charles VII to launch the very costly last campaigns of the Hundred Years War. Gascon resistance to the French, whom they regarded as an unwelcome foreign power, was much more spirited than that of the Normans. The duchy of Aquitaine had, after all, been held by the rulers of England since 1152, unlike the recently conquered duchy of Normandy. The French succeeded in taking Bordeaux, Bayonne and the rest of the duchy by August 1451, but a Gascon resistance movement, centred upon Bordeaux and led by some exiled Gascon nobles as well as merchants, ship-owners and mariners, joined forces with an English expeditionary force under John Talbot, earl of Shrewsbury, in October 1452. Part of the duchy was recovered in Henry VI's name but this success was not to endure. A lack of reinforcements from England conspired with defections by some members of the Gascon nobility to bring French arms back into the duchy in the spring and summer of 1453. The siege-guns of Charles VII's masters of the artillery – the Bureau brothers – did their work against Anglo-Gascon strongholds and, with the defeat and death of Talbot at the head of an Anglo-Gascon army at Castillon on 17 July 1453, the death-knell of English Gascony was sounded. The city of Bordeaux held out for some months after the battle at Castillon, but that last bastion of support for the Lancastrian cause was forced into surrender on 19 October 1453. The Bordelais and Bayonnais then paid the penalty for their resistance to the sovereignty of Valois France.

The loss of the French possessions clearly made a deep impression upon the English as well as the Gascon subjects of the Lancastrian monarchy. First, the sheer loss of prestige and status on the European stage suffered by the English crown should not be underestimated. Henry V's achievement lay in ruins. Throughout the diplomatic encounters of the 1430s and 1440s Henry VI had never agreed to renounce his claim to the French throne; after 1453 that claim was more difficult to sustain. But the claim was not abandoned by the British monarchy until 1802 – when there was no French crown to renounce. After 1453, French conquest was in effect a *fait accompli*. Although campaigns were mounted, in the hope of recovering territory, to support the French title under Edward IV and, as we shall see, with surprising tenacity under Henry VIII, the cards were now more heavily stacked against the English.[21] Dissension, disorder and civil war at home in the later fifteenth century did not provide a stable base from which to launch expeditions and to mobilize military manpower for foreign campaigns. Second, many Englishmen found themselves dispossessed as a direct result of the débacles in France between 1449 and 1453. In 1452 Henry VI's government received a petition from those Englishmen who had fought for, but lost, their possessions in Normandy and Maine. They told the king (in French) that they

> have lost in … Normandy, into which they had withdrawn, in consequence of the recent conquest … by your said uncle of France [Charles VII] all that remained to them of their moveable goods, upon which depended the livelihood of themselves, their wives and children; and at present most of them are completely ruined and reduced to beggary, which is a sad matter, given the good and just right you have to the said county [of Maine] and duchy of Normandy.[22]

They requested the king either to compensate them adequately (as had been promised) or to make more determined efforts to recover his French inheritance. Allowing for the normal exaggeration of all petitioners, their words contained more than a grain of truth. These men, who had held lands and offices in Lancastrian France, may not have been 'reduced to beggary' by their loss, but they suffered severe blows to their pride as well as to their material fortunes. The most trenchant and forceful supporters of the war effort against France, such as Sir John Fastolf, knight, and lord of Caister castle, master of the household to John, duke of Bedford at Rouen and baron of Cilly-Guillaume, were not exceptional among their class. Many English knightly and gentry families were represented in Lancastrian France and had much to lose there. Their subsequent involvement in English civil war was not entirely unrelated to that fact.

What happened to the survivors of these defeats? Some of those who formed the remnants of Talbot's army after its defeat at Castillon in 1453 found their way back to England by way of the sole remaining outpost of Lancastrian power abroad – the Calais garrisons. Some continued to serve there and a command at Calais remained prestigious among the English officer-class until its final loss in the mid-sixteenth century.[23] Others came back in the followings of the lords and captains whom they had served in France. But our knowledge of their careers is as yet incomplete. A tiny minority of Englishmen remained in Valois France: Sir Richard Merbury, for instance, who had married a Frenchwoman, took the oath of allegiance to the French and became a counsellor and chamberlain to Charles VII. The Welsh captain John Edwards surrendered La Roche-Guyon to them and also took the oath, for he too had a French wife.[24] But the overwhelming majority of the dispossessed returned to England, some to serve the house of York against Lancaster in the so-called 'Wars of the Roses'; others remained in the Lancastrian camp. Having once fought the French together, they survived to fight each other at St Alban's, Barnet and Towton.

Other Englishmen, who held no landed property or goods and chattels in Lancastrian France, nevertheless had important mercantile and commercial connections with the former French possessions. The wine merchants (vintners), ship-owners and mariners who traded and carried Gascon wine evidently felt the loss of Guyenne acutely. During the first half of the fifteenth century about 75 per cent of shipping paying customs duties at the port of Bordeaux was owned and largely manned by Englishmen. A great vessel such as the *Trinity* of Dartmouth, with a tonnage of 400 tuns, a crew of eighty and a complement of nine guns, regularly made the crossing to Bordeaux in the annual convoy of about 120 ships which brought the Gascon vintage to England.[25] The French seizures of Guyenne in 1451 and 1453 immediately broke the English monopoly over the wholesale, retail and carrying trade in Gascon wine. An export figure of 12,000 tuns had been reached between 1444 and 1449; it declined to between 2,000 and 4,000 tuns during the 1450s and 1460s. Breton, Norman, Spanish and Hanseatic ships sailed into the breach left by the ending of the English monopoly. A surge of mercantile protectionism afflicted English ports and traders. In 1467, for example, the authorities at Bristol refused to unload Gascon wine from Spanish ships and some of the origins of the later protectionist Tudor Navigation Acts may be seen in such measures.[26] The Gascons were no longer subjects of the English crown, nor did English ship-owners and traders any longer enjoy a privileged position in the trade with Bordeaux. But that trade ultimately survived. There was good cause for complaint among the sea-faring communities of western England. It was no coincidence that the search for new markets and sources of supply – Iceland, the Baltic, Spain and the Americas – was led by the mariners of the English western ports, well schooled in ocean-going seamanship through their trade with south-west France.

It has been claimed that the collapse of English rule in France between 1449 and 1453 led to an important and decisive shift in English preoccupations and ambitions abroad.[27] As we have seen, the so-called 'continentalist' policy of the fourteenth and fifteenth centuries, it is argued, based upon claims to rights and territories overseas, was gradually to give way to the insularity of the Tudors, which rested upon English sea power. The Channel and Western Approaches were to become parts of a 'moat defensive' rather than highways of commerce and military activity. But this contrast can be heavily overdrawn. The contemporary tract known as the *Libel of English Policy* (*c.* 1436) already asserted the importance of England's 'moat' and the necessity of 'safely keeping the narrow seas'. It was particularly important to provide some degree of security for the narrowest sea of all, the English Channel, especially between the southern coastal ports and Calais.[28] With the loss of Harfleur, Cherbourg, Bordeaux and Bayonne, English 'barbicans', bridge-heads and points of entry into France were drastically reduced at a stroke. Apart from its essential role as an entrepot for English commerce with the mainland of north-west Europe, Calais possessed a wider significance. The establishment of a wool and cloth Staple (Etaple) there, through which all English exports passed, led to the creation of a permanent colony of English residents whose connections lay with the Low Countries rather than with France. Their colleagues and kinsmen in England acted as intermediaries between England and the continent. Families such as the Celys and the Donnes held administrative positions and maintained mercantile interests at Calais, while the lieutenancies exercised there by Warwick (the 'Kingmaker') and William, Lord Hastings, Chamberlain to Edward IV, also drew men towards the Low Countries in the service of these magnates.[29]

This tendency was furthered by the renewal of the Anglo-Burgundian alliance which had fallen apart in 1435. The Yorkist monarchy of Edward IV was supported by the Burgundians, and the alliance of the two houses was cemented and formalized by the marriage of Edward's sister, Margaret of York, to Charles the Bold, duke of Burgundy, in 1468. With Burgundian power behind it, England's hold on Calais was strengthened. Calais was the gateway to what are now termed the 'Burgundian' and then 'Spanish' Netherlands – Flanders, Brabant, Hainault, Holland, Zeeland and Luxembourg – and much diplomatic and commercial traffic continued to flow through it from England to Bruges, Brussels, Antwerp and the other great towns of the Low Countries. The collapse of Charles's regime in 1477, when he was defeated and killed by a coalition of his enemies at Nancy, did not sever the connection with England because his successors – the Austrian and Spanish Habsburgs – saw England as a useful partner in their conflicts with France. The economic interests of their Netherlandish territories were, moreover, still partly dependent upon English markets and sources of supply. A slow re-orientation of England's commercial and cultural relations with northern Europe certainly took place, in which the loss and abandonment of French lands and titles gave way to closer and more productive relationships with the Low Countries. William Caxton published books at Bruges before he set up his printing presses at London, and the close contacts between the Calais Staplers and the citizens and nobles of the Netherlandish towns brought cultural as well as economic benefits to England. At the level of aristocratic and courtly society Burgundian influences were also strong. A tendency to adopt the practices of the court of Burgundy continued into the reigns of Henry VII and Henry VIII.

Similar conclusions can be reached for the visual arts, literature and music.[30] English glass- and panel-painting were influenced by Netherlandish styles and sometimes produced by Flemish artists and craftsmen. At least two affluent Englishmen patronised Flemish painters: Edward Grimston, esquire, was portrayed by Petrus Christus in 1448 while Sir John Donne 'of Calais' commissioned a triptych from Hans Memling at Bruges in about 1480. Both works now hang in the National Gallery, London. Secular literature was also subject to the influence of themes drawn from chivalric romances, many of which had been reworked in prose form at and for the court of Burgundy. Sir Thomas Malory drew his *Le Morte D'Arthur* from a 'Frensshe boke' and the adaptation (and transformation) of all kinds of literature well known in the courts and cities of the Low Countries again kept England within a cultural milieu which owed much to continental sources. William Caxton's list of translations into English of both secular and religious books reads rather like the contents of a Burgundian library. The early humanism of the Low Countries was, moreover, soon to be carried to England by John Colet and Thomas More, and Erasmus was to find some sympathy for his views in England. The Burgundian Netherlands have been described as a 'way-station' in the dissemination of Italian humanistic ideas to northern Europe, and England was not untouched by this development.[31] In the efflorescence of the arts associated with the Burgundian lands in the later Middle Ages, music had also played a central part. Choral polyphony was a true 'ars nova' (new art-form) and composers such as Guillaume Dufay, Gilles Binchois and Jean Ockeghem both influenced, and were influenced by, English musicians such as John Dunstable and Robert Morton. The English chapel royal thus entered the Tudor period fully conversant with the polyphonic styles of the Netherlands.

Influences such as these – some of them reciprocal – ensured that England never became culturally isolated after the loss of her French possessions in the mid-fifteenth century. A strong vernacular literary culture certainly existed, as did a robust patriotism which was drawn upon by the Tudors, but this did not lead to isolationism. The first major breach between England and the European continent – the loss of England's remaining French dominions – certainly accelerated existing tendencies towards a sense of national identity which had developed during the Hundred Years War. But these were to some extent offset by closer links with the Low Countries, and by a strengthening of relations with the Dutch, as well as with the Protestant German states and the Baltic lands. The second great breach – the English Reformation – was to drive a wedge between Protestant England and Catholic France, Flanders and Spain which was to endure until the eighteenth century and beyond.[32] It is a commonplace of historical writing to remark that England's development was unique because the kingdom was, in large part, an island. There are nonetheless grounds for arguing that, even after her continental power-base had disappeared, England formed an outpost of north-west Europe inextricably linked by economic and cultural ties to the Atlantic seaboard of the European continent. It has been observed that, even after the defeat of the Spanish Armada in 1588, 'the whole campaign … emphasized how little … England could afford for strategic reasons to turn her back completely upon the continent'.[33] It remained imperative, as it had done for centuries and was to do so for many more, to ensure that the coastline of north-west Europe, from Brest to Bremen, was not held by a single power. And it was not long before involvement in European wars once again brought aggressive Englishmen across the Channel. Although the most active phase of the Hundred Years War had effectively ended at Castillon on 17 July 1453, English armies, though defeated at that time, never deserted the battlefields of Europe. And there was to be what has been called a 'second Hundred Years War' with France, marked by other famous battles. Castillon may in effect have brought the first Hundred Years War to a conclusion; but the second Hundred Years War was to end only in the fields south of Brussels on 18 June 1815.

8

Tudor Ambitions and the War with France

The immediate effects on the English monarchy and its subjects of the mid-fifteenth-century losses in France have already been outlined. Yet the adamant refusal of English kings and their counsellors to consider renunciation of their claim and title to the French crown requires further consideration. Under Edward IV, Henry VII and Henry VIII there was a readiness not only to keep the claim alive but to exploit it at every available opportunity. Besides the French throne, moreover, there was the claim to the hereditary Plantagenet lands within France. In 1511, Henry VIII rejected the advice of some of his counsellors not to make war and 'so that he might have more than one Title to invade France, sent to require his patrimonial Inheritance of Anjou, Guyenne, etc. and, in case of refusal, to denounce warre'.[1] The war with France simply did not cease in 1453. What was about to change was not the validity, nor justification, of the English claim either to the French throne or to hereditary possessions in France, but the political and subsequently the religious, or confessional, situation in north-west Europe. Valois-Plantagenet rivalry and conflict was to give way to Valois-Habsburg confrontation on a much wider European stage, which now extended from the Low Countries to Spain and the Italian peninsula. The revival and transformation of the medieval Empire under the Habsburg Emperors Maximilian I (1493–1519) and Charles V (1519–56), stemming in part from their acquisition of the Burgundian Low Countries and of Spain, brought a new force into the politics of north-west Europe. The Habsburg rulers of the Low Countries, often described by contemporaries as 'the Burgundians', now assumed and perpetuated, in heightened form, a traditional role of the house of Burgundy as an increasingly powerful opponent of French aims and ambitions. In this Franco-imperial power struggle, the English crown pursued a surprisingly consistent policy. It was a policy designed, above all, to prevent an alliance between France and the new Habsburg rulers of the Low Countries at any price. Henry VIII was as concerned as any of his predecessors to exploit discord between the occupants of the French throne and the heirs to the Burgundian inheritance in the Netherlands. If necessary, overtures could even be made to France for an alliance against the Habsburgs, should the Emperor not be seen to be supporting English interests. English aggression against France in some respects reverted to what it had been under Edward III rather than Henry V – a war of sporadic raids rather than one of sustained conquest and occupation. Although a re-creation of Lancastrian France may not have lain within the limits of the politically feasible at any given moment, no English ruler could ever afford to ignore or neglect the opportunities for intervention and trouble-making which the Valois-Habsburg conflict presented.

It has, however, been argued that the Yorkist and early Tudor successors of the Lancastrians merely indulged in sham war on the European stage, concerned only to exact a monetary return from the French as the price of truce and security, rather than to pursue their 'just cause and quarrel' to its conclusion.[2] The subjects of the English crown, especially in their higher reaches, had allegedly become more peaceably inclined, and the old bellicosity of the age of Talbot and Fastolf was a thing of the past. The facts, however, invite a more nuanced interpretation of the evidence. Sheer luck, miscalculation, misfortune and the role of chance seem more determinant of Yorkist and early Tudor foreign policy than any overall and carefully calculated scheme to profit financially from waging war – or merely threatening to wage it. Similarly, the notion that the English aristocracy had become less chivalrically inclined and, indeed, less militaristic at this time seems contradicted by much of the evidence. There was no dearth of English recruits for chivalric encounter and for continental campaigning in the early modern age – a tendency visible well into the reign of Elizabeth I, immortalized by Edmund Spenser, Sir Henry Lee and Sir Philip Sydney. Some, such as Sir Thomas Everingham, sought service with foreign powers. Everingham fought for Maximilian of Austria between 1477 and 1481, having seen action – in Burgundian service – at the disaster of Nancy in January 1477.[3] There were few years between 1509 and 1525 when English peers, knights and esquires were not engaged in the king's service on the European continent: expeditions and chivalric encounters took place in 1510 (Portugal), 1511 (Guelderland), 1512 (Navarre), 1513 (Thérouanne and Tournai), 1514 (Calais), 1520 (Field of the Cloth of Gold), 1522 (Brittany, Picardy and Artois), and 1523 (Hainaut and northern France). Subsequent renewal of war with France, in alliance with the Empire, in 1543–44, resulted in the taking of Boulogne. This had been preceded by an English raid into northern France, immediately to the south of the English Pale of Calais, which had all the characteristics of a fourteenth-century *chevauchée*. A contemporary description of Sir John Wallop's 'foray' from Calais of July–August 1543 through the countryside around St Omer, Thérouanne and Aire reads in a very similar manner to accounts of English raids during the fourteenth century, and echoes the tactics advocated against the 'rebel' Burgundians by Sir John Fastolf in 1435. The writer tells us that Wallop's host:

> marched to Lanerton [Landrethun-le-Nord], beinge within the French palle; and there
> mete with the lord Greay, capitayne of Hames castill, and ther birnt Lanerton, with the

number of 300 howses, and Campfer [Caffiers] with Finies [Fiennes] mylle, otherwise called a castill ... The said army marchid forward unto the abbey of Lyquies [Licques], six mylles from Fynies [Fiennes], spoylinge and birning all the way they wente.[4]

These terrorizing tactics replicated those adopted during a previous raid under Thomas Howard, earl of Surrey, in August–October 1522, when an English force of just under 2,000 men marched out of Calais into Picardy:

> brenynge many townes, castles and villages ... tyll they cam to Hedyng [Hesdin], and that towne they brenyd and leyd sege to the castle, but wan it not; from thens they went to the watar of Sum [Somme], brennynge and destroyenge, for to seke Frenchemen, but they durst not abyde them.[5]

Such passages demonstrate the close affinities between styles of warfare which were separated by two centuries. A degree of havoc could still be inflicted by this kind of English military terrorism on the French countryside. Sir John Fastolf had set out the techniques of raiding, albeit in a punitive context, in his *Articles and Instructions* of September 1435. The seasons chosen for destructive raids – summer and autumn – were identical, and Fastolf advised Henry VI's French council that an English force should operate from early June to late October

> landing for the first tyme at Cales [Calais] or at Crotay [Le Crotoy], as shalbe thoughte expedient; and so holding forthe there way thoroughe Artois and Picardie, and so thoroughe Vermandoys, Lannoys, Champaigne, and Bourgoyne, *brennyng and distruynge alle the lande as thei pas, bothe hous, corne, veignes, and alle treis that beren fruyte for mannys sustenaunce, and alle bestaile, that may not be dryven, to be distroiede.*[6]

The response of the French to such tactics was, as Howard's Breton expedition demonstrated, to sue for a truce, so 'that the English would leave off this kind of desultory, and cruell Warre, which tended onely to the burning of Villages, and ransacking the poore'.[7]

Despite the alleged advances brought by humanist educators and anti-chivalric polemicists to the growth of more 'civilian', if not civilized, values among the English aristocracy, they remained men trained to kill. The lists of those engaged at Calais and in the garrisons of the Pale, as well as those participating in expeditionary forces between 1453 and 1558 included many members of the English nobility, knighthood and gentry. They sometimes read like a roll-call of families well-known for their service during the Hundred Years War. A sword-bearing class, addicted to duelling and the defence of personal and family honour, was not the most obvious candidate for a life of peaceful co-existence, preferring the legal and diplomatic to the martial arts.[8] The experience of both foreign and civil war in the fifteenth century had left a deep and lasting impression on them: and that experience did not always lead to reluctance to take up arms.

The inter-connectedness of English and continental European politics at this time has recently been underlined; indeed it has perhaps been over-emphasized. Claims, for example, that it was largely as a result of foreign intervention that usurping dynasties were placed on the English throne in the fifteenth century can be safely dismissed as exaggerated. But 'the European nature … of English politics during the Wars of the Roses is something still not sufficiently stressed'.[9] Both Yorkist and Tudor regimes fuelled, exploited and benefited from the tensions between the houses of Habsburg and Valois, as well as between the French monarchy and the princes of France.[10] Hence a revival of the Anglo-Burgundian alliance after 1468, and its renewal as a compact with the new Habsburg rulers of the Low Countries after 1489, could be read as an admission by the English crown of its need for allies – who could, of course, be both expensive and unreliable – against France. Under Edward IV, English forces totalling 6,000 archers had been dispatched in 1472 to aid the anti-French coalition which he was in the process of constructing, together with the dukes of Brittany and Burgundy, against Louis XI of France. By the summer of 1475, a full-scale expedition was ready to be launched against France. A record of the composition of the English army in that year was headed: 'A declaracion aswell of capitengnes, theire speires and archers, reteigned wyth our sovereigne lord kyng Edward the iiijth in his servise of guerre into his duchie of Normandye and his realme of Fraunce'.[11]

There was no sign here of any retreat from the claims of the past. Nor was there much evidence of reluctance among the upper ranks of English society to participate in the campaign. Edward was accompanied by five dukes, one marquis, five earls, 12 barons, 14 knights banneret, 18 knights bachelor and 173 esquires and gentlemen, all bringing retinues with them.

This represented a very high turn-out of the English nobility and gentry, especially of those with court and household connections. The entire force totalled at least 11,450 combatants and was one of the largest English armies ever to invade France in the fourteenth and fifteenth centuries. Although the results of the campaign were conspicuously inglorious – there was no expected re-enactment of Agincourt – the benefits reaped by both Edward and his subjects were not negligible. A pension of 56,000 crowns from Louis XI, plus important commercial concessions which lifted restrictions upon English trade, justified the costs and efforts involved in mounting the campaign and rendered Edward independent of Parliamentary subsidies for the rest of his reign.[12] The treaty of 29 August 1475, which agreed the terms of a truce with Louis, was sealed with the seals of both monarchs. It is striking that Edward's seal, which he used for French affairs, bore the legend: 'Edwardus dei gratia rex Francie et Anglie et dominus Hibernie', with the quartered arms of England and France, just as that of Edward III had done.[13] Despite the agreement with France there was, again, no suggestion that the title to the French throne should be renounced.

How did the English come to terms with the loss of all their French possessions except Calais? And why (and how) did Calais survive in English hands until 1558? Its value to England was still commented upon by contemporary observers, even on the very eve of its loss. Giovanni Michele, the Venetian ambassador writing in 1557, could report to the Senate that:

> Calais and Guines [are] guarded by them (and justly) with jealousy, especially Calais, for this is the key and principal entrance to their dominions, without which the English would have no outlet from their own, nor access to other countries, at least none so easy, so short, and so secure; so much so that, if they were deprived of it, they would not only be shut out from the continent, but also from the commerce and intercourse of the world ... It is considered by everyone as an impregnable fortress, on account of the inundation with which it may be surrounded, although there are persons skilled in the art of fortification, who doubt that it would prove so if put to the test.[14]

In the event, Calais did not prove to be impregnable, despite its elaborate and extensive water-defences. Another Italian commentator, in his 'Relation of the Island of England', probably composed in c. 1496–7, had been similarly impressed by the provisions for Calais's defence, writing that it was:

> of about the size of Mestre [a small town on the Venetian *terra firma*], including all her suburbs, whose jurisdiction extends over three leagues of country, in every direction, being entirely surrounded by the French, excepting for one short league, which adjoins the county of Flanders. There are always about 800 chosen men, including horse and foot, on guard at Calais.[15]

He went on to tell his Venetian patron that he 'did not believe that the castle of St Peter at Rhodes is more strictly guarded against the Turks than Calais is against the French' ['ne io credo che il Castella di San Pietro de Rodiani sia guardato contro a Turchi con maggior diligentia, che sia guardato Cales contro il Franzesi'].[16] The writer drew an appropriate parallel between Calais and Berwick, both frontier fortresses closely guarded 'from ancient natural instinct', and he claimed that the costs of both were met from the proceeds of the Calais wool staple.[17] The expenditure which the safe-keeping of Calais entailed was heavy; and that expenditure showed no sign of any decrease. It has been demonstrated that 'between 1440 and 1460 more money was spent on the defences of Calais by land and sea than on any other military construction since the time of Edward I'.[18] There was to be no decline in the high level of expenditure incurred in times of war, or threat of war, until the final debacle. It has been estimated that Henry VIII spent an average of just over £1,000 per year on works at Calais between 1515 and 1525; between 1538 and 1547 he was spending an average of just over £15,000 per year, while Edward VI's government spent an average of about £5,000 per year between 1547 and 1553.[19] Sums of this magnitude could not be raised from

Calais' own resources. It could not pay for itself, and thus received substantial subsidies from English sources, especially (after 1536) from the proceeds of the sale of dissolved monastic lands through the Court of Augmentations.

Under Edward IV, a determined effort had been made to bring expenditure on Calais under control, and to attempt to meet the costs of fortification, and other works there, from its own revenues. It was not therefore surprising that the bulk of the financial responsibility for Calais was to be passed to the resident Staplers as a result of an Act of Retainer in 1466. What made Calais and the Pale so costly to maintain was not only the need to keep walls, towers, bastions and bulwarks in good repair, but the constant demands made by the upkeep and improvement of the water-defences. Calais relied upon its elaborate system of water-courses, sluices and 'plashes' (or large ponds) to defend it against French attack, above all from the south-west. As Michele pointed out in 1557, the 'inundation with which it may be surrounded' formed its best, if most drastic, means of defence. By opening the sluices and flooding the countryside to the south-west, the lieutenant or deputy could in effect create a huge inland lake across which no attacking or besieging force could cross. But the extensive network of sea-walls, canals, ditches, dykes and sluice-gates required constant vigilance and repair if the combined effects of scouring by rivers and streams, and the ebb and flow of the sea-tide, were not to destroy them for ever. In 1439–40, the castle and harbour themselves were in imminent danger of being swept away after the sea-wall at Newneham Bridge – a strategically vital strongpoint – was breached. Calais was a port built on marshland – not unlike King's Lynn or Bruges – and thus entirely reliant on imported building stone, lime, timber and all the other materials necessary to keep its fortifications and buildings in a decent state of repair.[20] By the fifteenth century many of its walls and towers were constructed of brick, which could be produced locally. Yet the costs of supplying it with provisions, as well as with materials such as prefabricated parts for jetties and bulwarks, mainly from England, combined with the perennial problems of maladministration and corruption among those responsible for so doing, remained very high. But the price, or so it was thought, was worth paying.

Calais was, in effect, unlike the other French territories of the English monarchy, with one significant exception – the Gascon dominions. Both Calais and the Gascon lands were directly annexed to the English not the French crown. Although English common law and other usages did not apply there, neither territory had formed part of the judicial, administrative and fiscal systems of the English-occupied French kingdom. In neither case, for instance, had appeals gone to the Lancastrian Parlement at Paris, but were heard either by a local sovereign court (as at Bordeaux) or at Westminster. Calais and the Pale, as we have seen, were essentially English and became more markedly so after the loss of the other continental possessions. As David Grummitt has shown, 'a more belligerent and distinctly English identity in the Pale' is discernable, suggested by a sharp rise in the number of letters of denization granted to non-English residents, between 1453 and 1485.[21] By 1543, a policy of virtual ethnic cleansing had been imposed, and resident aliens were expelled altogether from both the town and the Pale. This was in part a product of post-Reformation suspicions about the religious affiliations of non-English inhabitants. It was unknown for a Frenchman or Fleming, without letters of denization, to hold office at Calais. In circumstances that were not entirely dissimilar, the burgesses of the Welsh borough of Conway under Henry VIII could assert that 'it is no more meet for a Welshman to bear any office in Wales ... than it is for a Frenchman to be an officer at Calais'.[22] The administrative personnel at Calais had always been predominantly English although, before the 1450s, men born within the English crown's French dominions – including Normans and Gascons – were not excluded from office. Even after the loss of the other French possessions, Gascon exiles such as Gaillard de Durfort, lord of Duras, served as marshal of the garrison, and there were 30 Gascons, all subjects of the English crown, on its strength in 1466. By the early years of the sixteenth century, moreover, the tendency towards 'Anglicization', evident from the 1450s onwards, had ensured that English was the language of the Pale's law courts and administration. An equation between ethnic and linguistic identity was increasingly gaining ground, and the prescription (1536) that 'the Englisshe language used within this Realme of England' should be spoken in the parishes of Calais and the Pale endorsed the principle.

Although it could, and did, act as a cultural as well as an economic entrepot, Calais thus remained an outpost of Englishness. After 1536, it sent two elected representatives to the English parliament. Before that date, members of the Company of the Staple had served as MPs for English shires and boroughs, and often represented the interests of Calais, presenting petitions on behalf of the burgesses and Staplers. It was increasingly dependent upon supplies and provisions, including meat and corn, from the south coast of England and, besides the Staplers (finally and permanently established there in 1423), was governed and administered, under the king's Deputy, by a network of inter-related resident English families – the Whethills, Wingfields, Garneys, Banasters and others.[23] In 1533, the oath 'whereby the King's Deputy of Calais is always sworn' prescribed that 'ye shall swear that ye shall be good and true to our liege lord King Henry the eight and his heirs kings of England as long as ye shall live'.[24] The Calais Statutes of 1535–6 added the king's other titles – king of France and lord of Ireland – to the royal style, but the English title preceded them. Unlike the documents and coins issued for Henry VIII's recently conquered towns of Tournai (1513–14) and Boulogne (1544), which treated them unequivocally as parts of Henry's titular French crown, all instruments of government and jurisdiction relating to Calais followed usages common to the dominions of the English crown, such as

Wales, Ireland and the former Gascon lands. It was not without justification and a strong sense of realism that the Lancastrian Sir Thomas Findern, lieutenant of Guînes (1451–60), set up at Camfrere [Caffiers], on the western boundary of the Calais Pale 'a post ... hanging from the same by a Cheyne a sword, where upon these wordes were graven: "no man be so hardy to take me awaye, ffor this ys the right pale between Ingland and Ffraunce".[25] The true boundary of the English kingdom thus lay across the English Channel: Calais was a true barbican or outwork.

In January 1558, that barbican of England was finally lost to French arms. Lord Wentworth surrendered the town and garrison of Calais itself on 8 January. The worst fears of what would result from its loss were voiced by Michiel Surian, Venetian ambassador to Philip II, writing from Brussels on that day, when he told the Doge and Senate that as the news

> is of greater importance than any other intelligence that could be heard at this present time, so has it very greatly troubled everybody here, both on account of the actual loss and the subsequent detriment; the French, on the other hand, having made the greatest possible acquisition in these parts, well nigh expelling the English from Flanders, and depriving them of that port which rendered them masters of the Channel, and of a fortress which they held in such great account, and giving them such vast repute, they being thus enabled to harass France and Flanders, and all these States at any time.[26]

Two remaining strong-points still had to be taken. Lord Grey of Wilton's beleaguered force marched out honourably from Guînes on 21 January after a hard-fought defence of that fortress. The smaller stronghold at Hammes was the last English possession on French soil to be lost when its captain, Lord Dudley, hearing of the fall of Guînes, saved the lives of himself and his men by simply slipping away with them into imperial Flanders. International politics played their part in the *débacle*. English alignment with Habsburg Spain against its French enemy had substantially reduced the opportunities for independent English action on the European mainland. The marriage of Mary I to Philip II of Spain had brought an increasingly anti-French stance in its wake. Marian foreign policy was thus as likely to be determined in Madrid as at Westminster. War with France, actively sought by Philip of Spain, had been precipitated in April 1557 by an attack on Scarborough by the rebel Thomas Stafford, allegedly with French support. The depleted Calais garrisons, manning defective defences, faced with a lack of military support from England, were soon forced to capitulate to French besieging forces. The story was not an entirely unfamiliar one. Under-manned garrisons, attempting to hold fortified places in less-than-perfect states of repair and maintenance, inadequately supported with funds and victuals from England, had been a commonplace and perennial feature of the waging of war during the previous two centuries. In October 1533, Lord Lisle, as the King's Deputy at

Calais, wrote to Thomas Cromwell that 'this, the King's town … hath been long in great necessity for lack of victual out of England' and told him that:

> I and the King's Council here do think that, among many necessaries, nothing may be more necessary than victuals. For, blessed be our Lord, if this town were in necessity and peril of enemies, if it shall please the King to cause it to be provided of men and victual, it needeth not to fear the Great Turk, [if] he were as nigh a neighbour as France or Flanders is.[27]

His complaint echoed those of many of his predecessors, and of others engaged in the task of defending the continental outposts of the English crown.

In 1404, for example, the English captain of the castle at Fronsac in the Bordelais, Sir William Faringdon, constable of Bordeaux, petitioned the king's council in England. He told them that there was

> very little revenue from the surrounding countryside called the Fronsadais, which country is otherwise entirely destroyed, and the said knight has pledged all the goods that he has, plate, cups, jewels and even the king's livery collar, to guard and sustain the said castle … and to give [the garrison] something to eat … without sufficient wages for 120 combatants or otherwise he is unable to hold and defend the said castle against the French, which castle is head of all Guienne, for if all the other fortresses of Guienne were lost, which God prevent, they could be recovered by way of the said castle of Fronsac.

> ['poy de revenu du paiis environ appelle Fronsades, la quele paiis est tout outrement destruyt, et le dit chivaler ad mys en gage toutz ses biens quant qil avoit, platz, tassez, oplantz, et unquore le coler du Roy, pour garder et soustener le dit chastel … et pour leur donner a manger … sanz gages suffisantz pour le dit chastel pour 120 combatanz ou autrement il ne puet tenir ne garder le dit chastel contre les Frraunceois, le quiel chastel est chef de tout Guyenne, car si toutz lez autrez forteressez de Guyenne furent perduz, que Dieu deffend, ils purrount estre recouvere par le dit chastel de Fronsac.][28]

The litany of complaint reverberated through the petitioning process which, although subject to customary exaggeration by the petitioners, often contained more than a grain of truth. Although the Lord Deputy and the Calais Council could maintain in 1533 that the place was 'never so poor since it was first English',[29] their grievances against the government at home (that is, at Westminster) had been commonplace in the repertoire of dialogue between 'central' and 'local' administrations for a long time. One of the very last missives to be sent from England's continental possessions was the letter dated 4 January 1558, in which Lord Grey, writing from the castle at Guînes, 'most assured English even to the death', told Queen Mary that

> The French have won Newnhambridge, and thereby entered into all the low country and the marishes between this and Calais. They have also won Rysbank, whereby they be now masters of that haven [of Calais]. And this last night past they have placed their ordnance

of battery against Calais, and are encamped upon St Peter's Heath before it. So that I am clean cut off from all relief and aid, which I looked to have both out of England and from Calais, and know not how to have help by any means either of men or victuals ... For lack of men out of England, I shall be forced to abandon the town, and take in the soldiers thereof for the defence of the castle.[30]

The duke of Guise and his army had been enabled to break into the English Pale from the South-West, because Lord Deputy Wentworth and the Calais council had not resolved to open the sluices and flood the countryside until it was too late. Had they done so in good time, Calais might never have fallen in 1558. The Venetian ambassador to the French court reported that the king, Henry II, had spoken to him about the Lord Deputy's 'mistakes', one of which was that

he did not flood the fields as he could have done, because he did not choose to deprive himself of next summer's crops by swamping the sowed *possessioni et campi* to his own detriment, and that of the principal inhabitants of the town [Calais], through loss of the harvest.[31]

To release so great a volume of salt water into the countryside of the English Pale would indeed have rendered it effectively sterile, and Henry II's account is to some extent confirmed by Wentworth's own despatch to Queen Mary on 2 January, at 10 p.m., when he wrote that '[he] would also take in the salt water about the town, but cannot do so, as it would infect the water wherewith they brew ... therefore [he] makes all the haste he can therein, and howsoever the matter goes must shortly be forced to let in the salt water'.[32]

It was too late. The French easily took Sangatte, Newneham Bridge and, most fatefully of all, the Rysbank opposite the harbour of Calais, from which they proceeded to demolish sections of the castle walls by artillery bombardment. The castle was the weakest link in the defences of the town and port – it was in effect a thirteenth-century stronghold only minimally adapted to meet the demands of sixteenth-century siege warfare. In 1556, the Privy Council in England had, tardily, addressed the issue. The castle was thought to be 'a place (as it nowe is) more apte to give th'ennemye an entrye to the towne thenne to defende the towne or itselfe'.[33] They were to be proved right, but nothing was done about the situation before the final collapse. The town's and the Pale's great bulwarks, gun platforms, bastions and water-defences which had cost so much time, effort and expense to create and improve, particularly during the 1540s, fell without a shot being fired. A parsimonious attitude on the part of the Marian government, worthy of the most cheese-paring of accountants, had proved fatal to the retention of England's last continental possession. Calais was lost for reasons very similar to those which led to the loss of Normandy and Gascony in the mid-fifteenth century: among them, inadequate support in men, money and provisions from the government in England and, having already lost the diplomatic initiative, capitulation in the face of superior forces concentrated at a decisive point.

It has been claimed that the 'logic of history' simply prevailed in this case. But how did that logic operate? 'It was the logic of history that the expanding power of France should recover a French stronghold, and the French gain was real'.[34] But it could, conversely, be argued that history has little logic about it – the existence of enclaves, anachronisms and anomalies within the modern world of nation-states disproves this idea. Examples could be cited from Andorra to Luxemburg, from Monaco to Gibraltar, from Vatican City to Lichtenstein, and from Limburg to Schleswig-Holstein. Whatever the material effects of the loss of Calais were (and contemporaries reckoned them considerable), it was 'a body blow to the early Elizabethan polity' in terms of dishonour alone.[35] Cardinal Pole, writing to Philip II on 10 January 1558, called it a 'sudden and grievous catastrophe'.[36] Calais had, since the Lancastrian losses of the mid-fifteenth century, been seen by England's rulers more as 'a principal member and chief jewel of our realm' than as an anachronistic and dispensable relic of a lost French kingdom.[37] Had it been retained after 1558, it would, while keeping its own administration and customs, undoubtedly have been fully incorporated (as was Wales) into the realm of England. The Tudor monarchy's claim to land and title in France now became a card in the diplomatic pack, to be played as and when opportune for English interests. An account of a discussion among Henry VIII's counsellors in 1511 on relations with France, the papacy and the Empire set out the case for and against an interventionist continental policy. Those in favour of prosecuting war with France opined that: 'It was probable his [Henry's] subjects in France retained still a due memory not onely of their allegiance, but of the benefit received from the crown of England; Besides, that in France their never wanted discontented Persons, who would joyn with his Forces'.[38]

Henry took their advice. Even those counsellors opposed to such a course of action felt that the king's 'Title indeed in France, especially to the hereditary Provinces, was undoubted' and that the time was propitious. The threat of an English descent upon the French coast, as in 1513–14, from Boulogne to Bayonne, therefore remained a real and live issue in Anglo-French relations until the final abandonment of the French title and arms in 1802.

Tudor historians were once wont to emphasize the radical changes which, they argued, took place in the 1530s whereby an Imperial kingship of England consolidated the peripheries and outer regions of the kingdom into a unitary state.[39] Franchises and liberties were, it is argued, suppressed and the Councils of the North and of Wales sought to impose English common law, while the Calais Act of 1536 brought the town and Pale into a more tightly centralized programme of reform by Parliamentary statute.[40] But it has recently been pointed out that most of the provisions of the 1536 Act can be traced back into the fifteenth century, if not before.[41] The notion of an 'Imperial' crown of England thus begins to look rather familiar when later medieval evidence is considered. In a paean of praise for the British Empire, J. E. C. Bodley could write that 'Henry [VIII]'s imperial yearnings' were no doubt a relic of the time, only seventy years before his birth, when, after Agincourt, the English Crown was for the last time paramount on French territory.[42] The application of the epithet 'imperial' to the crown, though it had no reference to domains beyond the ocean, was an assertion of the idea that England was destined to be not a self-contained country but the metropolis of an Empire. Fortunately for the history of our people, the domination of the English Crown over great regions of the European continent was never renewed'. England was indeed destined not to be a 'self-contained country' because it could not afford to be so. The benefits, or disadvantages, occasioned by the ending of English tenure of European continental territories were controversial issues at the time of their loss, and remained so. In 1511 Henry VIII's council had been divided on the issue: those who opposed an attack on France at that time recalled the lack of success experienced by English arms in the mid-fifteenth century, despite the occupation of Normandy and alliances with Brittany and Burgundy.

English public finances had been bled white, they claimed, by the war with France and they concluded (in terms worthy of the Venetian senate):

> Let us therefore (in God's Name) leave off our attempts against the *Terra firma*. The naturall scituation of Islands seems not to sort with Conquests in that kind. England alone is a just Empire. Or, when we would inlarge our selves, let it be that way we can, and to which it seems the Eternall Providence hath destin'd us; which is, by the Sea. The Indies are discovered, and vast Treasure brought from thence every day. Let us therefore bend our endeavours thitherwards.[43]

It is noteworthy that even those who opposed intervention in France did not dismiss the inevitability of the fact that the English would seek to 'inlarge' themselves. The debate over expansion of England's territories, interests and influence was soon to be shaped by the rise of these other modes of overseas dominion in the form of colonies and dependencies of a more far-flung nature. The very notion of an 'Imperial' crown lent an outward-looking aspect to the English monarchy. Overseas ambitions could not simply be abandoned by a maritime trading power. It was not to be long before adventurism and expansion, now predicated increasingly upon command of the oceans, again became a characteristic aspect of England's relations with a wider world.

The unitary English nation-state was therefore, once again, to become merely one component within a larger aggregation of countries and peoples, bound together only by allegiance to an Imperial crown. In 1542, Henry VIII assumed the title of king in Ireland (where he and his predecessors had previously been merely lords). The lordship was united to the Imperial crown of England while, in 1543, English common law was finally established in Wales. Henry's proclamation of kingship over Ireland, however, was moved by the eminently pragmatic concern that a mere 'lord' could not be fully sovereign over the Church in Ireland and would thereby have to acknowledge papal supremacy. Henry also began a renewed assault upon the Scots throne at this time – but this probably sprang from his desire to prevent Scottish aid to France in the conflict which he sought with Francis I in the 1540s. The unification of the British Isles was not an item on Henry VIII's political agenda. In that respect he differed little from his medieval predecessors. Some measures were clearly taken to improve the administration and finances of the Welsh and Irish lands. But Calais still remained outside all such attempts to impose a degree of legal and institutional uniformity on the 'peripheral' regions of the kingdom. The franchises of Guînes, Marck and Oye, as well as the customs of the town of Calais itself, were preserved until the end of English rule. Had the Gascon dominions remained in English hands after 1453, they would undoubtedly have enjoyed similar immunity, as they had done for centuries before. A fundamental misconception about the nature of English authority and its institutional structures within the continental possessions of the English crown has thus tended to distort historical writing. When married to concepts of the rise of the unitary nation-state, teleological interpretations tend to dominate historical analysis. It seems that historians have found it difficult to conceive of regimes which, although they united their territories under one rule, did not necessarily seek to impose or promote centralized or uniform modes of government, law or administration within them all. To be a 'member and joint' of the Imperial crown of England did not necessarily bring institutional uniformity in its wake.

Similarly, a robust patriotism, expressed in the vernacular language of the English, has sometimes been seen as a primary characteristic of Tudor 'insularity'. But French speech and a more general francophone culture continued to be acquired and cultivated among the English aristocracy. The ancient enmity was offset and balanced by fraternization. In September–December 1518, for instance, large gatherings of English nobles and gentry, most of them in the service of the royal household, assembled during the festivities which attended the visit of an 80-strong French embassy to the court of Henry VIII. Among them was the French-speaking Arthur Plantagenet, Lord Lisle, bastard son of Edward IV of England who was to become Lord Deputy at Calais in 1533.[44] His very names seem to epitomize both the chivalric and continental role of the English monarchy. The members of the Calais garrison known as 'Spears' (i.e. those men-at-arms, often of noble or gentle birth, equipped as heavy cavalry and commanding units equivalent to the French *lance*) were generally of good birth and included, in the musters of 1533–4 and 1539–40, representatives of the families of Bourchier, Broke, Browne, Hall, Hastings, Talbot and Willoughby.[45] Among the office-holders at Calais at the same time were Lords Berners, Lisle, Howard, Maltravers, Grey of Wilton and Cobham, together with knights such as Sir John Wallop, Sir Robert Wingfield, Sir Edward Ryngeley and Sir Christopher Garneys. The Deputies of Calais shared many characteristics with their immediate neighbours in both French and imperial service. Correspondence between Lord Lisle and his 'bon voisin et parfaict amy' ['good neighbour and perfect friend'] Oudart du Biez, French seneschal of Boulogne, was generally extremely cordial, and was conducted on both sides entirely in French. It was perhaps easier to be good neighbours at this particular time, in the wake of the Anglo-French truces which followed the peace treaties of 1525 and 1527. But similarly good relations, again conducted through the medium of the French language, were maintained with the imperial captain of Gravelines, Anthoine Brusset. Du Biez would send Lisle gifts such as boar's heads and pieces of venison, which were reciprocated, while co-operation and compromise over such matters as safe-conducts, piracy, the seizure of prizes off the coast, border raids, the pursuit and extradition of criminals and suchlike activities were the stuff of daily life in a frontier zone. In one boundary dispute, which concerned the limits of the English Pale, the location of certain meadows was at issue. Reference was made in Lisle's correspondence with Oudart du Biez to the treaty of Brétigny (1360) which added Guînes, where the disputed lands were located, to the Pale.[46] But Lisle assured Du Biez (in French) that:

> I have not come hither to begin any strife nor any kind of injury, but to employ myself in all things to the uttermost of my power to the maintenance of the good peace and amity which there is betwixt the Kings our masters, and to set aside all occasions that I might find contrary thereto and to conduct myself with you as a good neighbour and friend, if you will so regard me.[47]

A similarly amicable tone characterized his correspondence with the emperor's captain at Gravelines, from whom Lisle received 58 surviving letters during his seven-year tenure of the Deputyship.[48] Letters to and from both these correspondents often alluded to hunting, falconry, horses, dogs and the appreciation of wines – themes upon which aristocrats across Europe were always happy to dwell. These common social assumptions about ways of life overrode all political and national divisions between the protagonists resulting from their masters' quarrels. The Lisles (Lord and Lady) also formed genuine friendships with members of the northern French and Flemish nobility, reflected in letters revealing 'a degree of familiarity and warmth which seems to ignore any national boundaries', especially between the female representatives of these families.[49] Such common cultural and social connections were perpetuated by more formal and ceremonial events such as the Field of the Cloth of Gold in 1520, at which Lisle was again found among the select group present during Henry VIII's interviews with both Francis I of France and the Emperor Charles V. A similar exchange of lavish courtly hospitality and entertainment accompanied Henry's interviews with Francis I at Boulogne and Calais in October 1532, at which Lisle was again present.[50] The fundamental (and symbolic) significance of Calais as an English possession was emphasized on 27 October 1532 when a chapter of the Order of the Garter was held there, and both Anne de Montmorency and Philippe Chabot, lord of Brion and Admiral of France, were elected to the Order. In these higher echelons of Anglo-French society there can be little doubt that a knowledge of spoken, if not of written French, was both widespread and essential.

A comparison, however, between mid-fifteenth- and sixteenth-century practices is revealing. Henry VI, for example, certainly spoke very good French: during the peace negotiations with a French embassy at Westminster in July 1445, the archbishop of Rheims addressed Henry 'in French, because it had been thus agreed between them, and they (the French envoys) had ascertained that the king of England understood it well, and moreover the earl of Suffolk had so advised'[51] ['en Francois, pour ce que ainsi avoit este conclut entre euls, et avoient sceu que le roy Dangleterre lentendoit bien, et aussi lavoit conseille le comte de Suffolk']. But the chancellor of England replied to the address in Latin, not in French, thereby adopting Henry V's practice in such cases. There is also confirmatory evidence from June 1433 during a meeting with Burgundian envoys: even as a boy of 12 Henry VI was proficient in French, as the Burgundians reported to Philip the Good that 'the said king ... asked us very graciously, and in the French language, how you were, and where you were'[52] ['le quel roy ... nous demanda tres gracieusement et en langaige Francois, comment vous le faisies, et ou vous estiez']. We have already noted the reasonable proficiency in French of Edward IV ('assez bon francois') during his interview with Louis XI at Picquigny (August 1475).[53] Consumption of chivalric and courtly literature, moreover, in its original French versions, continued to characterize the reading habits of the English upper classes. But there were signs that, by the 1520s, the English vernacular language had gained much fuller acceptability in court circles, as well as a wider and perhaps more monoglot readership, when Lord Berners published his translation of Froissart's *Chronicles* (1524–5). The existence of a larger audience, among both the country gentry and urban laity, encouraged translators, publishers and printers to produce, and profit from, printed versions of tried and tested texts. Berners' translation of Froissart was the first attempt to render the most popular and widely disseminated account of 'the honourable and noble adventures of feats of arms, done and achieved by the wars of France and England' into the English language.[54] And it was undertaken by express royal command. The rubric at the beginning of Berners' first volume read: 'translated out of Frenche into our maternal englysshe tonge by Johan Bourchier, knight, lorde Berners: at the commaundement of oure moost highe redouted soverayne lorde kyng Henry the viii, kyng of Englande and of Fraunce'.[55]

Berners was Lord Deputy of Calais from 1520 to 1526, and again from 1531, dying there on 16 March 1533. His translations from the French included not only Froissart but also an Arthurian *Hystorye of the moost noble and valiaunt Knyght Arthur of lytell Brytayne*; the romance of *Huon of Bordeaux*; and the *Golden Book of Marcus Aurelius*, from a French version. Berners tells us in his Preface to the *Chronicles* that he had:

> read diligently the four volumes or books of sir John Froissart of the country of Hainault, written in the French tongue, which I judged commodious, necessary and profitable to be had in English, sith they treat of the famous acts done in our parts, that is to say, in England, France, Spain, Portugal, Scotland, Bretayne, Flanders and other places adjoining; and specially thay redound to the honour of Englishmen. What pleasure shall it be to the noble gentlemen of England to see, behold and read the high enterprises, famous acts and glorious deeds done and achieved by their valiant ancestors?[56]

His allusion to 'our parts' encompassed all the theatres of war and conquest in which England's rulers had been engaged during the later Middle Ages. Members of the English nobility and gentry were clearly his intended primary readership; but knowledge of French sufficient to enable them to read Froissart was, he implied, not necessarily within their grasp. A presumption of bilingualism, made in previous centuries, could no longer be made. In 1317 the 'mother tongue' of an English knight serving in Aquitaine was said to be French; by 1524 that mother tongue was assumed to be English.[57] Yet if Englishmen were to participate fully in the cultural, social and political world of their continental contemporaries, knowledge of French was essential. This could be achieved in a number of ways, including periods of residence and the boarding of children in France.[58] But there was also an increasing number of printed manuals, grammars, dictionaries and phrasebooks produced for the instruction of English pupils from the late fifteenth century onwards. The fourteenth-century treatise of Walter of Bibbesworth, and the *Liber Donati*, had offered instruction in Anglo-Norman, but times had changed. The establishment of English as the mother tongue of the highest echelons of English society heightened the need and demand for works which, as did that of Master Giles Duwes in *c.* 1533, permitted Englishmen to 'lerne to rede, to pronounce and to speke French trewly'.[59] The emphasis on the spoken word is interesting.

The learning of French in early- and mid-sixteenth-century England was evidently very common. For example, Jacques Peletier du Mans could observe that 'en Angleterre, a moins entre les Princes et en leurs cours, ilz parlent Francois en tous leurs propos' ['in England, at least among the Princes and in their courts, they speak French in all their affairs'].[60] It was therefore quite normal for members of the more ambitious English nobility and gentry to be taught French, as it 'began to emerge as a key international vernacular in the sixteenth century'.[61] In 1530, Master John Palsgrave, educated at Corpus Christi College, Cambridge and at the University of Paris, published his *Esclarcissement de la langue francoyse*.[62] This was a thoroughgoing attempt to produce a manual which set out French pronunciation, morphology and syntax, employing illustrative examples from a wide range of sources and usages. Palsgrave had been French tutor to Henry VIII's sister Mary at the time of her short-lived marriage in 1514 to Louis XII of France and her subsequent union with Charles Brandon, duke of Suffolk. Henry was himself a fluent French-speaker. Palsgrave was anxious to assure the king, to whom he dedicated his work, that he was 'desirous to do some humble service unto the nobilite of this victorious realme, and universally unto all the other estatz of this my natyfe countrey'.[63] He concluded his compendious treatise, which ran to 473 folios, with the wish that his labours:

> maye nat onely be commodyouse and profytable unto the nobylyte of this realme (the more soner by the menes herof in their tender age to attayne unto ye knowledge of this tonge) but also maye be moche vayllable unto all other persones of this noble realme, of what estate or condyscions so ever they be.[64]

A knowledge of French, especially of the spoken language, was therefore thought to be a desirable acquisition among a primarily English-speaking population. Palsgrave was particularly concerned to stress that a reading of his great work in its entirety was an essential pre-requisite for those with certain kinds of professional aspiration and that:

> if any of our nation be desyrous to be exquisyt in the Frenche tong, and by traycte of tyme covyte to come unto such parfyte knowledge therin that he may be able to do servyce in the faict of secretarishype, or otherwyse in those partyes to have further charge, or to use amongest them the fait of marchandyse, he should … read over all thre bookes by order.[65]

Trade, bureaucracy and foreign service all called for proficiency in written as well as spoken French. To illustrate good practice, it was significant that Palsgrave selected examples from the past – Alain Chartier and the *Roman de la Rose* – as well as a contemporary author Jean Lemaire de Belges.[66] 'Correct' French was clearly based upon the courtly language of the medieval past as well as the Renaissance present. Among Palsgrave's many examples of the use of French verbs some contained topical allusions, well known to all those who had served in Henry VIII's wars with France. Thus, under 'to besiege', he gave the example 'on les assiegea au chasteau de Hedyn: they were beseged in the castell of Hedyn' (Hesdin, 1522).[67] Closer cultural links between England and France had been fostered by the period of peace which marked the central years of Henry VIII's reign. But in times of both peace and war, relations between the two near-neighbours continued to be very close. And the language in which so many of those relations were conducted and expressed remained French.

9

The Aftermath

On 22 December 1562, the last active defender of England's role as a European land power was buried in the parish church of Cheshunt, Hertfordshire. William, Lord Grey of Wilton, KG, had held out valiantly against overwhelming odds at the castle of Guînes, in the marshland just south of Calais, in January 1558. The terms of its surrender, which he negotiated, stipulated that he and his fellow officers should become prisoners but that the rest of the garrison should go free.[1] After his release, and the payment of a ransom of 24,000 crowns to the French, he returned to hold office on another frontier of the English kingdom as Lord Warden of the East Marches towards Scotland and governor of Berwick. He was accorded a full heraldic funeral, attended by both Garter and Norroy kings-of-arms, and the 'greate banner of his armes', which was carried before his hearse, bore quartered achievements representing no less than ten noble families. These included those of Grey of Codnor, Grey of Ruthyn, Longchamp, Clare, La Vache, Talbot and Hastings – all of whom had seen their members serving in the wars of the English in France over the previous three centuries and beyond. Grey's funeral sermon was preached by Michael Reniger, one of the queen's chaplains, 'wherin he much comendyd the worthye servyce fro tyme to tyme don, as in Fraunce as in Scotland, by the defunct'.[2] Continuities were therefore broken in 1558 rather than in 1453. In many respects, crucial changes in both English foreign policy and English attitudes towards the kingdom's security, such as the essential role of naval power, took place between 1525 and 1560. Although Elizabeth I was strongly urged by some of her counsellors in the later 1560s to recover Calais and its Marches she never did so, and nor did her successors. Whatever the royal will might have been, however, it did not always command the support of all members of the Commons in Parliament. On the very morrow of Calais' fall, the Venetian ambassador to Philip II, then at Brussels, told the Doge and Senate that

> It is heard from England that it having been proposed in Parliament to provide for the recovery of Calais, many members said that the times were so bad, that before undertaking a war which might be the ruin of the kingdom, the matter should be well considered; and that if the French have taken Calais, they thus took nothing from the English, but recovered what was their own; so should this opinion be that of the majority, but little assistance can be hoped for from these people.[3]

Resistance to the crown took many forms, and reluctance – if not refusal – to vote subsidies for foreign wars became a recurrent theme in relations between English monarchs and their Parliaments. Henry VIII's reign perhaps witnessed the last examples of that partnership of crown and subjects in the pursuit of European territorial overseas ambitions which Edward III had inaugurated. In 1558, a long history of English intervention in mainland Europe, conducted from a continental territorial base, was to come to an end.

The previous four centuries had witnessed many changes in the relationship between the kingdom of England and its continental neighbours. Yet since the Angevin accession of 1154, there had been no time at which the English ruling house was not in possession of territory on the mainland of continental Europe. The centres of gravity of this much-ramified power structure shifted in the course of time. A fundamentally Francocentric power had already become more anglocentric by the mid-thirteenth century. But the linear progression over time towards an entirely England-centred, England-dominated and unitary nation-state was not an unbroken one. From Edward III to Henry VIII, the pursuit of continental power-bases and the vindication of claims to both title and land in France were subject to the constant ebb and flow tide of political events. Assertiveness, interventionism or withdrawal fluctuated as the balance of forces changed and as opportunities expanded or contracted. Yet there was never a time when the tenure of continental possessions, by whatever means and on whatever terms, was not an intrinsic element in that bundle of claims, rights and obligations which were inherited by those who wore the English crown. The English monarchs had also been dukes, counts and other lords, ruling a composite assemblage of territories. After 1340, when Edward III severed all feudal ties with the Valois house of France, they ceded sovereignty to no other power within their various dominions. Yet both before and after that date it was not by virtue of their English kingship that they had exercised authority in each one of their separate and discrete possessions. They were lords in Ireland; counts in Ponthieu; kings (of France) in those regions which they had occupied after conquest; and dukes in Aquitaine. There was no centralized, centripetal structure of empire. Notions of 'metropole' and 'periphery', the stock-in-trade of students of imperialism, often seem wide of the mark in this context. England's medieval empire was a ramshackle aggregation of territories and peoples, of different ethnic origins, historical traditions and cultural characteristics. Its government and administration, given the problems of communication over time and distance, necessarily relied upon a substantial measure of devolution and delegation. The extensive vice-regal, vice-ducal and vice-comital powers given to its major representatives in the various territories simply acknowledged the impossibility of creating, and sustaining, a truly centralized regime. This was not a papacy. Westminster was not Rome (nor was it Avignon). English kings might have had Napoleonic dreams, but dreams they remained.

As a result of the gradual re-orientation of England's continental aims and ambitions, which had of necessity to follow the loss of its residual French possessions, further important changes undoubtedly took place. The decline, and ultimate collapse, of a territorial power base across the Channel gave added rationale and impetus to the extension and consolidation of English supremacy over other regions of the British Isles. In the longer term, England was not to retain, nor seek to restore, its position as a land power on the mainland of continental Europe. Only Gibraltar (1704) and the island of Malta (1800) were subsequently acquired. Gibraltar, on its tiny peninsula, was to remain England's only land base in continental Europe. It served, very much as Calais had done, to control a vital sea-passage, but in a very different strategic theatre, at the western entry to the Mediterranean. England's retreat from its role as a continental land power was not entirely a product of choice and there were many who lamented the unfavourable conjunction of events which had led to the collapse in France. Hindsight might suggest that, by way of compensation for this loss of a European overseas 'empire', it was predictable that a renewed bid for English hegemony over the rest of the British Isles might be made. That said, it could not be claimed that this stemmed from any coherent policy of unification. Nor was the resulting polity anything more than an aggregation of peoples rather than a united kingdom in the form that was to evolve between 1707 and 1801. The English nation-state certainly advanced but did not yet include the whole of the British Isles, for the Scots jealously guarded and retained their independence. But, amid the changes, there were also elements of continuity. English policy towards the European mainland never became truly insular, because it could not afford to be so. The need to keep a watchful eye upon England's nearest continental neighbours continued to exercise the minds, and tax the ingenuity, of its rulers and their advisers. Thomas Howard, duke of Norfolk, told Lord Lisle, manning the Calais redoubt in December 1533, that Henry VIII's 'pleasure was [that] ye should have a vigilant Eye and respect to the fashion of the Emperor's subjects in the Low Countries'.[4] He was to discharge a similar function with regard to the king of France's subjects. With the subsequent loss of Calais, the need to maintain a constant English presence at the French and other European courts, and to infiltrate the entourage of the politically powerful in both France and the Low Countries, became even more imperative.

We have seen how the need to prevent the coastline of northern France and the Low Countries, and its immediate hinterland, from falling into the hands of a single dominant power had been a powerful determinant of English strategy over a long period of time. The creation, and retention, of English bases in those regions was an important part of this strategy. The fall of Calais, immediately preceded by the cession of more recently acquired strong points such as Tournai and Boulogne, demanded a radical re-thinking of this approach. The costs of maintaining a presence on the European mainland were very high. Parsimonious and cash-strapped English governments were tempted to look elsewhere to find means of ensuring a comparable degree of influence abroad, and of providing for England's security against invasion. This had become all the more pressing as a result of the breach with Catholic Europe in the 1530s. France and Spain – both Catholic powers – had somehow to be kept not only at arm's length but apart. The heavy costs to England of maintaining a physical presence on the north and west coasts of France were now compounded by the need to build a system of gun emplacements, artillery forts and bulwarks on the English south and east coasts to meet the threat, both actual and imagined, of Catholic invasion. By the end of 1540, 24 new forts had been garrisoned, and bastioned defences were being thrown up around coastal towns. When the expenses of guarding the marches towards Scotland were also added to these demands, the figure became enormous. A statement drawn up in *c.* 1553 calculated that, since 1539, £120,675 had been spent on the defences of Calais; £181,179 on English coastal fortifications; and £27,457 on the Scottish border.[5] This represented a total average annual expenditure of about £25,330. As an alternative line of conduct, greater recourse could be had to the apparatus of diplomacy. The rise of resident ambassadors and their legations enabled Englishmen to lie (and spy) abroad at rather less overall cost than that of strong points which could often degenerate into 'muddy redoubts' and precariously held outposts, however up-to-date their defensive works might have been.[6] At Calais, Tournai and Boulogne existing fortifications had to be modernized and new, expensive works were also required. Landward as well as seaward defences had to be put in place. The strides made in gunnery and siegecraft over the century between 1430 and 1530 necessitated the radical redesign of fortifications, both for defence and to house artillery. Angle-bastions, ramparts along which guns could be run, and massive bulwarks (French: *boulevard*; Dutch: *bollewerk*) became a *sine qua non* in the repertoire of the military architect and engineer. Castles and town defences became essentially artillery forts and gun-platforms. Changes in the nature of warfare thus, in part, dictated political and diplomatic strategies.

England's role may well have become that of a third party, or third player, in the new power-struggles of the age, but its part in the drama was not necessarily perceived to be a minor one. In October 1518, Cardinal Wolsey's multilateral peace treaty, drawn up at London, set out and defined a new role for the kingdom in European politics and diplomacy. England was to act as a third party, or middleman, between France and the Empire, pledged to take the offensive against either of the other powers if they should act against the tenor of the treaty. The English thus in effect held not the balance but the imbalance of power in their hands – a position much sought after by Wolsey. The plan failed, but left an enduring legacy in which England's role as a third party in major European conflicts at least potentially offered it the opportunity to exercise a relatively powerful influence. The opportunities to play an independent role and to avoid absorption by either France or Spain were there to be taken. Thus the loss of continental possessions did not necessarily mean that England was reduced to a position of relative weakness or insignificance. After the breach with Rome, moreover, papal mediation of disputes was totally unacceptable to the English. As we have seen, this was not the first time that the arbitrating and mediating role of the papacy had been rejected by them; during the Great Schism (1378–1417) the diplomatic intervention of popes and cardinals had been effectively outlawed. But in the 1530s the outright and permanent denial of papal supremacy changed the balance of forces for ever. Above all, there were to be no more English cardinals or careerists within the Church, playing what was often seen as a double game between papacy and monarchy. With no more Beauforts, Kemps, Poles or Wolseys in the College of Cardinals, a significant source of diplomatic manoeuvring was eliminated at a stroke. England became independent of their machinations. The 'Anglicization' of the Church in England, which had begun during the fourteenth century, was simply furthered and carried to its logical conclusion under Henry VIII.

The ensuing conflict with Spain, determined partly on religious and confessional lines, meant that the age-old enmity against France was now – but only for a time – a secondary characteristic of English foreign policy. The heat generated by the centuries-old conflict with France was to some extent reduced as England's defensive and aggressive priorities shifted towards the Iberian Peninsula and the Atlantic. It is arguable whether or not 'for two centuries after the end of the Hundred Years War, Anglo-French relations mattered less for both sides'.[7] Yet retention of the title 'king of France' in the English royal style until 1802 served as a constant reminder of ancestral claims and might still be used to justify descent upon the French coast at any point and at any time. The receipt, admittedly intermittent, of the French pension, first awarded to Edward IV in 1475, was dependent on the maintenance of an English claim to the French throne: if it had been renounced there would have been nothing to commute or buy off. Henry VIII, in a moment of chivalrous *bonhommie* and rare diplomatic tact, told Francis I in 1520, during the Field of the Cloth of Gold meetings that his English and French royal styles were merely 'titles given me which are good for nothing'.[8] Francis replied, with commendable finesse:

> Mon Frère, now that you are my friend, you are King of France, King of all my possessions, and of me myself; but without friendship I acknowledge no other King of France than myself, and thus, with the aid of our Lord God, do I hope to be able to defend and preserve this kingdom for myself and my successors.[9]

It was a eulogy of the sovereignty of friendship, framed as a conceit whereby one friend was granted possession of the other, and it was reciprocated in suitably ardent terms by Henry. But Henry's actions, both previous and subsequent, totally belied his assertion that his French title was 'good for nothing'. A second Crécy, Poitiers, Agincourt or Verneuil was denied him, but his determination to revive old claims and renew the Hundred Years War never died. It was not for want of interest, effort and expenditure – from his attempt to build up alliances against France to the close personal oversight of his works of fortification at Calais, Tournai and Boulogne – that his schemes failed. It was not for nothing that he shared a first name with his illustrious forebear.

A 'second Hundred Years War' with France was to erupt only after 1689 and would last until 1815. English arms never at any time deserted European battlefields. Battles fought in the Low Countries, from Oudenaarde (1708) to Waterloo, kept the power of France at bay and prevented the coastline of north-west Europe, from Brest to Bremen, from falling into the hands of a single master, whether that was Louis XIV or Napoleon Bonaparte. England's naval resources were meanwhile deployed to similar ends. But they were employed not only to defend the island fortress but to keep open, police and guard the vital sea ways linking it with its neighbours. Only sea power, arguably rediscovered and certainly re-organized under Henry VIII in the 1540s, would enable England to defend itself against the ever-present threat of invasion from Catholic France or Spain; to control the Narrow Seas and effectively to impede Spain from communicating with the Spanish Netherlands; and, similarly, to attempt to cut off France's sea passage to its ally since 1295, Scotland. The injunction of the *Libel of English Policy* (c.1436) thus continued to be of critical relevance to England's all-important relations with continental Europe:

> Cherish merchandise, keep the admiralty,
> That we be masters of the narrow sea.[10]

Whether that sea was likened to a wall, or a moat, with or without barbicans and outworks, the sea-girt isle which it protected continued to play a major part in the politics, diplomacy and trade patterns of continental Europe. The surrounding sea remained a highway, as it had always been. The Channel could, as John Le Patourel often observed, have bound the Norman kings' lands and lordships together rather than keeping them apart, as did both the Mediterranean and the Irish Sea at other times and in other contexts.[11] Throughout the period with which this book is concerned, England formed part of a 'trans-Channel polity', of varying and fluctuating size. It shared many things with its continental neighbours. Even its Janus-like predicament was by no means unique. Although they were not islands in a physical sense, England's closest overseas neighbours to some extent shared that predicament. The principalities of the Low Countries looked out, on one side, towards the kingdom of France; on the other, towards the German Empire. France itself gazed out, on the one hand, on the Latin cultures of Spain and Italy; on the other, towards the Germanic world. Even within the French kingdom, there was dichotomy and diversity: between *langue d'oïl* and *langue d'oc*, between the north, centre and Midi, and between regions of written and customary law. The welding together of modern, unitary, centralized political nations, with their foundation-myths, imagined histories and claims to exceptionalism is a relatively recent phenomenon. As part of that myth-making, the story of the English island-fortress and its progress towards nationhood is a stirring one. But that does not always make it good history.

The Anglo-French conflicts of our period have often been seen as a formative influence in giving both the English and the French a pronounced sense of their own identity. Michelet's dictum on the positive contribution made by war with England to France's awareness of nationhood could equally well be applied in reverse: by seeing the French at such close quarters, the English felt they were English. Yet this sense of national identity, or national consciousness, was offset, especially among the upper ranks of both societies, by constant interaction and an active cosmopolitanism. Aggressive rivalry, even a sense of hereditary enmity, was counter-balanced by mutual observance of agreed conventions in warfare, diplomacy, social intercourse and intellectual life. This remained the case for a very long time. It would be a distortion of the evidence to claim that the end of the Hundred Years War and the rise of a new era of religious conflict ushered in a totally new political and ideological world. England's decline, and ultimate withdrawal, as a continental European land power did not put an end to its very close involvement in European warfare, politics and culture. There was constant traffic of all kinds between England and France. Continuities with the distant past remained, some infused with new life long after they had passed from living memory.

As we have seen, the concept of England as a 'hereditary enemy' of France, already regarded as 'ancient' in 1436, was alive in 1962 and its legacy is still with us. The Joan of Arc legend, and the uses to which it has been put, provides us with an object lesson in how the medieval past of two modern nations can still play a vital part in the formation and perpetuation of national myths: unless and until the reality behind such myths can be presented to the widest possible audience in both countries, collective belief in distorted history will continue to make its baleful influence felt. Yet deliberately to forget unhelpful history, which can either contradict or confirm the sacred nostrums and articles of faith of nationalist or chauvinist sentiment, would again be to sacrifice truth to myth. The surprise in both countries, which recently (2007) greeted the news that in 1955–6, as well as in the desperate days of 1940, a joint Franco-British state had been envisaged, even including French membership of the British Commonwealth, demonstrates the strength of the idea of an ancient enmity and an unbridgeable gulf between the two nations. A pronounced sense of national identity has in both countries tended to erase all memory of periods in which substantial parts of France were held by the English crown. It is as if the union of the two kingdoms which created Lancastrian France had never been. But yesterday's ancient enemies are, however reluctantly, today's allies: there will probably never be another Hundred – let alone Six Hundred – Years War between England and France. Nothing is pre-ordained in history, but the risk of another armed conflict of any kind is in effect non-existent. Yesterday's enemies may even become tomorrow's friends.

Notes

Notes to Chapter 1: England and its Neighbours

1 See J. G. Zimmermann, *Vom Nationalstolze*, 4th edn. (Zurich, 1768), p. 177, translated as *Essay on National Pride*, tr. S. H. Wilcocke (London, 1797), pp. 116–17 and see above, p. ii. The author was a distinguished Swiss physician. For a recent study of Anglo-French, and Franco-British, relations of all kinds from the seventeenth to twentieth centuries see R. and I. Toombs, *That Sweet Enemy: The French and the British from the Sun King to the Present* (London, 2006).

2 Zimmermann, *Essay on National Pride*, pp. 35–6.

3 Philippe de Commynes, *Mémoires*, ed. J. Calmette and G. Durville (Paris, 1925), ii, pp. 207–8.

4 Quoted by R. and I. Tombs, *That Sweet Enemy*, p. 605.

5 Paris, Archives Nationales, K.64, no. 7 (8 January 1436): 'noz anciens ennemis les Anglois'.

6 See, for examples: AN, K.65, no. 6 (1439); K.67, nos. 3 (1441), 16 (1442); K.69, nos. 1 (1451), 13 (1454): 'noz anciens ennemis et adversaires les Anglois'.

7 *Rot.Parl.*, iii, p. 36b and above, p. ix.

8 For a good and very influential example see H. E. Marshall, *Our Island Story: A Child's History of England* (London, 1905).

9 For a trenchant statement of the view that 'Britain' is not a 'European' country, according to received and conventional definitions of Europe, see J. G. A. Pocock, 'Deconstructing Europe', in *The Question of Europe*, ed. P. Gowan and P. Anderson (London, 1997), pp. 297–316.

10 T. Garton Ash, *Free World* (London, 2005), pp. 196, 200 and, for an application of his notion of the Janus-like character of modern Britain to the medieval English kingdom, see below, pp. 3–4.

11 *Cal. S. P. Venetian, 1202–1509*, ed. Rawdon Brown, i (London, 1864), p. lxxii.

12 *The Sun*, Waterloo Day, 18 June 2004.

13 J. G. A. Pocock, 'British History: A Plea for a New Subject', *Journal of Modern History*, 47 (1975), pp. 606–7.

14 N. Saul (ed.), *England in Europe, 1066–1453* (London, 1994), p. 19.

15 See Marshall, *Our Island Story*, Ch. 1.

16 R. R. Davies, *The First English Empire: Power and Identity in the British Isles, 1093–1343* (Oxford, 2000), pp. 44–53. For a development of the notion of Anglo-Norman, and subsequently English, hegemony over the 'Atlantic archipelago' into the modern period,

see Pocock, 'British History: A Plea for a New Subject', pp. 617–19 and his 'The new British History in Atlantic Perspective: An Antipodean Commentary', *American Historical Review*, 104 (1999), pp. 490–500, esp. 493–4.

17   Davies, *First English Empire*, p. 30.

18   J. Dunbabin, *Charles I of Anjou: Power, Kingship and State-Making in Thirteenth-century Europe* (Harlow, 1998), pp. 27–9.

19   Dunbabin, *Charles I of Anjou*, p. 29.

20   Dunbabin, *Charles I of Anjou*, pp. 30–2.

21   R. Frame, *The Political Development of the British Isles, 1100–1400* (Oxford, 1990), p. 20.

22   *Calendar of Documents Preserved in France, Illustrative of the History of Great Britain and Ireland, 918–1206*, ed. J. H. Round (London, 1899), p. xxxi.

23   *The War of Saint-Sardos (1323–1325): Gascon Correspondence and Diplomatic Documents*, ed. P. Chaplais (London, 1954), p. 1.

24   See also R. B. Wernham, *Before the Armada: The Growth of English Foreign Policy, 1485–1566* (London, 1966), pp. 11–26.

25   Wernham, *Before the Armada*, p. 11.

26   N. A. M. Rodger, *The Safeguard of the Sea: A Naval History of Britain, 660–1649* (London, 1997), p. 175.

27   Sir Thomas Gray of Heaton, *Scalacronica*, ed. A. King (Surtees Society, cxxix, Woodbridge, 2005), pp. 136, 139.

28   Davies, *First English Empire*, p. 3.

29   *Saint-Sardos*, p. 4.

30   *Saint-Sardos*, p. 3 (6 Dec. 1323).

31   *Saint-Sardos*, p. 6.

32   See P. Chaplais, 'The Chancery of Guyenne, 1289–1453', in his *Essays in Medieval Diplomacy and Administration* (London, 1981), pp. viii, 64.

33   See M. W. Doyle, *Empires* (Ithaca and London, 1986), pp. 19–30; also, for a thesis which takes up the notion of an England-centred British Isles and develops it widely, see Pocock, 'British History: A Plea for a New Subject', esp. pp. 605–10.

34   J. H. Elliott, 'A Europe of Composite Monarchies', *P&P*, 137 (1992), pp. 48–71; and for a recent comparative study of early modern empires and their frameworks, see his *Empires of the Atlantic World: Britain and Spain in America, 1492–1830* (New Haven and London, 2006), esp. Ch. 5.

35   Davies, *First English Empire*, p. 20.

36   Marshall, *Our Island Story*, p. 177.

37   Wernham, *Before the Armada*, p. 11.

38   M. C. E. Jones, *Ducal Brittany, 1364–1399* (Oxford, 1970), pp. 143–4.

39   See Rodger, *Safeguard of the Sea*, p. 100.

40   P. Chaplais, *English Diplomatic Practice in the Middle Ages* (London, 2003), and TNA (PRO), SC 1/31, no. 72.

41   *PPC*, vi, p. 69.

42   *The Lisle Letters*, ed. M. St. Clare Byrne, 6 vols (Chicago and London, 1981), i, pp. 595–6.

43   Chaplais, *English Diplomatic Practice*, pp. 220–1 for examples; and see above, pp. 18–19.

44   3 July 1281: *Treaty Rolls*, I, no. 170.

NOTES TO PAGES 13–19

45 *Foedera*, II.ii, p. 1151: February 1341.

46 *Saint-Sardos*, p. 1.

47 *Saint-Sardos*, p. 1 and also p. 16.

48 *Saint-Sardos*, pp. 56–8: September 1324.

49 See Chaplais, *English Diplomatic Practice*, pp. 172–3, 215–16 for Hartung von Klux, KG (1411–40) and the lord of Cuijk in the 1290s.

50 See Chapter 6.

51 N. Desmarets, *L'ancienne jonction de l'Angleterre à la France ou le Détroit de Calais: Sa Formation par la Rupture de l'Isthme* (Paris, 1751), p. 87.

52 D. Gordon, *Making and Meaning: The Wilton Diptych* (London, 1993), pp. 57–8.

53 Bede, *Ecclesiastical History of the English People*, ed. B. Colgrave and R. Mynors (Oxford, 1979), p. 15.

54 *Metrical Chronicle*, ed. W. A. Wright (RS, London, 1887), I, ll. 1–5.

55 *The Libelle of Englyshe Polycye: A Poem on the Use of Sea-power, 1436*, ed. G. F. Warner (Oxford, 1926), ll. 1092–7.

56 *Libelle*, ll. 20–1.

57 G. M. Trevelyan, *English Social History* (London, 1944), p. 1.

58 Trevelyan, *English Social History*, p. xii.

59 See J. Campbell, 'The United Kingdom of England: The Anglo-Saxon Achievement', in *Uniting the Kingdom? The Making of British History*, ed. A. Grant and K. J. Stringer (London, 1995), pp. 31–47; for a critique of views which attribute ideas of 'nationality' to early medieval states, see P. Geary, *The Myth of Nations* (Princeton, 2002), pp. 15–40, 155–7.

60 See Doyle, *Empires*, pp. 30–47; Le Patourel, *Norman Empire*, pp. 319–24, 353–4; Davies, *First English Empire*, pp. 142–5, 169–71, 190–203.

61 See *Regesta Regum Scottorum*, ed. G. W. S. Barrow (Edinburgh, 1971), ii, Introduction.

62 *Cal. S. P. Venetian, 1581–91* (London, 1894), viii, pp. 345–6; cited in Wernham, *Before the Armada*, p. 19.

63 TNA (PRO), SC1/37, no. 94.

64 *Rot. Parl.*, iii, p. 36b.

65 *Libelle*, l. 811.

66 F. W. Brooks, *The English Naval Forces, 1199–1272* (London, 1932), pp. 80–94.

67 See, for example, *Saint-Sardos*, pp. 72–3.

68 Rodger, *Safeguard of the Sea*, pp. 116, 125–6.

69 Rodger, *Safeguard of the Sea*, p. 105.

70 Rodger, *Safeguard of the Sea*, p. 130.

71 Beckington, *Journal*, pp. 184–5.

72 See Chaplais, *English Diplomatic Practice*, pp. 221, 149, n. 483; Le Patourel, *Norman Empire*, pp. 163–72.

73 Trabut-Cussac, *L'Administration Anglaise*, pp. xvi–xvii.

74 *Lisle Letters*, ii, no. 148.

75 *Lisle Letters*, i, pp. 551–2.

76 *Saint-Sardos*, pp. 82, 107–8.

77 *Treaty Rolls*, I, p. 101, no. 234: Nov. 1294; Chaplais, *English Diplomatic Practice*, pp. 95–6, 148–9.

78   *Cal. S. P. Venetian*, I, p. 6.

79   Frame, *Political Development of British Isles*, p. 61.

80   See J. C. Holt, *Colonial England, 1066–1215* (London, 1997), pp. 1–24; H. Thomas, *The English and the Normans: Ethnic Hostility, Assimilation and Identity* (Oxford, 2003), pp. 1–25.

81   See Le Patourel, *Norman Empire*, pp. 330–4.

82   Frame, *Political Development of British Isles*, p. 25 and map.

83   See J. O. Prestwich, 'War and Finance in the Anglo-Norman State', *TRHS*, 5th ser., 4 (1954), pp. 19–43; W. L. Warren, 'The Myth of Norman Administrative Efficiency', *TRHS*, 5th ser., 34 (1984), pp. 113–32.

84   See D. J. A. Matthew, *The Norman Monasteries and their English Possessions* (Oxford, 1962), pp. 108–20.

85   See R. W. Southern, 'England's First Entry into Europe', in his *Medieval Humanism and Other Studies* (Oxford, 1970).

86   See, for example, P. Hyams, 'The Common Law and the French Connection', *Anglo-Norman Studies*, 4 (1981), pp. 77–92; P. Brand, *The Making of the Common Law* (London, 1992).

87   See J. C. Holt, 'Politics and Property in Early Medieval England', *P&P*, 57 (1972), pp. 3–52; F. M. Powicke, *The Loss of Normandy* (2nd edn.; Manchester, 1960), pp. 303–6.

Notes to Chapter 2: The Angevin Empire and the Kingdom of France

1   This chapter attempts to summarize the major conclusions reached by historians – both recent and less recent – of the Angevin empire, and to serve as an introduction or prelude to the more detailed study of the period from 1259 onwards which follows.

2   See Powicke, *Loss of Normandy*, pp. 328–58; J. Gillingham, *The Angevin Empire* (2nd edn.; London, 2001), pp. 119–25.

3   See J. Le Patourel, *Feudal Empires: Norman and Plantagenet* (London, 1984), viii, pp. 289–308.

4   See Chaplais, *Studies in Medieval Diplomacy and Administration*, II, pp. 132–5; Gillingham, *Angevin Empire*, pp. 123–5.

5   See Le Patourel, 'The Plantagenet Dominions', VIII, pp. 295–7; Gillingham, *Angevin Empire*, pp. 72–5.

6   Chaplais, *English Diplomatic Practice*, pp. 69–74.

7   Walter Map, *De Nugis Curialium*, ed. M. R. James (Oxford, 1914), pp. 242–6; Chaplais, *English Diplomatic Practice*, p. 73.

8   Davies, *First English Empire*, p. 145.

9   Thomas, *The English and the Normans*, p. 67.

10   See Le Patourel, 'Norman Barons', in *Feudal Empires*, VI, pp. 3–29; Davies, *First English Empire*, pp. 19–21; Holt, 'Politics and Property', pp. 24–32.

11   See D. Bates, 'England and Normandy after 1066', *EHR*, 104 (1989), 34–45; Holt, 'Politics and Property', pp. 10–22.

12   See, for example, T. Evergates, *Feudal Society in Medieval France: Documents from the County of Champagne* (Philadelphia, 1993), pp. xix–xxi; D. M. Nicholas, *Medieval Flanders* (London, 1992), pp. 77–89.

13 See the studies on this theme in D. Bates and A. Curry (eds), *England and Normandy in the Middle Ages* (London, 1994).

14 Frame, *Political Development of the British Isles*, p. 40.

15 See C. W. Hollister, 'Normandy, France and the Anglo-Norman Regnum', *Speculum*, 51 (1976), 202–42; Gillingham, *The Angevin Empire*, pp. 12–21.

16 See Powicke, *Loss of Normandy*, pp. 9–12; Y. Renouard, 'Essai sur le rôle de l'empire angevin dans la formation de la France et de la civilisation française aux xiie et xiiie siècles' in his *Etudes d'Histoire Médiévale* (Paris, 1968), pp. 849–61.

17 Renouard, 'Essai sur le rôle de l'empire angevin', pp. 858–60.

18 Le Patourel, 'The Plantagenet Dominions', in *Feudal Empires*, VIII, p. 298; *Norman Empire*, pp. 268–71, 275.

19 Chaplais, *English Diplomatic Practice*, pp. 69–70.

20 See the studies included in M. Aurell (ed.), *Culture politique des Plantagenet* (Poitiers, 2003); and *Noblesses de l'espace Plantagenet (1154–1224)* (Poitiers, 2001), esp. pp. 67–78.

21 See Aurell, *Culture politique des Plantagenet*, pp. 1–26, 205–76; A. Chauou, *L'ideologie Plantagenet. Royauté arthurienne et monarchie politique à la cour Plantagenêt (xiie–xiiie siècles)* (Rennes, 2001).

22 Frame, *Political Development of the British Isles*, p. 32; G. Spiegel, 'The Cult of St Denis and Capetian Kingship', *Journal of Medieval History*, 1 (1975), 43–69.

23 See Spiegel, 'The Cult of St Denis', pp. 66–9; C. Beaune, *Naissance de la nation France* (Paris, 1985), pp. 113–27.

24 For a recent account of the culture of the Angevin world see M. Auréll, 'La cour Plantagent: entourage, savoir et civilité' in M. Aurell (ed.), *La cour Plantagenêt, 1154–1224* (Poitiers, 2000). The plaque (Le Mans, Musée Tessé) is illustrated in colour in G. Duby, *Le Moyen Age: De Hugues Capet à Jeanne d' Arc, 987–1460* (Paris, 1987), p. 240.

25 See Le Patourel, 'The Plantagenet Dominions', viii, pp. 295–6. Le Patourel calculated that he spent an estimated 176 months in Normandy, 84 months in other French lands and 154 months in England, Wales and Ireland.

26 See J. C. Holt, 'The End of the Anglo-Norman Realm', *Proceedings of the British Academy*, 61 (1975), pp. 223–65.

27 See M. Clanchy, *England and its Rulers, 1066–1272* (London, 1983) pp. 111–18; Gillingham, *Angevin Empire*, pp. 7–8, 117–19.

28 See F. Barlow, *Thomas Becket* (London, 1968), pp. 27–32.

29 See M. Strickland, *War and Chivalry: The Conduct and Perception of War in England and Normandy, 1066–1217* (Cambridge, 1996), pp. 109, 128–9, 151–2; D. Crouch, *William Marshal: Court, Career and Chivalry in the Angevin Empire* (London/New York, 1990) provides the best recent account of the Marshal's career in English.

30 See Powicke, *Loss of Normandy*, pp. 303–7. The best recent guide to work on the loss of Normandy and its effects is S. Church (ed.), *King John: New Interpretations* (Woodbridge, 1999), especially the contributions by Barratt, Gillingham and Power.

31 See Holt, 'End of the Anglo-Norman Realm', pp. 223–65; Powicke, *Loss of Normandy*, Appendix II ('The Division of the Norman Baronage'), pp. 328–58.

32 See Matthew, *Norman Monasteries*, pp. 72–6, 97–9.

33 See above, pp. 4, 20.

34   Powicke, *Loss of Normandy*, p. 303.

35   Frame, *Political Development of British Isles*, p. 44.

36   For a detailed account, see R. C. Stacey, *Politics, Policy and Finance under Henry III, 1216–1245* (Oxford, 1987), pp. 160–200.

37   For an excellent recent survey, drawing upon archaeological, architectural and documentary evidence, see M.-P. Baudry, *Les Fortifications des Plantagenêts en Poitou, 1154–1242* (Paris, 2001), esp. pp. 99–124.

38   See M. K. James, 'Les activités commerciales des negoçiants en vins gascons en Angleterre à la fin du Moyen Ages', *Ec.H.R*, 65 (1953), pp. 35–49; Y. Renouard, *Etudes d'histoire médiévale*, 2 vols (Paris, 1968), i, pp. 297–336; ii, pp. 1019–34.

39   See Stacey, *Politics, Policy and Finance*, pp. 237–9, 255–7.

40   See H. Ridgeway, 'King Henry III and the "Aliens", 1236–1272', *Thirteenth-century England*, ii, pp. 65–82; 'William de Valence and his "familiares"', *Historical Research*, 65 (1992), pp. 239–57.

41   TNA (PRO), E. 175/2/5/1.

42   See below, pp. 41, 44–5.

Notes to Chapter 3: Aquitaine and the French Wars

1   *AMB*, v, *Livre des Coutumes*, ed. H. Barckhausen (Bordeaux, 1890), pp. 607–9.

2   See Chaplais, 'Le traité de Paris ...' in his *Essays in Medieval Diplomacy and Administration*, ii, pp. 121–2. Also see Map.

3   Le Patourel, 'Kings and Princes in fourteenth-century France', p. 159.

4   'La Guyenne est rattachée pour trois siècles à la domination d'outre-Manche' ['Aquitaine was attached for three centuries to a cross-Channel domination']: C. Dartigue, *Histoire de la Guyenne* (Paris, 1950), p. 51.

5   M. W. Labarge, *Gascony, England's First Colony, 1204–1453* (London, 1980), p. xii.

6   AN, J.654, no.10, m. 3r.

7   See E. A. Benians, J. Butler and C. E. Carrington (eds), *Cambridge History of the British Empire* (Cambridge, 1959), iii, p. 200.

8   Ibid., pp. 473–5.

9   Trabut-Cussac, *L'Administration anglaise*, pp. 290–1.

10   *Rot. Parl.*, i, p. 98, col. 1.

11   Davies, *First English Empire*, p. 28; J. F. Lydon in *A New History of Ireland: Medieval Ireland, 1169–1534*, ed. A. Cosgrove (Oxford, 1981), ii, pp. 194–5; W. H. Waters, *The Edwardian Settlement of North Wales* (Cardiff, 1938), pp. 14–15; R. A. Griffiths, *The Principality of Wales in the Later Middle Ages. I. South Wales, 1277–1536* (Cardiff, 1972), pp. 35–44. For similar practices in the financial administration of the earldom of Chester see P. H. W. Booth and A. D. Carr, *Account of Master John de Burnham the Younger, chamberlain of Chester, of the Revenues of the Counties of Chester and Flint, 1361–62* (Stroud, 1991), pp. xxiii–xxxviii.

12   *Documents illustrative of the History of Scotland, 1286–1306*, ed. J. Stevenson (Edinburgh, 1870), ii, p. 164.

13   *Rot. Parl.*, i, p. 309.

14 Trabut-Cussac, *L'Administration anglaise* ..., pp. 298–303; Waters, *Edwardian Settlement of North Wales*, pp. 22–4.

15 See *Gascon Register A*, ed. G. P. Cuttino (London, 1975), i, pp. 206–9.

16 Ormrod, 'English State', p. 209.

17 See, for examples, Trabut-Cussac, *L'Administration anglaise* ..., pp. 292–5, 303–6.

18 See Rodger, *Safeguard of the Sea*, p. 119; J. Bernard, *Navires et gens de mer à Bordeaux (vers 1400–vers 1550)*, i (Paris, 1968), p. 399.

19 E. M. Carus-Wilson and O. Coleman, *England's Export Trade, 1275–1547* (Oxford, 1963), pp. 203–4.

20 M. K. James, 'Fluctuations of the Anglo-Gascon wine trade in the fourteenth century', *EcHR*, 2nd ser., 4 (1951), pp. 191–2.

21 G. L. Harriss, *King, Parliament and Public Finance*, p. 523.

22 TNA (PRO), E.101/161/16 and 17.

23 Rodger, *Safeguard of the Sea*, pp. 125–6.

24 For a recent synthesis see M. Prestwich, *Plantagenet England, 1225–1360* (Oxford, 2005), pp. 165–8.

25 *Cal.Charter Rolls,I, 1225–1257*, pp. 386, 389.

26 *CPR, 1247–58*, p. 141.

27 W. M. Ormrod, 'The English State and the Plantagenet Empire, 1259–1360', in *The Medieval State*, ed. J. R. Maddicott and D. M. Palliser (London, 2000), p. 198.

28 Davies, *First English Empire*, pp. 142–5; Thomas, *The English and the Normans*, pp. 224–38.

29 Davies, *First English Empire*, pp. 29–30.

30 *Saint Sardos*, p. 67; see also E. A. R. Brown, 'Gascon Subsidies and the Finances of the English Dominions, 1315–24', *Studies in Medieval and Renaissance History*, 8 (1971), pp. 33–146.

31 Ormrod, 'English State', p. 201.

32 See above, pp. 38–9.

33 See above, pp. 37–8.

34 *St-Sardos*, p. 107.

35 Davies, *First English Empire*, p. 28.

36 Davies, *First English Empire*, p. 173.

37 *RG*, I, Supplément (1896), p. xix.

38 H. Jenkinson, 'The Great Seal of England: Deputed or Departmental Seals', *Archaeologia*, 85 (1935), pp. 307–8.

39 Bémont, *RG*, II, pp. i–iii; Davies, *First English Empire*, p. 28.

40 Jenkinson, 'The Great Seal', p. 314; Chaplais, 'Chancery of Guyenne', p. 62.

41 Davies, *First English Empire*, p. 173.

42 Chaplais, 'Chancery of Guyenne', p. 64.

43 Jenkinson, 'The Great Seal of England', pp. 314–16.

44 Lydon, *New History of Ireland*, ii, pp. 194–5; Jenkinson, 'The Great Seal', pp. 320–22; pl. xciii (1–3).

45 Waters, *Edwardian Settlement of North Wales*, pp. 22–4, 162–3; Waters, *Edwardian Settlement of Wales*, pp. 14–15; Davies, *England's First Empire*, p. 28.

46 Jenkinson, 'The Great Seal', pls xciii (1–3); xcv (1–2).

47   Ibid., p. 320, and pl. xciii (1–5).

48   Chaplais, 'Chancery of Guyenne', pp. 63–4; 'Le sceau de la cour de Gascogne', pp. 20–21.

49   Chaplais, 'Le sceau de la cour de Gascogne', pls. i and ii.

50   Jenkinson, 'The Great Seal', pp. 323–4.

51   H. Jenkinson, 'A Seal of Edward II for Scottish Affairs', *Antiq. Journal*, 11 (1931), pp. 229–39; Davies, *First English Empire*, pp. 28–9.

52   Davies, *First English Empire*, p. 173.

53   Frame, *Political Development of British Isles*, p. 139.

54   *Cal. S.P. Venetian*, i, p. 8.

55   Davies, *First English Empire*, p. 178.

56   Davies, *First English Empire*, pp. 173–80.

57   *EHD, 1189–1327, iii*, ed. H. Rothwell (London, 1975), p. 542.

58   Grummitt, 'Calais and the Crown', pp. 47–8.

59   Viscount Dillon, 'Calais and the Pale', *Archaeologia*, 53 (1892), pp. 289–388.

60   *King's Works*, i, pp. 434–5.

61   Grummitt, 'Calais and the Crown', p. 48.

62   Dillon, 'Calais and the Pale', pp. 296–7, 308–9.

63   Chaplais, *English Diplomatic Practice*, pp. 143.

64   Jenkinson, 'The Great Seal', p. 309 and pl. lxxxix (5–6).

65   See Le Patourel, 'Kings and princes', pp. 155–6.

66   See R. Barber, *Edward, Prince of Wales and Aquitaine* (1978), p. 177.

67   Capra in *Histoire de Bordeaux: Bordeaux Médiéval II*, p. 384.

68   See P. Chaplais, 'Some Documents Regarding the Fulfilment and Interpretation of the Treaty of Brétigny (1361–1369)', *Camden Miscellany*, xix, pp. 1–84; E. Perroy, 'Charles V et le traité de Brétigny', *MA*, 38 (1928), pp. 255–81.

69   Tout, *Chapters*, v, pp. 300–306, 347–8, 365–7, 375–8, 413–15, 427–8.

70   See the map of the principality published by Capra in *Histoire de Bordeaux: Bordeaux médiéval II*, carte 9. For the homages see Trabut-Cussac, *Livre des Hommages*, pp. 70–117.

71   Barber, *Edward, Prince of Wales and Aquitaine*, p. 177.

72   Capra in *Histoire de Bordeaux: Bordeaux Médiéval II*, p. 384; Tout, *Chapters ...*, v, pp. 289–400, esp. pp. 300–6, 347–8, 365–7.

73   F. Bériac, 'Une principauté sans chambre des comptes ...', in *La France des Principautés*, ed. P. Contamine and O. Matteoni (Paris, 1996), p. 108.

74   Ibid., pp. 119–21; TNA (PRO), E.101/179/9.

75   Bériac, 'Une principauté sans chambre des comptes ...', pp. 119–20.

76   See *Lists and Indexes, xxxv, Foreign Accounts Various*, pp. 42, 145; D. Green, *The Black Prince* (Stroud, 2001), pp. 85–6, 101–6.

77   See T. Thornton, 'Taxing the King's Dominions', in *Crises, Revolution and Self-Sustained Growth*, eds R. Bonney and W. M. Ormrod (Stamford, 1998), pp. 103–17.

78   Rymer, *Foedera*, III, ii, p. 667.

79   See *Le Livre des Hommages d'Aquitaine*, ed. J.-P. Trabut-Cussac (Bordeaux, 1955), pp. 70–117, and the map of the distribution of homages in *Histoire de Bordeaux: Bordeaux Médiéval II*, carte 9.

80   Rymer, *Foedera*, III, ii, p.668.

81 Ibid., p. 668.

82 Ibid., p. 810.

83 See J. B. Henneman, *Royal Taxation in Fourteenth-century France: The Development of War Financing, 1322–1356* (Princeton, 1971), pp. 3–12, 281–3.

84 See *Histoire de Bordeaux: Bordeaux Médiéval II*, pp. 398–9; E. Perroy, 'Edouard III et les appels gascons en 1368', *Annales du Midi*, 61 (1948–9), pp. 91–6.

85 See G. Loirette, 'Arnaud-Amanieu, sire d'Albret et l'appel des seigneurs gascons en 1368', in *Mélanges d'Histoire offerts à Charles Bémont* (Paris, 1913), pp. 317–40; Perroy, 'Edouard III et les appels gascons', pp. 91–3; P. Tucoo-Chala, *Gaston Fébus et la Vicomté de Béarn, 1343–1391* (Bordeaux, 1960), pp. 81–92.

86 Tucoo-Chala, *Gaston Febus*, pp. 90–91.

87 ATG, A.56, fos. 30r–31v; Tucoo-Chala, *Gaston Fébus*, pp. 90–2.

88 ATG, A.132: letter to lord of Severac, 31 May 1368.

89 Rymer, *Foedera*, III, ii, p. 941.

90 6 March 1373: Rymer, *Foedera*, III, ii, p. 972.

91 Green, *Black Prince*, p. 117.

92 Green, *Black Prince*, pp. 107, 109.

93 See above, p. 42.

94 See R. Favreau, 'Comptes de la sénéchaussée de Poitou', *BEC*, 117 (1959), pp. 74–6; Chaplais, 'Some Documents …', pp. 22–45, 36–9.

95 Chaplais, 'Some Documents …', pp. 6–9.

96 Bériac, 'Une principauté sans Chambre des Comptes …', pp. 108–9; Chaplais, 'Chancery of Guyenne', p. 87.

97 Bériac, 'Une principauté sans Chambre des Comptes …', p. 108.

98 *Rot. Parl.*, ii, p. 310.

99 See Perroy, 'Eduard III et les appels gascons', pp. 95–6; Loirette, 'Arnaud-Amanieu d'Albret et l'appel des seigneurs gascons', pp. 336–40.; *AHG*, i, p. 137.

100 *AHG*, i, p. 137.

101 Montesquieu, *Spirit of the Laws*, p. 145.

102 See A. Curry, 'L'administration financière de la Normandie anglaise: continuité ou changement?' in *La France des principautés*, pp. 92, 99.

103 *The Rous Roll*, ed. C. D. Ross (Gloucester, 1980), nos 63–4.

104 Transcription of the original inscription around the tomb-chest by the author, July 2006.

105 *The Rous Roll*, no. 50.

106 Rodger, *Safeguard of the Sea*, pp. 143–7.

107 See G. Hutchinson, *Medieval Ships and Shipping* (London, 1994), pp. 27–31, 156–7, 166.

108 For another view see M. H. Keen, 'The End of the Hundred Years War: Lancastrian France and Lancastrian England', in *England and her Neighbours, 1066–1453: Essays in Honour of Pierre Chaplais*, eds M. Jones and M. Vale (London, 1989), pp. 299, 307–11.

109 See *English Suits Before the Parlement of Paris, 1420–1436*, ed. C. A. J. Armstrong and C. T. Allmand (Camden 4th ser, London, 1982), esp. Appendix II.

110 Frame, *Political Development of the British Isles*, p. 179.

111 See M. Vale, 'The End and Aftermath of the Hundred Years War', in *England in Europe*, pp. 155–7.

Notes to Chapter 4: Allies, Mediators and the French Enemy

1 Edward Herbert, lord of Cherbury, *The Life and Raigne of King Henry the Eighth* (London, 1649), p. 7.
2 J. G. Black (ed.), 'Edward I and Gascony in 1300', *EHR*, 17 (1902), p. 525.
3 See *Cal.S.P. Venetian, I*, pp. cxxxii–cxxxiv, 16–18, 30–2, 35–6.
4 *Cal.S.P. Venetian, I*, p. 38.
5 For what follows see Chaplais, *English Diplomatic Practice*, pp. 44, 51–2.
6 See Chaplais, *English Diplomatic Practice*, p. 51; Powicke, *Loss of Normandy*, p. 81.
7 *Letters and Papers*, ii, II, p. 433.
8 *Gesta Henrici Quinti*, ed. F. Taylor and J. S. Roskell (Oxford, 1975), p. xxv.
9 See C. M. Crowder, *Unity, Heresy and Reform*, p. 115.
10 Ibid., p. 116.
11 Ibid., pp. 108–9.
12 Ibid., p. 121.
13 E. F. Jacob, 'Theory and Fact in the General Councils of the Fifteenth Century', in his *Essays in Later Medieval History* (Manchester, 1968), pp. 135–7; Crowder, *Unity, Heresy and Reform*, pp. 150–2.
14 Crowder, *Unity, Heresy and Reform*, p. 151.
15 Jacob, 'Theory and Fact', p. 137.
16 J. G. Dickinson, *The Congress of Arras, 1435: A Study in Medieval Diplomacy* (Oxford, 1955), pp. 89–90.
17 Ibid., pp. 25–6.
18 Ibid., p. 28.
19 *Letters and Papers*, ii, II, pp. 431–2.
20 Ibid., ii, II, p. 527.
21 Ibid., ii, II, p. 528.
22 *English Suits before the Parlement of Paris*, ed. Armstrong and Allmand, p. 1.

Notes to Chapter 5: English Identity: Language and Culture

1 W. Stubbs, *Select Charters* (Oxford, 1870, revised edn, 1895, repr. 1960), pp. 2–3.
2 T. F. Tout, *France and England: Their Relations in the Middle Ages and Now* (Manchester, 1922), p. 96.
3 Ibid., p. 83.
4 See above, p. 16.
5 T. C. W. Blanning, *The Culture of Power and the Power of Culture* (Oxford, 2002), p. 279.
6 T. Turville-Petre, *England the Nation: Language, Literature and National Identity 1290–1340* (Oxford, 1996), p. 8.
7 See below, pp. 89–90, 92–3.
8 See Vale, *Origins of the Hundred Years War*, p. 5.
9 See above, p. 15.
10 *Metrical Chronicle*, ii, ll. 7537–43. I have modernized the Middle English original.

11   See Vale, *Origins of the Hundred Years War*, p. 5, n.16.

12   See Chaplais, *English Diplomatic Practice*, p. 127.

13   F. Hingeston, *Royal and Historical Letters*, i, pp. 357–8.

14   Chaplais, *English Diplomatic Practice*, p. 133.

15   Rymer, *Foedera*, ix, p. 658 (Dec. 1418).

16   Ibid., ix, pp. 656–7.

17   M.-J. Arn, 'Two MSS, One Mind: Charles d'Orléans and the Production of Manuscripts in Two Languages', in M.-J. Arn (ed.), *Charles d'Orléans in England (1415–1440)* (Woodbridge, 2000), p. 78.

18   Commynes, *Mémoires*, ii, p. 53.

19   Ibid., ii, p. 65.

20   Beckington, *Correspondence*, ii, p. 205.

21   J. Catto, 'Written English', *P & P*, 178 (2003), pp. 24–59.

22   For the 'high' Middle Ages (eleventh to thirteenth centuries) and the rise to hegemony of French culture see the observations of R. W. Southern in his *The Making of the Middle Ages* (London, 1953), pp. 14–16, 17–25.

23   For more extended discussion of what follows see Vale, *Princely Court*, pp. 282–8.

24   See, for the following section, Vale, *Princely Court*, pp. 287–94.

25   Binski, *Westminster Abbey and the Plantagenets*, p. 166.

26   Vale, *Origins of the Hundred Years War*, pp. 23–6.

27   For this, and what follows, see M. C. Prestwich, '*Miles in Armis Strenuus*: The Knight at War', *TRHS*, 6th ser., 5 (1995), pp. 218–19.

28   TNA, SC.1/13, no. 12 (14 October 1279); 13/38 (undated). See Vale, *Origins of the Hundred Years War*, p. 34.

29   K. B. McFarlane, 'Had Edward I a "Policy" Towards the Earls?', in his *The Nobility of Medieval England* (Oxford, 1973), pp. 248–67.

30   See, for example, some contributions to *The Medieval State*, esp. pp. 1–24, 197–214.

31   See Blanning, *The Culture of Power*, pp. 29–40, and esp. 316–19.

32   See the work of Frédérique Lachaud, including her 'Liveries of robes in England, *c.* 1200–*c.* 1330', *EHR*, 111 (1996), pp. 279–98 and, above all, her 'Textiles, Furs and Liveries: a Study of the Material Culture of the Court of Edward I (1272–1307)' (unpub. Oxford D.Phil. thesis, 1992).

33   See D. J. A. Matthew, *The Norman Monasteries and their English Possessions* (Oxford, 1962), pp. 19–22.

34   For this, and what follows see Matthew, *Norman Monasteries*, pp. 81–6.

35   For what follows see: *Art and the Courts: France and England from 1259 to 1328*, eds P. Brieger, P. Verdier and M. F. Montpetit, 2 vols (Ottawa, 1972), i, no. 98; M. Harrison, 'A Life of St Edward the Confessor in the Early 14th Century Stained Glass at Fécamp in Normandy', *JWCI*, 16 (1965), pp. 22–37; *Les Vitraux de Haute-Normandie*, eds M. Callias Bey, V. Chausse, F. Gatouillat and M. Hérold (Corpus Vitrearum medii aevi, Recensement des vitraux anciens de la France), 6 (Paris, 2001), pp. 22–3, 303–10.

36   See P. Verdier, 'Témoignages artistiques des mariages franco-anglais au début du xive siècle', *Bulletin Monumental* (1973), pp. 137–45.

37   *Les Vitraux*, p. 305.

38 See P. Binski, *Westminster Abbey and the Plantagenets: Kingship and the Representation of Power, 1200–1400* (New Haven and London, 1995), pp. 54, 56–7; cf. Harrison, 'A Life of St Edward', pp. 35–7.

39 *Art of the Courts*, ii, p. 175.

40 Matthew, *Norman Monasteries*, pp. 81, 83–5.

41 Harrison, 'A Life of St Edward', p. 31; P. Binski, *The Painted Chamber at Westminster* (London, 1986), pp. 36–43.

42 *Les Vitraux*, pp. 22–3.

43 For what follows, see Binski, *Westminster Abbey and the Plantagenets*, pp. 56–7.

44 *King's Works: The Middle Ages*, i, p. 133.

45 For much of what follows, see Binski, *The Painted Chamber at Westminster*, pp. 63–6, 105–12; and *Westminster Abbey and the Plantagenets*, pp. 90–120.

46 J. C. Holt, 'The End of the Anglo-Norman Realm', *Proceedings of the British Academy*, 61 (1975), pp. 223–65, esp. pp. 263–5.

47 See J. Vale, *Edward III and Chivalry* (Woodbridge, 1982), Ch. 5; H. L. Collins, *The Order of the Garter, 1348–1461* (Oxford, 2000).

48 See Binski, *Westminster Abbey and the Plantagenets*, pp. 107–8.

49 See Binski, *Westminster Abbey and the Plantagenets*, pp. 165–6, 171–4; Vale, *Princely Court*, pp. 250–3.

50 Binski, *Painted Chamber*, pp. 88–93.

Notes to Chapter 6: The Legend of Joan of Arc

1 See above, pp. ix, 1.

2 Amid a vast secondary literature in English, one of the best accounts of the aftermath and legacy of Joan of Arc's career remains Marina Warner, *Joan of Arc: The Image of Female Heroism* (New York, 1981); the French-language literature on the subject is too large even to be presented in summary form here, but a recent synthesis can be found in M. Winock, *Jeanne d'Arc* in P. Nora (ed.), *Les lieux de Mémoire*, iii (Paris, 1992).

3 William Stubbs, *The Constitutional History of England in its Origin and Development* (5th edn, Oxford, 1896), iii, p. 275.

4 Stubbs, *Constitutional History*, p. 276.

5 G. L. Harriss, *Shaping the Nation: England, 1360–1461* (Oxford, 2005), p. 587.

6 See Joan's letter to the English (22 March 1429) where she refers to the prospect of the 'fairest deed that has ever been done for Christianity', i.e. a joint Anglo-French crusade to recapture the Holy Places: C. Taylor (ed.), *Joan of Arc: La Pucelle* (Manchester, 2006), p. 76; for Henry V, see E. F. Jacob, *Henry V and the Invasion of France* (London, 1947), p. 191.

7 See the articles by J. Dalarun and M. Winock in the special number ('Jeanne d'Arc: une passion française') of the popular French historical review *Histoire*, 210 (May 1997). The documentation of the beatification and canonization processes is to be found in *Sacra Ritum Congregatione, eminentissimo ac reverendissimo domino Card. Lucido Maria Parocchi relatore: Aurelianen: Beatificationis et Canonizationis servae Dei Joannae de Arc, Pucellae*

Aurelianensis nuncupatae: Positio super introductione causae (Rome, 1893); *Positio super virtutibus* (Rome, 1901); *Novissima Positio super virtutibus* (Rome, 1903).

8　Geary, *Myth of Nations*, p. 15.

9　See P. Contamine, 'Jeanne d'Arc dans la mémoire des droites', in J.-F. Sirinelli (ed.), *Histoire des droites en France* (Paris, 1992).

10　Bruno Mégret, deputé of l'Isère, on 7 May 1987 (cited, with Jean-Marie Le Pen on http://fr.wikipedia.org/wiki/Jeanne d'Arc: naissance d'un mythe).

11　For a review of current thinking see D. A. Bell, 'Recent Works on Early Modern French National Identity', *Journal of Modern History*, 68 (1996), pp. 84–113.

12　Bell, 'Recent Works', p. 86.

13　See P. S. Lewis, 'War Propaganda and Historiography in Fifteenth-century France and England', *TRHS*, 5th ser., 15 (1965), pp. 1–21; C. Taylor, 'War, Propaganda and Diplomacy in Fifteenth-century France and England', in *War, Government and Society in Late Medieval France*, ed. C. T. Allmand (Liverpool, 2000), pp. 70–91.

14　A. Lang, *The Maid of France: Being the Story of the Life and Death of Jeanne d'Arc* (London, 1908), p. 285.

15　A. France, *Jeanne d'Arc* (Paris, 1908), ii, pp. 86–9.

16　J.-B.-J. Ayroles, *La Vraie Jeanne d'Arc*, 5 vols (Paris, 1890–1901), i, pp. 120–5.

17　For what follows, and for a summary of his career, see *Procès de condamnation de Jeanne d'Arc*, ed. P. Tisset and Y. Lanhers, 3 vols (Paris, 1960, 1970–1), ii, pp. 394–5.

18　See the incontrovertible evidence of the original French minute of the session on 12 May in *La minute française des interrogatoires de Jeanne la Pucelle*, ed. P. Doncoeur and Y. Lanhers (Melun, 1956), pp. 246–7. This document formed the basis upon which the formal Latin trial record was drawn up – by Courcelles himself.

19　See M. G. A. Vale, *Charles VII* (London, 1974), p. 214.

20　See C. Taylor (ed.), *Joan of Arc: La Pucelle*, pp. 292–3 for his deposition to the rehabilitation process.

21　See J. Michelet, *Jeanne d'Arc*, ed. G. Rudler, 2 vols (Paris, 1925); P. Contamine, 'Jules Quicherat, historien de Jeanne d'Arc', in his *De Jeanne d'Arc aux Guerres d'Italie* (Orléans, 1994), pp. 179–93.

22　Michelet, *Jeanne d'Arc*, i, pp. 7–8.

23　Michelet, *Jeanne d'Arc*, i, p. 9.

24　Michelet, *Jeanne d'Arc*, ii, p. 7. This theme is taken up and examined by Colette Beaune in her *Jeanne d'Arc* (Paris, 2004), pp. 379–85.

25　J. Quicherat (ed.), *Procès de condamnation et de réhabilitation de Jeanne d'Arc*, 5 vols (Paris, 1841–9).

26　Ayroles, *Vraie Jeanne d'Arc*, i, p. 616. Pere Ayroles was also the author of a book entitled *L'Université de Paris au temps de Jeanne d'Arc et la cause de sa haine contre la libératrice* (Paris, 1902).

27　Cited by W. S. Scott, *Jeanne d'Arc: Her Life, her Death, and the Myth* (London, 1974), Appendix E: 'The Changing Image of Jeanne d'Arc in English Opinion', p. 169.

28　E. Perroy, *The Hundred Years War* (London, 1962), p. 288. The bracketed interpolations are mine.

29　Perroy, *Hundred Years War*, pp. 288–9.

30   E. F. Jacob, *The Fifteenth Century, 1399–1485* (Oxford, 1961), pp. 251–2.

31   See the extracts from the depositions made at the rehabilitation trial in Taylor (ed.), *Joan of Arc: La Pucelle*, pp. 290–4, 304–48.

32   Lang, *The Maid of France*, p. vii.

33   Quoted in Scott, *Jeanne d'Arc*, p. 172.

34   T. Douglas Murray, *Jeanne d'Arc, Maid of Orléans, Deliverer of France: Being the Story of her Life, her Achievements, and her Death, as Attested on Oath and Set Forth in the Original Documents* (London, 1903).

35   Harriss, *Shaping the Nation*, p. 563.

36   Beaune, *Jeanne d'Arc*, p. 385.

37   My translation. For another (very similar) version see Taylor, *Joan of Arc: La Pucelle*, p. 221.

Notes to Chapter 7: The Fall of Lancastrian France

1   This chapter is a slightly revised version of my contribution entitled 'The End and Aftermath of the Hundred Years War', in *England in Europe, 1066–1453*, ed. N. Saul (London, 1994), pp. 151–62.

2   See M. Vale, 'The Last Years of English Gascony, 1451–1453', *TRHS*, 5th ser., 19 (1969), pp. 119–38.

3   See P. Geary, *The Myth of Nations* (Princeton, 2002), p. 13.

4   For an analytical account which puts as much emphasis on conditions in mid-fifteenth century England as in France, see M. H. Keen, 'The End of the Hundred Years War: Lancastrian France and Lancastrian England', in *England and her Neighbours, 1066–1453: Essays in Honour of Pierre Chaplais*, eds M. Jones and M. Vale (London, 1989), pp. 297–311.

5   *Paston Letters*, ed. J. Gairdner (London, 1872), i, no. 103.

6   See below, pp. 116–20

7   For the 'peace congress' at Arras (1435) which in many ways marked the beginning of English diplomatic failures see above, pp. 64–5, 70–1.

8   Montesquieu, *The Spirit of the Laws*, eds A. M. Cohler, B. C. Miller, H. W. S. Stone (Cambridge, 2005), p. 243.

9   See 'Sir John Fastolf's Report' (1435) in *Letters and Papers*, ed. Stevenson, ii, pp. 575–85.

10   See R. Vaughan, *Philip the Good*, pp. 98–114.

11   See, for a series of pioneering studies of English military occupation and organization in Normandy, R. A. Newhall, *The English Conquest of Normandy, 1416–1424: A Study in Fifteenth-century Warfare* (New Haven, 1924); *Muster and Review: A Problem of English Military Administration, 1420–1440* (Cambridge, MA, 1940); and 'Henry V's Policy of Conciliation in Normandy, 1417–1422', in *Anniversary Essays in Medieval History of Students of C. H. Haskins*, ed. C. H. Taylor (Boston, 1929). A more recent account is in A. Curry, 'The First English Standing Army? Military Organisation in Lancastrian Normandy, 1420–1450', in *Patronage, Pedigree and Power in Later Medieval England*, ed. C. D. Ross (Gloucester and Totowa, NJ, 1979).

12 See C. T. Allmand, *Lancastrian Normandy, 1415–1450: The History of a Medieval Occupation* (Oxford, 1983), pp. 234–40.

13 For a recent overview see Harriss, *Shaping the Nation*, pp. 58–66, 564–5, 571–2.

14 See J. L. Kirby, 'The Issues of the Lancastrian Exchequer and Lord Cromwell's Estimates of 1433', *BIHR*, 30 (1957), esp. pp. 147–8.

15 *The Governance of England by Sir John Fortescue,* ed. C. Plummer (Oxford, 1885), p. 114.

16 For an overall survey of English fiscality and taxation in the later Middle Ages see W. M. Ormrod, 'England in the Middle Ages', in *The Rise of the Fiscal State in Europe, c. 1200–1815*, ed. R. Bonney (Oxford, 1999), pp. 19–52.

17 See H. Kleineke, 'The Commission *de mutuo faciendo* in the Reign of Henry VI', *EHR*, 116 (2001), pp. 1–30; and Vale, *English Gascony*, pp. 120–1, 147–51.

18 See G. L. Harriss, 'Cardinal Beaufort, Patriot or Usurer?', *TRHS*, 5th ser., 20 (1970), pp. 129–48.

19 M. H. Keen and M. J. Daniel, 'English Diplomacy and the Sack of Fougeres in 1449', *History*, 54 (1974), pp. 375–91; C. Taylor, 'Brittany and the French Crown: The Legacy of the English attack upon Fougères (1449)' in *The English State*, pp. 243–57.

20 See, for what follows, Vale, 'Last years of English Gascony', pp. 119–38.

21 See below, pp. 111–15.

22 *Letters and Papers*, ed. Stevenson, ii, pp. 601–2. See also, for investment by Englishmen in Norman land, R. Massey, 'The Land Settlement in Lancastrian Normandy', in *Property and Politics: Essays in Later Medieval English History*, ed. A. J. Pollard (Gloucester, 1984), pp. 76–96.

23 See below, pp. 123–4.

24 For these and other examples see Allmand, *Lancastrian Normandy*, pp. 79–80.

25 Vale, *English Gascony*, pp. 152–3.

26 Ibid., pp. 13–20.

27 Wernham, *Before the Armada*, pp. 11–23.

28 See also below, pp. 134–5.

29 See D. Grummitt, '"One of the mooste pryncipall treasours belongyng to his Realme of Englande": Calais and the Crown, c.1450–1558', in *The English Experience in France, c. 1450–1558* (Aldershot, 2002), pp. 46–62.

30 For studies of Anglo-Netherlandish relations at this time see *England and the Low Countries in the Late Middle Ages*, ed. C. Barron and N. Saul (Stroud and New York, 1995); also the essays collected together in C. A. J. Armstrong, *England, France and Burgundy in the Fifteenth Century* (London, 1983).

31 For a thesis which sees the influence of the Burgundian/Habsburg Netherlands as a prime element in English Renaissance culture see G. Kipling, *The Triumph of Honour: Burgundian Origins of the Elizabethan Renaissance* (Leiden, 1977).

32 See below, pp. 111–12, 131–4.

33 Wernham, *Before the Armada*, p. 408.

Notes to Chapter 8: Tudor Ambitions and the War with France

1 Herbert of Cherbury, *Life and Raigne*, p. 19.
2 J. R. Lander, 'The Hundred Years War and Edward IV's Campaign in France', in *Tudor Men and Institutions: Studies in English Institutions and Law*, ed. A. J. Slavin (Baton Rouge, LA, 1952), pp. 70–100.
3 See E. L. Meek, 'The Career of Sir Thomas Everingham, "Knight of the North", in the Service of Maximilian, Duke of Austria, 1477–81', *Historical Research*, 74 (2001), pp. 238–48.
4 *Chronicle of Calais in the Reigns of Henry VII and Henry VIII to the Year 1540*, ed. J. G. Nichols (Camden Soc., London, 1846), pp. 211–12.
5 Ibid., p. 32.
6 *Letters and Papers*, ed. Stevenson, II.ii, p. 580. Italics mine.
7 Herbert of Cherbury, *Life and Raigne*, p. 25.
8 See, for a recent treatment of this very important theme, S. Anglo, *Martial Arts in Renaissance Europe* (New Haven and London, 2000), esp. pp. 1–5, 271–3.
9 C. Richmond, 'Patronage and Polemic', in *The End of the Middle Ages*, ed. J. L. Watts (Gloucester, 1998), p. 67.
10 See C. S. L. Davies, 'The Wars of the Roses in European context', in *The Wars of the Roses*, ed. A. J. Pollard (London, 1995), p. 177.
11 *Edward IV's French Expedition of 1475*, ed. F. P. Barnard (Oxford, 1925), fo. 1r.
12 See Ross, *Edward IV*, esp. pp. 234–8; Commynes, *Mémoires*, ii, pp. 27–8.
13 *Edward IV's French Expedition*, p. 146 and plate.
14 *Chronicle of Calais*, p. xxv.
15 *A Relation or Rather a True Account of the Island of England*, ed. C. A. Sneyd (Camden Soc., London, 1847), p. 45
16 Ibid., pp. 45–6.
17 Ibid., pp. 45, 50, 119.
18 *King's Works*, i, p. 432.
19 Ibid., iii, p. 361.
20 Ibid., i, pp. 426–7, 433–44.
21 'Calais and the Crown', in *English Experience in France*, pp. 54, 55–7.
22 P. R. Roberts, 'The Welsh Language, English Law and Tudor Legislation', *Transactions of the Cymmrodorion Society* (1989), p. 21; Davies, *First English Empire*, p. 198.
23 *Lisle Letters*, I, pp. 442–3, 447.
24 TNA (PRO), SP1/76, fo. 194r.
25 Grummitt, 'Calais and the Crown', p. 53.
26 *Cal.S.P.Venetian*, vi, p. 1415.
27 *Lisle Letters*, i, p. 643.
28 TNA (PRO), E.28/28, nos. 125, 126.
29 *Lisle Letters*, i, p. 548.
30 *A Commentary of the Services and Charges of William, Lord Grey of Wilton, KG, by his Son Arthur, Lord Grey of Wilton, KG*, ed. Sir P. Egerton (Camden Soc., London, 1847), pp. 51–2.
31 *Cal. S.P.Venetian*, vi, p. 1445: 6 Feb. 1558.

32 *Cal. S.P., Foreign, 1553–1558*, ed. W. B. Turnbull (London, 1861), p. 356.

33 *Acts of the Privy Council*, ed. J. L. Dasent *et al.*, 46 vols (1890–1964), v, p. 340.

34 J. D. Mackie, *The Earlier Tudors, 1485–1558* (Oxford, 1957), p. 558.

35 Grummitt, 'Calais and the Crown' in *English Experience in France*, p. 62.

36 *Cal. S.P. Venetian*, vi, p. 1421.

37 *Cal. S.P. Dom., Mary I, 1553–1558*, ed. C. S. Knighton (London, 1998), p. 81.

38 Herbert of Cherbury, *Life and Raigne*, p. 17.

39 G. R. Elton, *England under the Tudors* (London, 1955), pp. 175–7; A. F. Pollard, *Henry VIII* (London, 1951), pp. 290–304.

40 J. Guy, *Tudor England* (Oxford, 1988), pp. 174–6; S. Ellis, 'Crown, Community and Government in the English Territories, 1450–1575', *History*, 71 (1986), pp. 187–204.

41 Grummitt, 'Calais and the Crown', in *English Experience in France*, pp. 57–62.

42 J. E. C. Bodley, *The Coronation of Edward the Seventh: A Chapter of European and Imperial History* (London, 1903), pp. 324–5.

43 Cited in Rodger, *Safeguard of the Sea*, p. 18.

44 *Lisle Letters*, i, pp. 169–71.

45 Ibid., i, pp. 688–9.

46 Ibid., i, p. 481 (1534).

47 Ibid., i, pp. 481–2.

48 Ibid., i, pp. 671–2.

49 See D. Potter, 'The Lisles and their French Friends', in *The English Experience in France*, esp. pp. 200–5, 221–2.

50 *Lisle Letters*, i, pp. 249–52.

51 *Letters and Papers*, i, pp. 117–18.

52 Ibid., ii.I, pp. 218–30.

53 See above, p. 79.

54 Jean Froissart, *Chronicles*, ed. G. C. Macaulay (London, 1908), p. 1.

55 Ibid., p. xxvii.

56 Ibid., p. xxix.

57 Gilbert Pecche (1317): see Vale, *Origins of the Hundred Years War*, p. 5, n. 14 and references.

58 See Potter, 'The Lisles and their French friends', pp. 204–5.

59 J. Palsgrave, *L'Esclarcissement de la Langue Francoyse, 1530*, ed. R. C. Alston (Menston, 1969), p. iii.

60 J. Peletier du Mans, *Dialogue d'ortographe* (Paris, 1550), p. 60; cited in Potter, 'The Lisles and their French friends', p. 205.

61 Potter, 'The Lisles and their French friends', p. 205.

62 See above, n. 59.

63 Palsgrave, *L'Esclarcissement*, fo. A, iiir.

64 Ibid., fo. 473v.

65 Ibid., fo. iiir.

66 Ibid., fos.21v–30v.

67 Ibid., fo. 163v.

Notes to Chapter 9: The Aftermath

1 *A Commentary of the Services and Charges*, pp. 36–7.
2 'Ceremonial of the Funeral of William, Lord Grey of Wilton', in *A Commentary of the Services and Charges*, p. 63.
3 *Cal. S.P. Venetian*, vi, p. 1449: 12 February 1558.
4 *Lisle Letters*, i, p. 660.
5 See Bodleian Library, MS Bodley Add.D. 43.
6 *King's Works*, iii, p. 393.
7 R. and I. Tombs, *That Sweet Enemy*, p. 1.
8 *Cal. S.P. Venetian*, iii, p. 45; cited J. J. Scarisbrick, *Henry VIII* (Harmondsworth, 1971), p. 183.
9 *Cal. S.P. Venetian*, iii, pp. 45–6.
10 *Libelle*, p. 172.
11 See Le Patourel, *Norman Empire*, p. 172.

Bibliography

MANUSCRIPT SOURCES

Although this book depends heavily upon printed primary sources and published secondary literature, it also reflects many years of work in both British and French archives, above all in the former Public Record Office (now National Archives). Among the classes of document most heavily consulted there are the following:

Ancient Correspondence (SC 1)
Ancient Petitions (SC 8)
Chancery Miscellanea & Diplomatic Documents, Chancery (C 47)
Chancery, Gascon Rolls (C 61)
Chancery, Treaty Rolls (C 76)
Chancery, Norman Rolls (C 64)
Chancery, Roman Rolls (C 70)
Exchequer, Diplomatic Documents (E 30)
Exchequer, Treasury of the Receipt, Miscellaneous Books (E 36)
Exchequer, Accounts Various (E 101)
Exchequer, Foreign Accounts (E 364)
Exchequer, Pipe Rolls (E 372)
Exchequer, Issue Rolls (E403)
London, The National Archives (TNA, ex-PRO), SC 1/31; SC 1/37; E 175/2/5/1; E 101/161/16 and 17; E 179/9; SP 1/76; E 28/28, nos. 125, 126; SC 1/13/12; SC 1/13/38.
Montauban, Archives Départementales de Tarn-et-Garonne (ATG), A. 56, A. 132.
Oxford, Bodleian Library: MS Bodley Add.D. 43.
Paris, Archives Nationales: K.64, K.65, K.67, K.69.

PRIMARY SOURCES

A Commentary of the Services and Charges of William, Lord Grey of Wilton, KG, by his Son Arthur, Lord Grey of Wilton, ed. Sir P. Egerton (Camden Soc., London, 1847).
A Relation or rather a True Account of the Island of England ... about the year 1500, ed. C. A. Sneyd (Camden Soc., London, 1847).
Account of Master John de Burnham the Younger, chamberlain of Chester, of the Revenues of the counties of Chester and Flint, 1361–62, ed. P. H. W. Booth and A. D. Carr (Stroud, 1991).
Acts of the Privy Council, ed. J. L. Dasent *et al.*, 46 vols (1890–1964).

Archives Municipales de Bordeaux: Livre des Coutumes, ed. H. Barckhausen (Bordeaux, 1890).

Bede, *The Ecclesiastical History of the English People*, ed. B. Colgrave and R. Mynors (Oxford, 1979).

Calendar of Documents Preserved in France, Illustrative of the History of Great Britain and Ireland, i, 918–1206, ed. J. H. Round (London, 1899).

Calendar of State Papers and Manuscripts Relating to English Affairs, Existing in the Archives and Collections of Venice, i, 1202–1509 (London, 1864); *viii, 1581–1591* (London, 1894).

Calendar of State Papers, Domestic, Mary I, 1553–1558, ed. C. S. Knighton (London, 1998).

Calendar of State Papers, Foreign, 1553–1558, ed. W. B. Turnbull (London, 1861).

Calendars of Charter Rolls

Calendars of Close Rolls

Calendars of Patent Rolls

Chronicle of Calais in the Reigns of Henry VII and Henry VIII to the year 1540, ed. J. G. Nichols (Camden Soc., London, 1846).

Commynes, Philippe de, *Mémoires*, ed. J. Calmette and G. Durville, 3 vols (Paris, 1925).

Documents Illustrative of the History of Scotland, 1286–1306, ed. J. Stevenson, ii (Edinburgh, 1870).

Edward IV's French Expedition of 1475, ed. F. P. Barnard (Oxford, 1925).

English Historical Documents, iii, 1189–1327, ed. H. Rothwell (London, 1975).

English Suits before the Parlement of Paris, 1420–1436, ed. C. A. J. Armstrong and C. T. Allmand (Camden 4th ser., London, 1982).

Foedera, conventiones, litterae et cuiuscunque generis acta publica, ed. T. Rymer, 20 vols (London, 1704–35).

Fortescue, Sir John, *The Governance of England by Sir John Fortescue*, ed. C. Plummer (Oxford, 1885).

Froissart, Jean, *Chronicles*, ed. G. C. Macaulay (London, 1908).

Gascon Register A, ed. G. P. Cuttino, 3 vols (London, 1975).

Gesta Henrici Quinti, ed. F. Taylor and J. S. Roskell (Oxford, 1975).

Gray, Sir Thomas, of Heaton, *Scalachronica*, ed. A. King (Surtees Society, ccix, Woodbridge, 2005).

La minute française des interrogatoires de Jeanne la Pucelle, ed. P. Doncoeur and Y. Lanhers (Melun, 1956).

Le Livre des Hommages d'Aquitaine, ed. J.-P. Trabut Cussac (Bordeaux, 1959).

Letters and Papers Illustrative of the Wars of the English in France during the Reign of Henry VI King of England, ed. J. Stevenson, 2 vols (London, 1861–4).

Map, Walter, *De Nugis Curialium*, ed. M. R. James (Oxford, 1914).

Official Correspondence of Thomas Bekynton, ed. G. Williams, 2 vols (London, 1872).

Palsgrave, J., *L'Esclarcissement de la Langue Françoyse, 1530*, ed. R. C. Alston (Menston, 1969).

Paston Letters, ed. J. Gardner, 3 vols (London, 1872).

Peletier du Mans, J., *Dialogue d'ortographe* (Paris, 1550).

Proceedings and Ordinances of the Privy Council of England, ed. N. H. Nicolas, 7 vols (London, 1827–34).

Procès de condamnation de Jeanne d'Arc, ed. P. Tisset and Y. Lanhers, 3 vols (Paris, 1960, 1970–1).

Procès de condamnation et de réhabilitation de Jeanne d'Arc, ed. J. Quicherat, 5 vols (Paris, 1841–9).

Regesta Regum Scottorum, ii, ed. G. W. S. Barrow (Edinburgh, 1971).

Rôles Gascons, ed. F. Michel, C. Bemont, Y. Renouard, 4 vols (Paris and London, 1885–1964).

Rotuli Parliamentorum, ed. J. Strachey *et al.*, 6 vols (London, 1783).

Royal and Historical Letters during the Reign of Henry IV, ed. F. C. Hingeston, i (London, 1860).

Select Charters, ed. W. Stubbs (Oxford, 1870; revised edn., 1895; repr. 1960).

'Some documents regarding the fulfilment and interpretation of the treaty of Brétigny (1361–1369)', ed. P. Chaplais (*Camden Miscellany*, xix, London, 1952), pp. 1–84.

The *Libelle of Englyshe Polycye: A Poem on the Use of Sea-power, 1436*, ed. G. F. Warner (Oxford, 1926).

The Lisle Letters, ed. M. St Clare Byrne, 6 vols (Chicago and London, 1981).

The Metrical Chronicle of Robert of Gloucester, ed. W. A. Wright, 2 vols (London, 1887).

The Paston Letters, 1422–1509, ed. J.Gairdner, 3 vols (London, 1910).

The Rous Roll, ed. C. D. Ross (Gloucester, 1980).

The War of Saint-Sardos (1323–1325). Gascon Correspondence and Diplomatic Documents, ed. P. Chaplais (Camden third series, lxxxvii, London, 1954).

Treaty Rolls, preserved in the Public Record Office, i (1234–1325), ed. P. Chaplais (London, 1955); *ii (1337–1339)*, ed. J. T. Ferguson (London, 1972).

SECONDARY AUTHORITIES

Allmand, C.T., *Lancastrian Normandy, 1415–1450: The History of a Medieval Occupation* (Oxford, 1983).

Anglo, S., *Martial Arts in Renaissance Europe* (New Haven and London, 2000).

Armstrong, C. A. J., 'The Golden Age of Burgundy', in A. G. Dickens (ed.), *Courts of Europe: Politics, Patronage and Royalty, 1400–1800* (London, 1977), pp. 55–75.

—*England, France and Burgundy in the Fifteenth Century* (London, 1983).

Arn, M.-J., 'Two MSS, One Mind: Charles d'Orléans and the Production of Manuscripts in Two Languages', in M.-J. Arn (ed.), *Charles d'Orléans in England (1415–1440)* (Woodbridge, 2000), pp. 61–78.

Art and the Courts: France and England from 1259 to 1328, ed. P. Brieger, P. Verdier and M. F. Montpetit, 2 vols (Ottawa, 1972).

Aurell, M. (ed.), *La Cour Plantagenêt, 1154–1224* (Poitiers, 2000).

—(ed.), *Noblesses de l'espace Plantagenêt, 1154–1224* (Poitiers, 2001).

—(ed.), *Culture politique des Plantagenêt* (Poitiers, 2003).

Ayroles, J.-B.-J., *La Vraie Jeanne d'Arc*, 5 vols (Paris, 1890–1901).

—*L'Université de Paris au temps de Jeanne d'Arc et la cause de sa haine contre la libératrice* (Paris, 1902).

Bachrach, B., 'The Idea of Angevin Empire', *Albion*, 10 (1978), pp. 293–9.

Barber, R., *Edward, Prince of Wales and Aquitaine* (London, 1978).

Barlow, F., *Thomas Becket* (London, 1968).

Barratt, N., 'The English Revenues of Richard I', *EHR*, 116 (2001), pp. 635–56.

—'The Revenues of John and Philip Augustus Revisited', in S. Church (ed.), *King John: New Interpretations* (Woodbridge, 1999).

Bartlett, R., *England under the Norman and Angevin Kings 1075–1225* (Oxford, 2000).

Bates, D., 'The Rise and Fall of Normandy, c.911–1204', in D. Bates and A. Curry (eds), *England and Normandy in the Middle Ages* (London, 1994).

Bates, D. and Curry, A. (eds), *England and Normandy in the Middle Ages* (London, 1994).

Bates, D., 'England and Normandy After 1066', *EHR*, 104 (1989), pp. 34–45.

Baudry, M.-P., *Les Fortifications des Plantagenêts en Poitou, 1154–1242* (Paris, 2001).

—(ed.), *Les Fortifications dans les domaines Plantagenêts xiie–xive siècles* (Poitiers, 2000).

Bautier, R-H., 'Conclusion. "Empire Plantagenêt" ou "Espace Plantagenêt". Y-eut-il une civilisation du monde Plantagenêt'?, *CCM*, 29 (1986), pp. 139–47.

Beaune, C., *Jeanne d'Arc* (Paris, 2004).

—*Naissance de la nation France* (Paris, 1985) [translated as *The Birth of an Ideology: Myths and Symbols of Nationhood in Later Medieval France* (Berkeley, 1992)].

Bell, D. A., 'Recent Works on Early Modern French National Identity', *Journal of Modern History*, 68 (1996), pp. 84–113.

Benions, E. A., J. Butler and C. E. Carrington (eds), *The Cambridge History of the British Empire*, iii (Cambridge, 1959).

Benton, J. F., 'The Court of Champagne as a Literary Center', *Speculum*, 36 (1961), pp. 551–91.

Bériac, F., 'Une principauté sans chambre des comptes ni échiquier: l'Aquitaine, 1362–70', in P. Contamine and O. Matteoni (eds), *La France des Principautés: Les Chambres des Comptes, xive et xve siècles* (Paris, 1996), pp. 105–22.

Bernard, J., *Navires et gens de mer à Bordeaux (vers 1400–vers 1550)*, 3 vols (Paris, 1968).

Binski, P., *The Painted Chamber at Westminster*, Society of Antiquaries occasional paper, 9 (London, 1986).

—*Westminster Abbey and the Plantagenets: Kingship and the Representation of Power, 1200–1400* (New Haven and London, 1995).

Black, J. G., 'Edward I and Gascony in 1300', *EHR*, 17 (1902), pp. 518–27.

Blanning, T. C. W., *The Culture of Power and the Power of Culture: Old Regime Europe, 1660–1789* (Oxford, 2002).

Bodley, J. E. C., *The Coronation of Edward the Seventh: A Chapter of European and Imperial History* (London, 1903).

Boussard, J., 'Les influences anglaises dans le développement des grandes charges de l'empire Plantagenêt', *Annales de Normandie*, 5 (1955), pp. 215–31.

—'Philippe Auguste et les Plantagenêts' in R. H. Bautier (ed.) *La France de Philippe Auguste: le temps des mutations* (Paris, 1982).

Bradbury, J., *Philip Augustus, king of France, 1180–1223* (London, 1998).

Brand, P., *The Making of the Common Law* (London, 1992).

Brooks, F. W., *The English Naval Forces, 1199–1272* (London, 1932).

Brown, E. A. R., 'Gascon subsidies and the finances of the English dominions, 1315–24', *Studies in Medieval and Renaissance History*, 8 (1971), pp. 33–146.

Campbell, J., 'The United Kingdom of England: The Anglo-Saxon Achievement', in A. Grant and K. J. Stringer (eds), *Uniting the Kingdom? The Making of British History* (London, 1995), pp. 31–47.

Carpenter, D., *The Minority of Henry III* (London, 1990).

—*The Struggle for Mastery. Britain 1066–1284* (London, 2003).

Carus-Wilson, E. M. and Coleman, O., *England's Export Trade, 1275–1547* (Oxford, 1963).

Catto, J., 'Written English: The Making of the Language, 1370–1400', *Past & Present*, 178 (2003), pp. 24–59.

Chauou, A., *L'idéologie Plantagenêt: royauté arthurienne et monarchie politique dans l'espace Plantagenêt (xii–xiiie siècles)* (Rennes, 2001).

—'The Chancery of Guyenne, 1289–1453', in J. Conway Davies (ed.), *Studies Presented to Sir Hilary Jenkinson* (Oxford, 1957), 61–96 [reprinted in his *Essays in Medieval Diplomacy and Administration* (London, 1981), pt VIII].

Chaplais, P., 'Le Sceau de la Cour de Gascogne ou Sceau de l'Office de Sénéchal de Guyenne', *AM*, 67 (1955), 19–29 [reprinted ibid., pt VII].

—*English Diplomatic Practice in the Middle Ages* (London, 2003).

—*Essays in Medieval Diplomacy and Administration* (London, 1981).

Church, S. D. (ed.), *King John: New Interpretations* (Woodbridge, 1999).

Clanchy, M., *England and its Rulers, 1066–1272* (London, 1983).

Colley, L., *Britons: Forging the Nations, 1707–1837* (London, 2003).

Collins, H. L., *The Order of the Garter, 1348–1461* (Oxford, 2000).

Colvin, H. M. *et al.* (eds), *The King's Works*, 6 vols (London, 1963–82).

Contamine, P., 'Jules Quicherat, historien de Jeanne d'Arc', in *De Jeanne d'Arc aux Guerres d'Italie* (Orleans, 1994).

—'Jeanne d'Arc dans la memoire des droites', in J.-F. Sirinelli (ed.), *Histoire des droites en France* (Paris, 1992).

Cosgrove, A., *A New History of Ireland, vol. II. Medieval Ireland, 1169–1534* (Oxford, 1981).

Coulson, C., 'Fortress Policy in Capetian Tradition and Angevin Practice: Aspects of the Conquest of Normandy by Philip II', *Anglo-Norman Studies*, 6 (1983), pp. 13–38.

Crouch, D., *The Image of Aristocracy in Britain, 1000–1300* (London, 1992).

—*William Marshal: Court, Career and Chivalry in the Angevin Empire, 1147–1219* (London and New York, 1990).

Crowder, C. M. D., *Unity, Heresy and Reform, 1378–1460: The Conciliar Response to the Great Schism* (London, 1977).

Currin, J. M., '"The King's Army into the Parties of Bretaigne": Henry VII and the Breton Wars, 1489–91', *War in History*, 7 (2000), pp. 379–412.

Curry, A., 'L'administration financier de la Normandie anglaise: continuité ou changement?', in P. Contamine and O. Matteoni (eds), *La France des principautés: Les Chambres des Comptes, xive et xve siècles* (Paris, 1996), pp. 83–103.

—'The First English Standing Army? Military Organisation in Lancastrian Normandy, 1420–1450', in C. D. Ross (ed.), *Patronage, Pedigree and Power in Later Medieval England* (Gloucester and Totowa NJ, 1979), pp. 193–214.

Dartigue, C., *Histoire de la Guyenne* (Paris, 1950).

Davies, C. S. L, 'The Wars of the Roses in European Context', in A. J. Pollard (ed.), *The Wars of the Roses* (London, 1995).

—'Henry VIII and Henry V: The Wars in France', in J. Watts (ed.), *The End of the Middle Ages* (Gloucester, 1998), pp. 236–52.

Davies, R. R., *The First English Empire: Power and Identity in the British Isles, 1093–1343* (Oxford, 2000).

Desmarets, N., *L'ancienne junction de l'Angleterre à la France ou le Détroit de Calais: Sa formation par la Rupture de l'Isthme* (Paris, 1751).

Dickinson, J. G., *The Congress of Arras, 1435: A Study in Medieval Diplomacy* (Oxford, 1955).

Dillon, Viscount, 'Calais and the Pale', *Archaeologia*, 53 (1892), pp. 289–388.

Doyle, M. W., *Empires* (Ithaca and London, 1986).

Duby, G., *Le Moyen Age: De Hugues Capet à Jeanne d'Arc, 987–1460* (Paris, 1987).

Dumas, F., 'La monnaie dans les domaines Plantagenet', *CCM*, 29 (1986), pp. 53–9.

Dunbabin, J., *Charles I of Anjou: Power, Kingship and State-Making in Thirteenth-century Europe* (Harlow, 1998).

Eickels, K. van, '"Homagium" and "Amicitia": Rituals of Peace and their Significance in Anglo-French Negotiations of the Twelfth Century', *Francia*, 24 (1997), pp. 133–40.

Elliott, J. H., 'A Europe of Composite Monarchies', *Past & Present*, 137 (1992), pp. 48–71.

—*Empires of the Atlantic World: Britain and Spain in America, 1492–1830* (New Haven and London, 2006).

Ellis, S., 'Crown, Community and Government in the English Territories, 1450–1575', *History*, 71 (1986), pp. 187–204.

Elton, G. R., *England under the Tudors* (London, 1955).

Everard, J., *Brittany and the Angevins: Province and Empire, 1158–1203* (Cambridge, 2000).

Evergates, T., *Feudal Society in Medieval France: Documents from the County of Champagne* (Philadelphia, 1993).

Favreau, R., 'Comptes de la sénéchaussée de Poitou', *BEC*, 117 (1959)

Frame, R., *The Political Development of the British Isles, 1100–1400* (Oxford, 1990).

France, A., *Jeanne d'Arc*, 2 vols (Paris, 1908).

Garton Ash, T., *Free World* (London, 2005).

Geary, P., 'Living with Conflicts in Stateless France: A Typology of Conflict Management Mechanisms, 1050–1200' in P. Geary (ed.), *Living with the Dead in the Middle Ages* (Ithaca, NY, 1994).

—*The Myth of Nations: The Medieval Origins of Europe* (Princeton, 2002).

Gillingham, J., *The English in the Twelfth Century: Imperialism, National Identity and Political Values* (Woodbridge, 2000).

Gillingham, J., 'Richard I, Galley-warfare and Portsmouth: The Beginnings of a Royal Navy', in M. Prestwich, R. H. Britnell and R. Frame (eds), *Thirteenth-century England VI* (Woodbridge, 1997).

Gillingham, J., 'The Unromantic Death of Richard I', *Speculum*, 54 (1979), pp. 18–41.

—*The Angevin Empire* (2nd edn., London, 2001).

Gordon, D., *Making and Meaning: The Wilton Diptych* (London, 1993).

Green, D., *The Black Prince* (Stroud, 2001).

Griffiths, R. A., *The Principality of Wales in the Later Middle Ages. I. South Wales, 1277–1536* (Cardiff, 1972).

Grummitt, D., '"One of the Mooste Pryncipall Treasours Belongyng to his Realme of Englande": Calais and the Crown, c.1450–1558', in D. Grummitt (ed.), *The English Experience in France, c. 1450–1558* (Aldershot, 2002), pp. 46–62.

Gunn, S. J., 'The French Wars of Henry VIII', in J. Black (ed.), *The Origins of Wars in Early Modern Europe* (Edinburgh, 1987), pp. 28–51.

Guy, J., *Tudor England* (Oxford, 1988).

Hajdu, R., 'Family and Feudal Ties in Poitou, 1100–1300', *Journal of Interdisciplinary History*, 8 (1977), pp. 117–39.

—'Castles, Castellans and the Structure of Politics in Poitou, 1152–1271', *JMH*, 4 (1978), pp. 27–53.

Hallam, E. M., 'Royal Burial and the Cult of Kingship in England and France, 1060–1330', *JMH*, 8 (1982), pp. 359–80.

Harrison, M., 'A Life of St Edward the Confessor in the early 14th century Stained Glass at Fécamp in Normandy', *JWCI*, 16 (1965), pp. 22–37.

Harriss, G. L., *Shaping the Nation: England, 1360–1461* (Oxford, 2005).

—*Cardinal Beaufort* (Oxford, 1988).

—*King, Parliament and Public Finance to 1360* (Oxford, 1975).

Henneman, J. B., *Royal Taxation in Fourteenth-century France: The Development of War Financing, 1322–1356* (Princeton, 1971).

Herbert, Edward, Lord of Cherbury, *The Life and Raigne of King Henry the Eighth* (London, 1649).

Hollister, C. W., 'Normandy, France and the Anglo-Norman *Regnum*', *Speculum*, 51 (1976), pp. 202–42.

—'The Making of the Angevin Empire', *JBS*, 12 (1973), pp. 1–25.

Holt, J.C., 'Politics and Property in Early Medieval England', *Past & Present*, 57 (1972), pp. 3–52.

—'The End of the Anglo-Norman Realm', *Proceedings of the British Academy*, 61 (1975), pp. 223–65.

—*Colonial England, 1066–1215* (London, 1997).

Hutchinson, G., *Medieval Ships and Shipping* (London, 1994).

Hyams, P., 'The Common Law and the French Connection', *Anglo-Norman Studies*, 4 (1981), pp. 77–92.

Jacob, E. F., 'Theory and Fact in the General Councils of the Fifteenth Century', in *Essays in Later Medieval History* (Manchester, 1968), pp. 124–40.

Jacob, E. F., *Henry V and the Invasion of France* (London, 1947).

—*The Fifteenth Century, 1399–1485* (Oxford, 1961).

James, M. K., 'Fluctuations of the Anglo-Gascon Wine Trade in the Fourteenth Century', *EcHR*, 2nd ser., 4 (1951), pp. 170–96.

—'Les activités commerciales des negociants en vins gascons en Angleterre à la fin du Moyen Age', *AM*, 65 (1953), pp. 35–49.

'Jeanne d'Arc: une passion française', *Histoire*, Special issue, 210 (May 1997).

Jenkinson, H., 'A Seal of Edward II for Scottish Affairs', *Antiquaries Journal*, 11 (1931), pp. 229–39.

—'The Great Seal of England: Deputed or Departmental Seals', *Archaeologia*, 85 (1935), pp. 314–24.

Jones, M. C. E., *Ducal Brittany, 1364–1399* (Oxford, 1970).

Jouet, R., *Et la Normandie devint française* (Paris, 1983).

Keen, M. H and Daniel, M. J., 'English Diplomacy and the Sack of Fougères in 1449', *History*, 59 (1974), pp. 375–91.

Keen, M. H., 'The End of the Hundred Years War: Lancastrian France and Lancastrian England', in M. Jones and M. Vale (eds), *England and her Neighbours, 1066–1453: Essays in Honour of Pierre Chaplais* (London, 1989), pp. 297–311.

—*England in the Later Middle Ages* (London, 1979).

Kipling, G., *The Triumph of Honour: Burgundian Origins of the Elizabethan Renaissance* (Leiden, 1977).

Labarge, M. W., *Gascony, England's First Colony, 1204–1453* (London, 1980).

Laborderie, O. de, 'Richard the Lionheart and the Birth of a National Cult of St George in England: Origins and Development of a Legend', *Nottingham Medieval Studies*, 29 (1995), pp. 37–53.

Lachaud, F., 'Liveries of Robes in England, c.1200–c.1330', *EHR*, 111 (1996), pp. 279–98.

—'Textiles, Furs and Liveries: A Study of the Material Culture of the Court of Edward I (1277–1307)' (unpublished Oxford D.Phil. Thesis, 1992).

Lander, J. R., 'The Hundred Years War and Edward IV's Campaign in France', in A. J. Slavin (ed.), *Tudor Men and Institutions: Studies in English Institutions and Law* (Baton Rouge, 1952), pp. 70–100.

Lang, A., *The Maid of France: Being the Story of the Life and Death of Jeanne d'Arc* (London, 1908).

Le Patourel, J., *Feudal Empires: Norman and Plantagenet* (London, 1984).

—— *The Norman Empire* (Oxford, 1976).

Les Vitraux de Haute-Normandie, ed. M. Callias Bey, V. Chausse, F. Gatouillat and M. Hérold (Corpus Vitrearum medii aevi, Recensement des vitraux anciens de la France), 6 (Paris, 2001).

Lewis, P. S., 'War Propaganda and Historiography in Fifteenth-century France and England', *TRHS*, 5th ser., 15 (1965), pp. 1–21.

Loirette, G., 'Arnaud-Amanieu, sire d'Albret et l'appel des seigneurs gascons en 1368', *Mélanges d'Histoire offerts à Charles Bémont* (Paris, 1913), pp. 317–40.

Mackie, J. D., *The Earlier Tudors, 1485–1558* (Oxford, 1957).

Marshall, H. E., *Our Island Story: A Child's History of England* (London, 1905).

Martindale, J., 'The Sword on the Stone: Some Resonances of a Medieval Symbol of Power', *ANS*, 15 (1993), pp. 199–241.

—'"An Unfinished Business": Angevin Politics and the Siege of Toulouse, 1159', *ANS*, 23 (2000), pp. 115–54.

—*Status, Authority and Regional Power* (Aldershot, 1997).

Mason, E., '"Rocamadour in Quercy above All Other Churches: The Healing of Henry II', in *Studies in Church History*, xix, ed. W. Shiels (Oxford, 1982).

Massey, R., 'The Land Settlement in Lancastrian Normandy', in A. J. Pollard (ed.), *Property and Politics: Essays in Later Medieval History* (Gloucester, 1984), pp. 76–96.

Matthew, D. J. A., *The English and the Community of Europe in the Thirteenth Century* (Stenton Lecture, Reading, 1997).

—*The Medieval European Community* (London, 1977).

—*The Norman Monasteries and their English Possessions* (Oxford, 1962).

McCash, J. M. H., 'Marie de Champagne and Eleanor of Aquitaine: A Relationship Re-examined', *Speculum*, 54 (1979), pp. 698–711.

McFarlane, K. B., *England in the Fifteenth Century*, ed. G. L. Harriss (London, 1981).

—*The Nobility of Later Medieval England* (Oxford, 1973).

Meek, E. L., 'The Career of Sir Thomas Everingham, "Knight of the North", in the Service of Maximilian, Duke of Austria, 1477–81', *Historical Research*, 74 (2001), pp. 238–48.

Michelet, J., *Jeanne d'Arc*, ed. G. Rudler, 2 vols (Paris, 1925).

Montesquieu, C. de Secondat, Baron de, *The Spirit of the Laws*, ed. A. M. Cohler, B. C. Miller and H. W. S. Stone (Cambridge, 2005).

Moss, V., 'The Defence of Normandy, 1193–98', *ANS*, 24 (2001), pp. 145–61.

Murray, T. Douglas, *Jeanne d'Arc, Maid of Orléans, Deliverer of France: Being the Story of her Life, her Achievements, and her Death, as Attested on Oath and Set Forth in the Original Documents* (London, 1903).

Nelson, J. L. (ed.), *Richard Coeur de Lion in History and Myth* (London, 1992).

Nicholas, D. M., *Medieval Flanders* (London, 1992).

Nora, P. (ed.), *Les lieux de Mémoire*, iii (Paris, 1992).

Ormrod, W. M., 'The English State and the Plantagenet Empire, 1259–1360' in J. R. Maddicott and D. M. Palliser (eds) *The Medieval State* (London, 2000), pp. 197–214.

Paterson, L., *The World of the Troubadours: Medieval Occitan Society, c.1100–1300* (Cambridge, 1993).

Perroy, 'Charles V et la traité de Brétigny', *MA*, 38 (1928), pp. 255–81.

Perroy, E., 'Edouard III et les appels gascons en 1368', *AM*, 61 (1948–9), pp. 91–6.

—*The Hundred Years War* (London, 1962).

Pitte, D., 'Château-Gaillard dans la défense de la Normandie orientale, 1196–1204', *ANS*, 24 (2001), pp. 163–75.

Pocock, J. G. A., 'British History: A Plea for a New Subject', *Journal of Modern History*, 47 (1975), pp. 601–21.

—'Deconstructing Europe', in P. Gowan and P. Anderson (eds), *The Question of Europe* (London, 1997), pp. 297–317.

Pollard, A. F., *Henry VIII* (London, 1951).

Potter, D., 'The Private Face of Anglo-French Relations in the Sixteenth Century: the Lisles and their French friends', in D. Grummitt (ed.), *The English Experience in France, c. 1450–1558* (Aldershot, 2002), pp. 200–22.

Power, D. and Standen, N. (eds), *Frontiers in Question: Eurasian Borderlands, 700–1700* (Basingstoke, 1999).

Power, D., 'What Did the Frontier of Angevin Normandy Comprise?', *ANS*, 17 (1995), pp. 181–201.

Powicke, F. M., *The Loss of Normandy* (2nd edn.; Manchester, 1960).

Prestwich, J. O., 'War and Finance in the Anglo-Norman State', *TRHS*, 5th ser., 4 (1954), pp. 19–43.

Prestwich, M., *Plantagenet England, 1225–1360* (Oxford, 2005).

—— '*Miles in Armis Strenuus*: The Knight at War', *TRHS*, 6th ser., 5 (1995), pp. 201–20.

Renouard, Y. (ed.), *Bordeaux sous les Rois d'Angleterre* [*Histoire de Bordeaux III: Bordeaux Médi'val II*] (Bordeaux, 1965).

—— 'Essai sur le rôle de l'empire angevin dans la formation de la France et de la civilisation française aux xiie et xiiie siècles', in *Etudes d'Histoire Médiévale*, 2 vols (Paris, 1968), pp. 849–61.

Richmond, C., 'Patronage and Polemic', in J. L. Watts (ed.), *The End of the Middle Ages* (Gloucester, 1998).

Rickard, P., *Britain in Medieval French Literature, 1100–1500* (Cambridge, 1956).

Ridgeway, H., 'King Henry III and the "Aliens", 1236–1272', in P. R. Coss and S. D. Lloyd (eds), *Thirteenth-century England II* (Woodbridge, 1987), pp. 81–92.

—'William de Valence and his "familiares"', *Historical Research*, 65 (1992), pp. 239–57.

Rodger, N. A. M., *The Safeguard of the Sea: A Naval History of Britain, 600–1649* (London, 1997).

Saul, N. (ed.), *England in Europe, 1066–1453* (London, 1994).

Scarisbrick, J., *Henry VIII* (Harmondsworth, 1971).

Scott, W. S., *Jeanne d'Arc: Her Life, Her Death and the Myth* (London, 1974).

Southern, R. W., 'England's First Entry into Europe', in R. W. Southern (ed.), *Medieval Humanism and Other Studies* (Oxford, 1970).

—*The Making of the Middle Ages* (London, 1953).

Spear, D., 'Power, Patronage and Personality in the Norman Cathedral Chapters, 911–1204', *ANS*, 20 (1997), pp. 205–22.

—'The Norman Empire and the Secular Clergy, 1066–1204', *JBS*, 21 (1981–2), pp. 1–10.

Spiegel, G., 'The Cult of St Denis and Capetian Kingship', *JMH*, 1 (1975), pp. 43–69.

Stacey, R. C., *Politics, Policy and Finance under Henry III, 1216–1245* (Oxford, 1987).

Strickland, M., *War and Chivalry: The Conduct and Perception of War in England and Normandy, 1066–1217* (Cambridge, 1996).

Stubbs, W., *The Constitutional History of England in its Origin and Development*, 3 vols (5th edn.; Oxford, 1896).

Taylor, C., 'Brittany and the French Crown: The Legacy of the English Attack on Fougères (1449)', in *The English State: Essays Presented to James Campbell*, eds J. R. Maddicott and D. M. Palliser (London, 2000), pp. 243–57.

—'War, Propaganda and Diplomacy in Fifteenth-century France', in C. T. Allmand (ed.), *War, Government and Society in Late Medieval France* (Liverpool, 2000), pp. 70–91.

—*Joan of Arc: La Pucelle* (Manchester, 2006).

The Cambridge History of the British Empire, 8 vols (Cambridge, 1929–63).

Thomas, H., *The English and the Normans. Ethnic Hostility, Assimilation and Identity* (Oxford, 2003).

Thornton, T., 'Taxing the King's Dominions', in R. Bonney and W. M. Ormrod (eds), *Crises, Revolution and Self-Sustained Growth* (Stamford, 1998), pp. 103–17.

Tombs, R. and I., *That Sweet Enemy: The French and the British from the Sun King to the Present* (London, 2006).

Tout, T. F., *France and England: Their Relations in the Middle Ages and Now* (Manchester, 1922).

Trabut-Cussac, J.-P., *L'Administration anglaise en Gascogne sous Henry III et Edouard I de 1254 à 1307* (Geneva, 1972).

Trevelyan, G. M., *English Social History* (London, 1944).

Tucoo-Chala, P., *Gaston Fébus et la Vicomté de Béarn, 1343–1391* (Bordeaux, 1960).

Turner, R. V., 'Good or Bad Kingship? The Case of Richard Lionheart', *Haskins Society Journal*, 8 (1999), pp. 63–78.

—'Richard Lionheart and the Episcopate in his French Domains', *French Historical Studies*, 21 (1998), pp. 518–42.

—'The Problem of Survival for the Angevin Empire: Henry II's and his Sons' Vision Versus Late Twelfth-century Realities', *American Historical Review*, 100 (1995), pp. 78–96.

Turville-Petre, T., *England the Nation: Language, Literature and National Identity, 1290–1340* (Oxford, 1996).

Vale, J., *Edward III and Chivalry* (Woodbridge, 1982).

Vale, M., 'The End and Aftermath of the Hundred Years War', in N. Saul (ed.), *England in Europe, 1066–1453* (London, 1994), pp. 151–62.

—*The Princely Court: Medieval Courts and Culture in North-west Europe, 1270–1380* (Oxford, 2001).

—*Charles VII* (London, 1974).

—*English Gascony, 1399–1453* (Oxford, 1970).

—'The Last Years of English Gascony, 1451–1453', *TRHS*, 5th ser., 19 (1969), pp. 119–38.

Vaughan, R., *Philip the Good: The Apogee of Burgundy* (London, 1970; 2nd edn. 2002).

Verdier, P., 'Témoignages artistiques des mariages franco-anglais au debut du xive siècle', *Bulletin Monumental* (1973), pp. 137–45.

Vincent, N., 'William Marshal, King Henry II and the Honour of Châteauroux', *Archives*, 25 (2000), pp. 1–15.

—*Peter des Roches* (Cambridge, 1996).

—*The Holy Blood: King Henry III and the Westminster Blood Relic* (Cambridge, 2001).

Warner, M., *Joan of Arc: The Image of Female Heroism* (New York, 1981).

Warren, W. L., 'The Myth of Norman Administrative Efficiency', *TRHS*, 5th ser., 34 (1984), pp. 113–32.

Waters, W. H., *The Edwardian Settlement of North Wales* (Cardiff, 1938).

Weiler, B. and Rowlands, I., *England and Europe in the Reign of Henry III* (Aldershot, 2003).

Werner, K. F., 'Kingdom and Principalities in 12th-century France', in T. Reuter (ed. and trans.), *The Medieval Nobility* (Amsterdam, 1979).

Wernham, R. B., *Before the Armada: The Growth of English Foreign Policy, 1485–1566* (London, 1966).

Zimmermann, J. G., *Essay on National Pride* (trans. S. H. Wilcocke) (London, 1797).

Index